# THE
# PETER
# SEABROOK

# GOOD PLANT
## GUIDE

## Written by Peter Seabrook

## Edited by Peter McHoy
## and David Squire

**CASSELL**
London

## ACKNOWLEDGEMENTS

Many organizations and individuals have co-operated to make this book possible. In addition to the many nurserymen and seedsmen who have kindly helped with stockist information, the author and publishers particularly wish to thank the following individuals who have contributed their expertise in various areas, and who have made this a better book:

Philip Damp (National Dahlia Society)
Frederic Doerflinger (Bulb Information Desk)
Jack Harkness
Roy Heath
Jack Matthews
Ken Muir
Maurice Prichard
Brian Self (East Malling Research Station)

The publishers are grateful to the following for providing photographs:

David Hoy Publishing
Peter Seabrook
Michael Warren

Line illustrations by Eileen Ellott

CASSELL LTD
35 Red Lion Square, London WC1R 4SG
and at Sydney, Auckland, Toronto, Johannesburg
an affiliate of Macmillan Publishing Co. Inc., New York

Designed and produced for Cassell Ltd by
Intercontinental Book Productions
Berkshire House, Queen Street,
Maidenhead, Berkshire, SL6 1NF.
Copyright © 1981 Intercontinental Book Productions.

First Published 1981

ISBN 0 304 30736 X

Filmset by Vantage Photosetting Co. Ltd.
Southampton and London

Printed in Italy

# *Contents*

# Introduction

We are spoilt for choice in gardening; every year sees numerous exciting new varieties launched with great acclaim. Some stand the test of time, others are quickly superseded by even greater improvements.

Even when some plants are eliminated from consideration, there are still literally thousands of different plants for us to choose from to plant in our gardens. Thumb through the pages of Hilliers' catalogue and you will see 60 pages of rhododendrons alone, 1,100 different species and varieties, Scotts have more than 160 different apples, and Bressingham Gardens list in excess of 1,000 kinds of hardy border plants.

The selections here are considered the best available for ordinary everyday gardens. You may be surprised to see well-known and trusted names omitted from the lists. There are very good reasons for this, for what is the point in growing 'Ailsa Craig' tomato, 'Arran Pilot' potato, or 'James Scarlet Intermediate' carrot when we have much superior alternatives. That is not to say I do not recommend old varieties which still have a place; 'Tom Thumb' lettuce for example can be found in lists 100 years old and it still has no equal as an early small-hearted variety.

Sadly none of us can know it all, but the experience of many leading specialists has been sought to make the selection as accurate as possible.

No doubt in the final reckoning I will have made mistakes. We all have 'eyes for our own children' and it is impossible to leave out a few less common plants that have served me well. All seedsmen and raisers of new plants will have enthusiasm for, and confidence in, the results of their many years of work. Every effort has been made to eliminate such prejudiced opinion.

It is one thing to recommend the best plants to grow and quite another finding a good source of supply. Many of the more popular plants are freely available at most good retail nurseries, garden centres and garden shops. If you are unable to find a convenient local source of supply, however, then mail order sources are given here to help track down the better plants.

This one guide sums up more than 30 years of continuous plant assessment. There is no substitute for walking the bulb fields of Holland to sort out the better spring-flowering bulbs and summer-flowering corms and tubers. Braving the weather and walking rose fields in the rain, and checking summer-flowering annual trials after heavy storms, quickly shows which plants withstand rough weather.

We cannot expect the shop or garden centre assistant to know from personal experience all about the many different groups of plants as well as the uses of countless chemicals and pieces of garden equipment. This guide is the perfect crib and aid to memory.

The more experienced gardeners could well mark their copy up with the results of their comparative trials. Gardening never stands still, every season is different and every garden has different soils and conditions. Even so, if you are new to gardening or new to a certain group of plants, this selection will give a very good foundation from which to build the near perfect garden.

I say 'near perfect' because the whole challenge and fascination of this productive pastime is the knowledge that next year we can surely do better. Where a certain plant has served you well over many years, I am not suggesting it is dropped overnight. It is very strongly recommended, however, that you run a small trial of the kinds recommended here alongside the proven sowing or planting and see how this compares.

Watch the gardens in your locality to assess the merits of different trees, shrubs and other long-lived plants. That is just what I've been doing. Add to this the prompt from literally thousands of letters with gardening queries over the years, and you will see where experience has come for the selection.

At the outset it looked easy. After all, roses 'Peace' and 'Silver Jubilee' are quite outstanding, the tomato 'Gardeners' Delight' is the sweetest and tastiest you will have savoured. Every house should have the large-leaved decorative ivy and colourful, large-flowered clematis. The names of really good plants accumulate at tremendous speed and then the heart searching began, trying to decide just what to leave out.

After the lists were finished so much information on suitable soils, likely sizes, possible and best uses, and so on, all had to be neatly packed into a pocket-sized book. Life is all compromises, gardening is compromises, and this book is a compromise. It is also a distillation of information it would take more than half a working lifetime to accumulate.

It tells you what to buy and, just as important, what not to buy. Nurserymen and garden supplies retailers are trying to give value for money. They can never sell out completely, however, and care must be taken to see that you don't buy the leftovers. Once a plant has had a severe check to growth it will take a long time to recover, and some never really recover.

What looks more expensive with living plants is very often the best value for money in the long term. Correctly named stock of good variety, and vigorous young growth, is always a good buy.

# How to Use the Book

Over 1600 plants are described within the 136 pages of
this book – with cultural information and advice on
where to obtain every one of them. Space has even been
found to incorporate 28 full-colour illustrations. Such a
mass of information can only be crammed into a small-
format book like this if everything is condensed, and as
much advice as possible presented symbolically.

As far as possible the symbols have been carefully
selected to be committed to memory easily. Once the
book has been used a few times, there will be little need
to refer to the symbol list on the opposite page.

A typical entry is explained below:

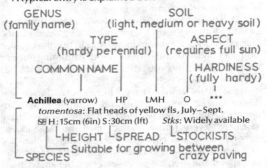

A key to abbreviations and symbols is given on the
opposite page. The stockists appear in individual
chapters. A plant is listed as widely available if stocked by
at least half the specialist suppliers.

With so many good plants to grow the list may still be
bewildering – to shortlist the very best plants in each
group, Peter Seabrook's personal favourites have been
highlighted in a second colour.

## Latin names

Latin names have been used throughout most of this
book – attractive though common names are, they are
not always accurate.

Even Latin names sometimes change, but it has been
the policy in this book to use those under which the
plant is most likely to be distributed commercially.

If you encounter a plant under a common name, and
you cannot find it in the relevant chapter, the common
name index on page 125 should enable you to track it
down.

In catalogues and when shopping for plants, the term
'cultivar' may be encountered. Technically this is a
variety raised in cultivation, as opposed to a naturally-
occurring variety. For simplicity the word variety has
been used for both throughout this book.

## KEY TO ABBREVIATIONS AND SYMBOLS

**Type of plant**

| | |
|---|---|
| D | Deciduous (autumn leaf-shedding) |
| E | Evergreen |
| HA | Hardy annual |
| HA(A) | Hardy annual, suitable for spring and autumn sowing |
| HB | Hardy biennial |
| HHA | Half-hardy annual |
| HP | Hardy perennial |

**Soil**

| | |
|---|---|
| H | Heavy/clay |
| L | Light/sandy |
| M | Medium loam |
| (A) | Requires an acid soil |
| (C) | Grows in chalk/lime soil |
| (D) | Prefers dry compost conditions |
| (M) | Requires a moist position, or compost |
| (P) | Benefits from peat incorporated at planting time |

**Fruit uses** *(after variety name)*

| | |
|---|---|
| C | Culinary (variety to cook) |
| D | Dessert (variety to eat uncooked) |

**Aspect**

| | |
|---|---|
| ○ | Full sun |
| ◑ | Partial shade |
| ● | Shade |

**Hardiness**

| | |
|---|---|
| *** | Hardy in British Isles |
| ** | May need protection in exposed areas |
| * | Tender |

**Uses and merits**

| | |
|---|---|
| ✕ | Recommended as cut flower |
| ▩ | Suitable for planting between crazy-paving |
| ▤ | Suitable for planting in dry stone wall |
| ♋ | Suitable for growing in pots or other containers |
| △ | Conifers, annuals or bulbs for the rock garden |
| ♚ | Suitable for naturalizing |
| ◌ | Responds well to growing under unheated glass |
| ❀ | Good ground-covering plant |
| ♨ | Fragrant flowers. For roses, ♨♨: very fragrant |
| ☡ | Attractive berries or other fruits |
| ◕ | Attractive autumn foliage |
| ⊘ | Particularly decorative leaves |
| ⟙ | Tree with weeping habit |
| ♠ | Suitable for planting as specimen tree in lawn |
| ① | Good exhibition variety |
| ✽ | Houseplant grown primarily for its flowers |
| ✳ | Vegetable or fruit recommended for freezing |
| Ｆ | Vegetable or fruit recommended for flavour |
| ⊠ | Herbaceous plant not requiring staking |
| Ⓑ | Tree or shrub with decorative bark or twigs |
| ℻ | $F_1$ hybrid. Such seed-raised plants are usually vigorous, uniform and more disease resistant. |

# Annuals and Biennials

Annuals are plants that grow, flower, seed and die in one year, while biennials are sown and grown one year to flower, seed and die the next. Some of the flowers chosen here are perennial, but are treated as annual or biennial for the best show in the garden.

The stars on the top line of each entry indicate the hardiness.

The initials HA (hardy annual), HHA (half-hardy annual), and HB (hardy biennial) indicate the best method of treatment rather than hardiness or type of plant.

## How to grow

**HA**: Sow the seeds outside in rows where you want them to flower. If you do not know what the flower seedlings look like, mix a little fast-germinating radish seed in with the flowers. The radishes come up quickly and indicate where the flowers will follow, allowing you to hoe between rows to control weeds. Some varieties (indicated by an 'A' in brackets) can be sown in September and overwintered in the garden to produce larger plants that

**HOW TO SOW HARDY ANNUALS**

Break the soil down finely, using a fork or garden rake.

Take out a drill with a hoe or trowel, using a garden line.

Roll seeds through the thumb and forefinger to sow evenly.

Use the feet to shuffle the soil back into the drill.

will flower earlier and have more and larger blooms. Where cloche protection is given overwinter, the results will be even better. Sow in rows the same distance apart as the spread. Larger kinds are better thinned to a distance half of the listed spread. They will then completely cover the soil, hiding the rows.

**HHA**: Sow in seed compost indoors and raise in warmth. Once well up the seedlings can be spaced out singly in pots or seed-boxes filled with potting compost and planted out when well established (8–10cm/3–4in high) and, for the very tender kinds, after any risk of frost. Most summer bedding plants are produced in this way.

**HB**: Sow outside in early summer, transplant to produce bushy plants, and transplant again into the flowering position in the autumn. Space the distance apart indicated by the spread dimension.

### Possible difficulties

While the seeds sold will produce flowers quite as attractive as the picture on the packet, incorrect cultural treatment can bring disappointment. Hardy annuals are better sown a little later in cold springs, so that the soil has a chance to warm. This encourages quick germination and stronger growth as a result.

Half-hardy annuals also need to get away to a good start, and most need really warm germination temperatures of the order 15–20°C (60–70°F). This is especially the case for begonias, impatiens, petunias and salvias.

### What to buy, how to keep

The higher priced seed packets will contain the better quality stock and are well worth the extra money. Surplus seed of most varieties will retain germination for a year if stored in an airtight tin in a cool place.

Seed saved from $F_1$ hybrids is likely to produce plants inferior to the original strain. While many flowers can be satisfactorily raised from seed you have saved yourself, the range of colours will deteriorate over two or three years on some varieties, and new seed should be purchased periodically to retain top quality flowers.

### Bedding plants – what to look for

If heated glass is not available, and summer-flowering bedding plants have to be bought in May or June, look for even, strong-growing, compact, rich green plants. Individually pot-grown plants may be more expensive but they can be planted wider apart, will suffer no root check, flower earlier and grow larger than plants grown close together in seed trays.

### If you want to know more . . .

Most of the specialist mail order seed companies provide free colour catalogues, which have much useful information. Several open their seed trial grounds to the public and a visit can be pleasurable and informative.

**Acroclinium**   HA   LMH   O   ***
*grandiflorum*: Pink or white daisy-like 'everlasting' fls.
✂ H:45cm (1½ft) S:38cm (15in)   *Stks*: Widely available

**Ageratum**   HHA   LMH   O–◑   *
'Blue Blazer': Very early, attractive deep blue 'powderpuffs'.
⊖▣ H:10cm (4in) S:15cm (6in)   *Stks*: Widely available
'Blue Danube': Low spreading, with lavender-blue fls.
⊖▣ H:18cm (7in) S:23cm (9in)   *Stks*: SS, TM, WU
'Blue Mink': Large heads of bluish-mauve fls.
⊖ H:20cm (8in) S:20cm (8in)   *Stks*: Widely available
'Spindrift': Early, with compact heads of white fls.
⊖▣ H:13cm (5in) S:15cm (6in)   *Stks*: SS, WU

**Agrostemma**   HA   LMH   O   ***
*milas*: Graceful stems of lilac-pink 5cm (2in) fls.
✂ H:75cm (2½ft) S:45cm (1½ft)   *Stks*: Widely available

**Alyssum**   HA   LMH   O   ***
'Carpet of Snow': Makes a creeping carpet of white fls.
⊠⊖ H:10cm (4in) S:15cm (6in)   *Stks*: Widely available
'Little Dorrit': More erect than 'Carpet of Snow'.
⊠⊖ H:15cm (6in) S:15cm (6in)   *Stks*: Widely available
'Oriental Night': Vigorous growth, and deep purple fls.
⊠⊖ H:10cm (4in) S:15cm (6in)   *Stks*: Widely available
'Snow Carpet' see 'Carpet of Snow'
'Wonderland': Sweetly-scented, bright deep-red fls.
⤶⊠⊖ H:7.5cm (3in) S:15cm (6in)   *Stks*: Widely available

**Amaranthus**   HA   LMH   O   ***
*caudatus* (love lies bleeding): Cascading long red tassels.
✂ H:75cm (2½ft) S:45cm (1½ft)   *Stks*: Widely available

**Anchusa**   HA(A)   LMH   O–◑   ***
*capensis* 'Blue Angel': Ultramarine-blue 'forget-me-not' fls.
H:23cm (9in) S:20cm (8in)   *Stks*: Widely available

**Antirrhinum** (snapdragon)   HHA(A)   LMH   O–◑   ***
'Coronette mixed': Clusters of lateral spikes. Mixed.
▣ H:25cm (10in) S:20cm (8in)   *Stks*: Widely available
'Little Darling': Wide colour range of freesia-like fls.
✂▣ H:30cm (1ft) S:20cm (8in)   *Stks*: Widely available
'Madame Butterfly': Double, azalea-like, florets. Mixed.
✂▣ H:60cm (2ft) S:30cm (1ft)   *Stks*: Widely available
'Regal Rust Resistant Mixed': Uniform habit, ideal bedder.
▣ H:45cm (1½ft) S:30cm (1ft)   *Stks*: Widely available

**Arctotis** (African daisy)   HHA   LMH   O   *
'Large-flowered Hybrids': Large, bright 'daisies'. Mixed.
✂ H:45cm (1½ft) S:30cm (1ft)   *Stks*: Widely available

**Aster**   HHA/HA   LMH   O–◑   **
'Duchess Mixed': Like incurving chrysanthemums.
✂ H:45cm (1½ft) S:30cm (1ft)   *Stks*: Widely available
'Milady': Weather-resistant, incurved fls. Mixed colours.
⊖ H:30cm (1ft) S:25cm (10in)   *Stks*: Widely available
'Pepite Mixed': Mounds of semi-double fls. in mixed colours.
H:30cm (1ft) S:25cm (10in)   *Stks*: Widely available
'Pinocchio Mixed': Compact. Small double fls. Mixed colours.
H:25cm (10in) S:20cm (8in)   *Stks*: Widely available
'Powder Puffs': 'Powderpuff'-like fls. Wilt-resistant. Mixed.
✂ H:45cm (1½ft) S:30cm (1ft)   *Stks*: DB, SS

---

**SOME ASTER TYPES**

'Duchess'

'Super Sinensis'

'Pepite'

---

'Princess Giant': Crested centre with plain petals. Mixed.
✕ H:75cm (2½ft) S:30cm (1ft)   *Stks:* GP, SS, WJ

'Super Princess': Quilled, weather-resistant fls. Mixed.
✕ H:60cm (2ft) S:30cm (1ft)   *Stks:* Widely available

'Super Sinensis': Single, wilt-resistant, mixed colours.
✕ H:60cm (2ft) S:30cm (1ft)   *Stks:* SS, WU

**Bartonia**    HA    LMH    ○    ***
*aurea*: Large, single, bright yellow fls.
H:45cm (1½ft) S:30cm (1ft)   *Stks:* Widely available

**Begonia**    HHA    LMH(P)    ○–●    *
'Non-stop Mixed' (tuberous): Many double fls. Bright colours.
▣ H:25cm (10in) S:30cm (1ft)   *Stks:* DB, TB, WU

*semperflorens* 'Cocktail': Deep bronze lvs. Many colours.
◒▣ H:20cm (8in) S:20cm (8in)   *Stks:* Widely available

*semperflorens* 'Danica': Bronze lvs. Large rose or red fls.
◒▣ H:30cm (1ft) S:25cm (10in)   *Stks:* Widely available

*semperflorens* 'Organdy': Neat plants. Mixed.
◒▣ H:15cm (6in) S:15cm (6in)   *Stks:* Widely available

**Bellis** (double daisy)    HB    LMH    ○–◑    ***
*perennis* 'Giant Double Super Monstrosa': Large, double fls.
◒ H:15cm (6in) S:18cm (7in)   *Stks:* SS, TB, WJ

*perennis* 'Pomponette': Small button-type, red, rose, white.
◒ H:10cm (4in) S:18cm (7in)   *Stks:* Widely available

**Calendula** (pot marigold)    HA(A)    LMH    ○–◑    ***
'Art Shades Mixed': Lovely colour range – yellow, cream, pink.
✕ H:60cm (2ft) S:30cm (1ft)   *Stks:* Widely available

'Family Circle': Compact, good colour range.
◒ H:20cm (8in) S:25cm (10in)   *Stks:* GP

'Fiesta Gitana': Compact, creamy-yellow to deep orange.
◒ H:20cm (8in) S:25cm (10in)   *Stks:* Widely available

'Geisha Girl': Incurving, with attractive orange fls.
✕ H:45cm (1½ft) S:30cm (1ft)   *Stks:* SS, TB, TM

'Gipsy Festival' see 'Fiesta Gitana'

'Orange King': Very large, double, orange fls.
✕ H:38cm (15in) S:30cm (1ft)   *Stks:* Widely available

'Radio': Quilled petals on fully double orange fls.
✕ H:60cm (2ft) S:30cm (1ft)   *Stks:* DB, SS, TB

**Calceolaria** (slipper flower)    HHA    LMH    ○    **
*rugosa* 'Sunshine': Yellow pouched fls. May overwinter.
◒▣ H:30cm (1ft) S:25cm (10in)   *Stks:* Widely available

**Campanula**    HB    LMH    ○–◑    ***
*calycanthema* 'Cup and Saucer Mixed': Pinks, mauves, blues.
H:75cm (2½ft) S:45cm (1½ft)   *Stks:* Widely available

**Candytuft**   HA(A)   LMH   O–◑   ***

'Fairy Mixed': Compact. White, pink and red to mauve.
H:20cm (8in) S:20cm (8in)   Stks: Widely available

'Giant Hyacinth-flowered': Hyacinth-like spikes. White.
🌱✂H:30cm (1ft) S:25cm (10in)   Stks: DB, TB, SS

'Red Flash': A really dazzling shade of crimson-carmine.
H:30cm (1ft) S:20cm (8in)   Stks: Widely available

**Celosia**   HHA   LM   O–◑   *

cristata (cockscomb): Crested heads in red, orange or yellow.
H:30cm (1ft) S:23cm (9in)   Stks: Widely available

plumosa: Feathery plumes of fls, July–Aug.
H:45cm (1½ft) S:30cm (1ft)   Stks: Widely available

**Centaurea** (cornflower)   HA(A)   LMH   O–◑   ***

cyanus 'Blue Diadem': Large, double, deep blue fls.
✂H:90cm (3ft) S:45cm (1½ft)   Stks: Widely available

cyanus 'Polka Dot Mixed': Bushy plants. Good colour range.
H:30cm (1ft) S:25cm (10in)   Stks: Widely available

cyanus 'Tall Double Mixed': Wide range of colours.
✂H:90cm (3ft) S:45cm (1½ft)   Stks: Widely available

**Cheiranthus**   HB   LMH   O–◑   ***

allionii (Siberian wallflower): Orange, wallflower-like fls.
🌱H:30cm (1ft) S:25cm (10in)   Stks: Widely available

cheiri see Wallflower

**Chrysanthemum**   HA   LMH   O   ***

'Court Jesters': Very bright colour range, many boldly zoned.
✂H:45cm (1½ft) S:30cm (1ft)   Stks: DB, TM

'Double Mixed': Bronze-yellow, edged other colours.
✂H:60cm (2ft) S:30cm (1ft)   Stks: SS, TB, WU

'Merry Mixed': Attractive single fls, multi-coloured.
✂H:75cm (2½ft) S:45cm (1½ft)   Stks: GP, TB

**Clarkia**   HA   LMH   O   ***

elegans 'Double Mixed': Slender stems of pink or red fls.
✂H:60cm (2ft) S:30cm (1ft)   Stks: Widely available

**Cleome** (spider flower)   HHA   LMH   O   *

'Rose Queen': Large clusters of spider-like pink fls.
H:75cm (2½ft) S:45cm (1½ft)   Stks: DB, SS, TB

**Convolvulus**   HA   LMH   O–◑   ***

minor 'Blue Flash': Blue and white flowers, yellow centres.
H:25cm (10in) S:20cm (8in)   Stks: Widely available

minor 'Royal Ensign': Ultra-marine fls with gold centres.
H:38cm (15in) S:30cm (1ft)   Stks: Widely available

**Coreopsis** (calliopsis)   HA   LMH   O   ***

'Sunray': Delightful double, yellow, rayed fls.
H:45cm (1½ft) S:30cm (1ft)   Stks: Widely available

**Cosmea** (cosmos)   HHA   LMH   O–◑   *

'Sensation Mixed': Pink or white fls like single dahlias.
H:90cm (3ft) S:45cm (1½ft)   Stks: Widely available

**Dahlia**   HHA (tubers will over winter)   LMH   O   *

'Coltness Hybrids': Dwarf, compact. Large single fls.
H:45cm (1½ft) S:30cm (1ft)   Stks: Widely available

'Dandy': Distinctive 'collarette' petal formation. Mixed.
H:60cm (2ft) S:30cm (1ft)   Stks: Widely available

'Redskin': Bronze lvs, double or semi-double fls. Mixed.
H:45cm (1½ft) S:30cm (1ft)   Stks: Widely available

'Rigoletto': Double fls in a range of very bright colours.
H:38cm (15in) S:30cm (1ft)   Stks: Widely available

**Dianthus** (carnation/pink)   HHA   LMH(C)   ○   ***
'Knight' series: Carnations in range of colours.
🌱✕▣ H:30cm (1ft) S:30cm (1ft)   *Stks*: WJ, WU

'Magic Charms': Single, serrated fls in bright colours.
▣ H:15cm (6in) S:15cm (6in)   *Stks*: Widely available

'Queens Court': Single fls in a wide range of bright colours.
▣ H:20cm (8in) S:20cm (8in)   *Stks*: DB, SS, WU

'Snow Fire': Large, single white fls with scarlet centres.
🏵▣ H:20cm (8in) S:18cm (7in)   *Stks*: TM, WU

**Digitalis** (foxglove)   HB   LMH   ○–●   ***
'Excelsior Hybrids': Tall spikes, fls surrounding the stem.
H:1.5m (5ft) S:45cm (1½ft)   *Stks*: Widely available

'Foxy': Dwarf foxgloves. Can also be treated as HHA.
H:90cm (3ft) S:45cm (1½ft)   *Stks*: Widely available

**Dimorphotheca**   HA   LMH   ○   *
*aurantiaca* hybrids: Bright daisy-like fls in various shades.
✕ H:30cm (1ft) S:25cm (10in)   *Stks*: Widely available

**Echium**   HA(A)   LMH   ○   ***
'Dwarf Hybrids': Mixture of blue, rose, lavender and white.
H:30cm (1ft) S:23cm (9in)   *Stks*: Widely available

**Eschscholzia** (Californian poppy)   HA(A)   LMH   ○   ***
'Art Shades': Semi-double, frilled, in a range of colours.
H:30cm (1ft) S:20cm (8in)   *Stks*: Widely available

'Ballerina': Fluted fls, in a brilliant range of colours.
H:25cm (10in) S:20cm (8in)   *Stks*: Widely available

**Gazania**   HHA (can be over wintered)   LMH   ○   *
'Hybrids Mixed': Daisy-like fls with contrasting zones.
H:30cm (1ft) S:30cm (1ft)   *Stks*: Widely available

**Geranium**   see page 84

**Godetia**   HA(A)   LMH   ○   ***
'Dwarf Double': Double fls in various shades, some striped.
H:25cm (10in) S:20cm (8in)   *Stks*: SM, TB

'Sybil Sherwood': Salmon-pink, with a delicate white border.
✕ H:60cm (2ft) S:30cm (1ft)   *Stks*: Widely available

'Tall Double': Double fls in a range of colours.
✕ H:60cm (2ft) S:30cm (1ft)   *Stks*: Widely available

---

**ORNAMENTAL GRASSES**

**Briza**   HA   LMH   ○   ***
*maxima*: Long, nodding spikes of green and white.
✕ H:45cm (1½ft) S:30cm (1ft)   *Stks*: Widely available

**Hordeum**   HA   LMH   ○   ***
*jubatum*: Silky, long-haired barley-like tassels.
✕ H:45cm (1½ft) S:30cm (1ft)   *Stks*: Widely available

**Lagurus**   HA   LMH   ○   ***
*ovatus*: Soft, woolly plumes carried on long stems.
✕ H:45cm (1½ft) S:30cm (1ft)   *Stks*: Widely available

**Setaria**   HA   LMH   ○   ***
*italica*: Large, graceful, nodding, green fl heads.
✕ H:45cm (1½ft) S:30cm (1ft)   *Stks*: DB, SS, TM

**Tricholaena**   HA   LMH   ○   ***
*rosea*: Long stems bearing fluffy, brown spikelets.
✕ H:45cm (1½ft) S:30cm (1ft)   *Stks*: Widely available

---

**Gypsophila**    HA(A)    LMH    ○    ***
*elegans* 'Covent Garden': Dainty sprays of large white fls.
✄ H:45cm (1½ft) S:38cm (15in)    *Stks*: Widely available

**Helichrysum** (Immortelle)    HA    LMH    ○    ***
'Bright Bikini': Low-growing and very free-flowering.
✄ H:30cm (1ft) S:25cm (10in)    *Stks*: Widely available
'Monstrosum': Colourful double 'everlasting' fls.
✄ H:90cm (3ft) S:45cm (1½ft)    *Stks*: Widely available
'Spangle Mixed': 'Everlasting' fls in many bright colours.
✄ H:30cm (1ft) S:30cm (1ft)    *Stks*: GP, WU

**Hibiscus**    HA    LMH    ○–◑    ***
*trionum*: Creamy-primrose fls, with a purple-black 'eye'.
H:38cm (15in) S:38cm (15in)    *Stks*: DB, SS, TB

**Impatiens**    HHA    LMH(P)    ○–◑
*(Can be over wintered in pots indoors)*
'Futura Mixed': Free-flowering. Fls in a wide colour range.
☺▣ H:23cm (9in) S:23cm (9in)    *Stks*: SS, TM, WU
'Imp': Large fls, in many delicate shades.
☺▣ H:23cm (9in) S:23cm (9in)    *Stks*: DB, SM, WU
'Zig-Zag': Attractive, large bi-coloured fls.
☺▣ H:15cm (6in) S:23cm (9in)    *Stks*: Widely available

**Ipomoea** (morning glory)    HHA    LMH    ○    *
'Heavenly Blue': Large sky-blue fls like open trumpets.
Climber.    *Stks*: Widely available
*rubrocoerulea* see 'Heavenly Blue'

**Kochia** (burning bush)    HHA    LMH    ○–◑    **
*trichophylla*: Oval green 'bushes' turning bronze/red.
H:60cm (2ft) S:30cm (1ft)    *Stks*: Widely available

**Larkspur**    HA(A)    LMH    ○–◑    ***
'Giant Imperial': Tall spikes of delphinium-like fls.
✄ H:1.2m (4ft) S:45cm (1½ft)    *Stks*: Widely available
'Hyacinth Flowered': Tall and short types. Dense fl spikes.
✄ H:30–75cm (1–2½ft) S:30–45cm (1–1½ft)    *Stks*: Wdly avail.
'Stock Flowered': Branching, dense spikes of stock-like fls.
✄ H:90cm (3ft) S:45cm (1½ft)    *Stks*: TB, WU

**Lavatera** (mallow)    HA(A)    LMH    ○–◑    ***
'Mont Blanc': Small bushes covered with pure white fls.
✄ H:60cm (2ft) S:38cm (15in)    *Stks*: Widely available
'Silver Cup': Rose-pink, shaded with scarlet and silver.
✄ H:75cm (2½ft) S:45cm (1½ft)    *Stks*: Widely available

**Leptosiphon**    HA    LMH    ○    ***
*hybridus*: Masses of tiny star-shaped fls in many colours.
△ H:7.5cm (3in) S:10cm (4in)    *Stks*: DB, SS, TB

**Limnanthes**    HA(A)    LMH    ○    ***
*douglasii*: Saucer-shaped yellow fls edged with white.
△ H:15cm (6in) S:20cm (8in)    *Stks*: Widely available

**Linaria**    HA(A)    LMH    ○–◑    ***
'Fairy Bouquet': Dainty spikes of small snapdragon-like fls.
△ H:15cm (6in) S:20cm (8in)    *Stks*: Widely available

**Linum** (flax)    HA    LMH    ○–◑    ***
*grandiflorum rubrum*: Brilliant crimson-scarlet fls.
H:38cm (15in) S:30cm (1ft)    *Stks*: Widely available

**Lobelia**    HHA    LMH    ○–◑    *
'Blue Cascade': Tumbling fls in shades of Cambridge blue.
☺ H:Trailing    *Stks*: Widely available

'Cambridge Blue': Soft, azure-blue fls on neat plants.
☻ H:15cm (6in) S:20cm (8in)   *Stks*: Widely available

'Crystal Palace': Rich, deep blue fls and bronze lvs.
☻ H:10cm (4in) S:15cm (6in)   *Stks*: Widely available

'Red Cascade': Rosy-red, white-eyed fls.
☻ H:Trailing   *Stks*: Widely available

'Rosamond': White-eyed, wine-red fls. Very neat plants.
☻ H:15cm (6in) S:20cm (8in)   *Stks*: Widely available

'String of Pearls': Light and dark blue, white, or carmine fls.
☻ H:10cm (4in) S:15cm (6in)   *Stks*: Widely available

**Lunaria** (honesty)   HB   LMH   ◑   ***
'Mixed': Purple or white fls. Seed pods used for decoration.
✕ H:60cm (2ft) S:30cm (1ft)   *Stks*: Widely available

'Purple': Purple fls, attractive silvery seed pods.
✕ H:60cm (2ft) S:30cm (1ft)   *Stks*: DB, TB, TM

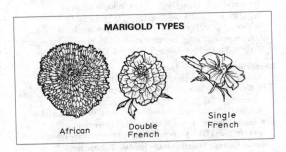

**MARIGOLD TYPES**

African     Double French     Single French

**Marigold (African)**   HHA   LMH   ○   *
'Climax': Available in mixed and separate colours.
▣ H:90cm (3ft) S:45cm (1½ft)   *Stks*: DB, SS, TB

'Gay Ladies Mixed': Compact. Early and very free-flowering.
☻▣ H:38cm (15in) S:30cm (1ft)   *Stks*: DB, SM, WU

'Jubilee Hybrids': Densely foliated hedge-type plants.
▣ H:60cm (2ft) S:30cm (1ft)   *Stks*: Widely available

**Marigold (African-French hybrids)**   HHA   LMH   ○   *
'Nell Gwynn': Single fls, bright golden-yellow with red centre.
▣ H:30cm (1ft) S:25cm (10in)   *Stks*: DB, SS, WU

**Marigold (French)**   HHA   LMH   ○   *
'Goldfinch': Large gold fls. Dark green lvs. Floriferous.
☻ H:25cm (10in) S:25cm (10in)   *Stks*: DB, SS, WU

'Honeycomb': Crested fls, marked with gold and brown.
☻ H:20cm (8in) S:25cm (10in)   *Stks*: Widely available

'Queen Bee': Attractive fls, brownish-red and yellow.
☻ H:25cm (10in) S:20cm (8in)   *Stks*: SS, WU

**Marigold (French, Dwarf Double)**   HHA   LMH   ○   *
'Boy-O-Boy Mixed': Tight, double fls in several shades.
☻ H:15cm (6in) S:20cm (8in)   *Stks*: Widely available

'Bolero': Bright, mahogany-red fls with gold markings.
☻ H:15cm (6in) S:20cm (8in)   *Stks*: Widely available

**Marigold (French, Single)**   HHA   LMH   ○   *
'Dainty Marietta': Compact plants. Yellow, crimson blotches.
☻ H:15cm (6in) S:15cm (6in)   *Stks*: DB, SS, WU

'Naughty Marietta': Golden fls with crimson blotches.
☻ H:30cm (1ft) S:30cm (1ft)   *Stks*: Widely available

**Matthiola**   HA   LMH   ○   ***
*bicornis* (night-scented stock): Small, lilac fls, open at night.
🌱 H:30cm (1ft) S:20cm (8in)   *Stks*: Widely available

**Mesembryanthemum**   HHA   LMH   ○   *
*criniflorum*: Large daisy-like fls, in various gay colours.
△ H:15cm (6in) S:15cm (6in)   *Stks*: Widely available

**Mimulus** (monkey flower)   HHA   LMH(M)   ○–●   ***
'Royal Velvet': Velvety, red fls, yellow throats spotted red.
🔲 H:25cm (10in) S:20cm (8in)   *Stks*: SS, WU

**Molucella** (bells of Ireland)   HA   LMH   ○–◖   **
*laevis*: Graceful stems covered with green funnel-shaped fls.
H:90cm (3ft) S:45cm (1½ft)   *Stks*: Widely available

**Myosotis** (forget-me-not)   HB   LMH   ○–◖   ***
'Blue Ball': Compact and ball-shaped. Bright indigo-blue fls.
H:15cm (6in) S:18cm (7in)   *Stks*: Widely available
'Royal Blue': Early flowering. Large, bright blue fls.
H:30cm (1ft) S:25cm (10in)   *Stks*: Widely available
'Ultramarine': Deep, ultramarine-blue fls. Neat and compact.
H:15cm (6in) S:18cm (7in)   *Stks*: DB, GP, TB

**Nasturtium**   HA   LMH   ○   **
'Alaska': Variegated lvs. Fls in many different colours.
H:30cm (1ft) S:30cm (1ft)   *Stks*: Widely available
'Climbing' ('Tall'): Full range of colours.
H:1.8m (6ft) S:60cm (2ft) (trailing)   *Stks*: Widely available
'Gleam Hybrids': Vigorous mixture of bright fls.
🌱◗ H:38cm (15in) S:38cm (15in)   *Stks*: Widely available
'Jewel Mixed': Mixed colours held well above lvs.
H:20cm (8in) S:25cm (10in)   *Stks*: Widely available
'Red Roulette': Fiery orange-red spurless fls, clear of lvs.
🌱◗ H:25cm (10in) S:25cm (10in)   *Stks*: Widely available

**Nemesia**   HHA   LMH   ○–◖   *
'Carnival': Large, weather-resistant fls in various colours.
◗ H:18cm (7in) S:15cm (6in)   *Stks*: Widely available

**Nigella** (love-in-a-mist)   HA(A)   LMH   ○–◖   ***
'Miss Jekyll': Clear cornflower-blue fls amid feathery lvs.
✄ H:45cm (1½ft) S:30cm (1ft)   *Stks*: Widely available
'Persian Jewels': Mixed colours – blue, rose, pink, white.
✄ H:45cm (1½ft) S:30cm (1ft)   *Stks*: Widely available

**Pansy**   HP   LMH   ○–◖   ***
'Clear Crystals Mixed': Medium-sized fls with clear colours.
◗ H:23cm (9in) S:23cm (9in)   *Stks*: Widely available
'Majestic Giants': Saucer-sized fls, in a mixture of colours
◗🔲 H:23cm (9in) S:23cm (9in)   *Stks*: Widely available
'Roggli Giant Mixed': Large fls. Mixed colours; good reds.
◗ H:20cm (8in) S:20cm (8in)   *Stks*: DB, SS, TM
'Sunny Boy': Huge, golden-yellow fls with dark blotches.
◗🔲 H:20cm (8in) S:20cm (8in)   *Stks*: DB, WU

**Papaver** (poppy)   HA(A)   LMH   ○–◖   ***
'Champagne Bubbles'(†): Iceland type, with large fls. Mixed.
🔲 H:60cm (2ft) S:30cm (1ft)   *Stks*: DB, TM, WU
'Paeony-flowered Double': Double poppies. Brilliant colours.
H:90cm (3ft) S:45cm (1½ft)   *Stks*: Widely available
'San Remo'(†): A large-flowered Iceland poppy; many colours.
✄ H:60cm (2ft) S:30cm (1ft)   *Stks*: SS

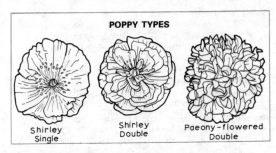

**POPPY TYPES**

Shirley
Single

Shirley
Double

Paeony-flowered
Double

'Shirley Double Mixed': Double poppies in many shades.
H:75cm (2½ft) S:60cm (2ft)    *Stks*: Widely available

'Shirley Single Mixed': Single poppies in pastel shades.
H:75cm (2½ft) S:60cm (2ft)    *Stks*: SS, TB

†: Really perennial, but best treated as biennial sown April to
August and given cloche protection over winter. The other
varieties listed can also be sown in late August or September,
but cloche protection is not so necessary.

**Petunia**    HHA    LMH    ○    *
### Double Grandiflora
'Pan American Double': Large double fls. Mixed.
❄☂▣ H:30cm (1ft) S:30cm (1ft)    *Stks*: GP, TB
### Double Multiflora
'Cherry Tart': Small double fls. Rose-pink with white.
❄☂▣ H:30cm (1ft) S:30cm (1ft)    *Stks*: Widely available
'Honeybunch': Clear salmon small double fls.
❄☂▣ H:30cm (1ft) S:30cm (1ft)    *Stks*: GP
### Grandiflora Single
'Blue Frost': Violet-blue fls with pure white edge.
☂▣ H:30cm (1ft) S:25cm (10in)    *Stks*: SS, WU
'Cascade Mixed': Early and free-flowering. Large fls.
☂▣ H:30cm (1ft) S:25cm (10in)    *Stks*: Widely available
### Multiflora
'Resisto Mixed': Bedding petunias to stand up to bad weather.
▣ H:30cm (1ft) S:25cm (10in)    *Stks*: Widely available

**Phacelia**    HA(A)    LMH    ○    ***
*campanularia*: Grey lvs. Lovely blue, bell-shaped fls.
H:23cm (9in) S:23cm (9in)    *Stks*: Widely available

**Phlox**    HHA    LMH    ○    *
*drummondii* 'Beauty Mixed': Densely-packed heads of fls.
☂ H:15cm (6in) S:20cm (8in)    *Stks*: Widely available

**Polyanthus** see Primula

**Primula** (polyanthus)    HB    LMH    ○–◑    **/***
'Crescendo'(***): Large fls, brilliant range of colours.
❄☂▣ H:25cm (10in) S:25cm (10in)    *Stks*: WU
'Pacific Giants'(**): Large fls. Good colour range, incl blue.
❄✕☂ H:25cm (10in) S:25cm (10in)    *Stks*: Widely available

**Rudbeckia** (black-eyed Susan)    HHA    LMH    ○–◑    ***
'Irish Eyes': Clear, golden-yellow fls, emerald-green eyes.
✕ H:45cm (1½ft) S:30cm (1ft)    *Stks*: SS
'Marmalade': Large, brilliant golden-orange fls.
✕ H:45cm (1½ft) S:30cm (1ft)    *Stks*: Widely available
'Rustic Dwarfs': Large fls in oranges and yellows.
✕ H:60cm (2ft) S:30cm (1ft)    *Stks*: Widely available

**Salvia**    HHA/HA    LMH    ○    *

'Carabiniere' (HHA): Scarlet-red spikes over deep green lvs.
⬱ H:38cm (15in) S:30cm (1ft)    *Stks*: SS

*farinacea* 'Victoria' (HHA): Long-flowering. Violet-blue.
H:75cm (2½ft) S:45cm (1½ft)    *Stks*: Widely available

'Flarepath' (HHA): Pure scarlet fls, dark green lvs
H:23cm (9in) S:30cm (1ft)    *Stks*: TM

*horminum* 'Bouquet Mixed': (HA): Blue/pink/white bracts.
✕ H:45cm (1½ft) S:30cm (1ft)    *Stks*: Widely available

**Saponaria** (soapwort)    HA(A)    LMH    ○    ***

*vaccaria*: Gypsophila-like sprays of pink fls.
✕ H:60cm (2ft) S:30cm (1ft)    *Stks*: Widely available

**Schizanthus** (poor man's orchid)    HHA    LMH    ○–◑    **

'Dwarf Bouquet Mixed': Compact plants in many colours.
⬱ H:30cm (1ft) S:20cm (8in)    *Stks*: Widely available

'Star Parade': Very compact plants. Excellent pot plant.
⬱ H:20cm (8in) S:20cm (8in)    *Stks*: DB, SS, WU

**Statice**    HHA    LMH    ○    *

*sinuata* 'Mixed Hybrids': 'Everlasting' fls in many colours.
✕ H:45cm (1½ft) S:30cm (1ft)    *Stks*: Widely available

*suworowii*: Long, tail-like spikes of rose-pink fls.
✕ H:45cm (1½ft) S:30cm (1ft)    *Stks*: DB, TM, WU

**Stocks**    HHA/HB    LMH    ○–◑    ***

'Beauty of Nice' (HHA): Vigorous, with many flowering stems.
⬱✕ H:45cm (1½ft) S:30cm (1ft)    *Stks*: DB, TB

'Brompton' (HB): Sow June–Aug. for May fls.
⬱✕ H:38cm (15in) S:30cm (1ft)    *Stks*: Widely available

'East Lothian' (HHA/HB): Almost perpetual-flowering.
⬱✕☉ H:38cm (15in) S:30cm (1ft)    *Stks*: Widely available

'Excelsior Columns' (HA(A)): Non-branching, quality spikes.
⬱✕ H:60cm (2ft) S:45cm (1½ft)    *Stks*: Widely available

Night-scented – see Matthiola bicornis

'Ten Week' (HHA): Good colour range; branching habit.
⬱ H:30cm (1ft) S:30cm (1ft)    *Stks*: Widely available

**Sweet pea** see page 90

**Sweet William**    HB/HP    LMH(C)    ○–◑    ***

'Auricula-eyed Mixed': Circles of different colours on each fl.
⬱✕ H:45cm (1½ft) S:30cm (1ft)    *Stks*: Widely available

'Indian Carpet': Compact, useful for bedding and edging.
⬱ H:15cm (6in) S:20cm (8in)    *Stks*: Widely available

**Tagetes**    HHA    LMH    ○    *

*signata* 'Golden Gem': Bushy plants, thickly studded with fls.
⬱ H:20cm (8in) S:15cm (6in)    *Stks*: Widely available

*signata* 'Lemon Gem': Bushy plants forming neat domes.
⬱ H:20cm (8in) S:15cm (6in)    *Stks*: Widely available

*signata* 'Paprika': Compact plants, crimson-red fls.
⬱ H:15cm (6in) S:15cm (6in)    *Stks*: Widely available

*signata* 'Tangerine Gem': Neat, bushy plants. Well-formed fls.
⬱ H:20cm (8in) S:15cm (6in)    *Stks*: Widely available

**Verbena**    HHA    LMH    ○    *

'Sparkle Mixed': Compact plants, free-flowering.
⬱ H:20cm (8in) S:20cm (8in)    *Stks*: Widely available

**Viola**    HB    LMH    ○–◑    ***

'Blue Heaven': Low-growing, with superb mid-blue fls.
⬱ H:15cm (6in) S:15cm (6in)    *Stks*: GP, SS, TM

'Large-flowered Mixed': Free-flowering, mostly self-colours.
❤ H:15cm (6in) S:15cm (6in)    *Stks*: Widely available

**Viscaria**    HA    LMH    O    ***
'Blue Angel': Dwarf and compact. Delightful azure-blue fls.
H:25cm (10in) S:20cm (8in)    *Stks*: DB

**Wallflowers**    HB    LMH(C)    O–◑    ***
'Blood Red': Very beautiful velvety-crimson fls.
🌱✕ H:45cm (1½ft) S:30cm (1ft)    *Stks*: Widely available
'Cloth of Gold': Large bright golden-yellow blooms.
🌱✕ H:45cm (1½ft) S:30cm (1ft)    *Stks*: Widely available
'Fair Lady Mixed': Excellent mixture. Very uniform.
🌱 H:30cm (1ft) S:25cm (10in)    *Stks*: Widely available
'Fire King': A striking shade of brilliant orange-red.
🌱✕ H:45cm (1½ft) S:30cm (1ft)    *Stks*: Widely available
'Scarlet Bedder': Compact plants. Bright crimson-scarlet fls.
🌱 H:30cm (1ft) S:25cm (10in)    *Stks*: Widely available

**Xeranthemum**    HA    LMH    O    ***
'Double Mixed': Everlasting-type fls in various shades.
✕ H:60cm (2ft) S:45cm (1½ft)    *Stks*: Widely available

**Zinnia**    HHA    LMH    O    *
'Cut and Come Again': Medium-sized double fls. Mixed.
🌱 H:38cm (15in) S:30cm (1ft)    *Stks*: SS
'Envy': Large green double or semi-double fls.
✕ H:60cm (2ft) S:45cm (1½ft)    *Stks*: Widely available
'Lilliput Mixed': Neat, button-like double fls.
✕ H:25cm (10in) S:30cm (1ft)    *Stks*: GP, SS, TB
'Persian Carpet': Double and semi-double, many bicoloured.
H:30cm (1ft) S:25cm (10in)    *Stks*: Widely available
'Peter Pan': Large, fully double fls, in many different colours.
❤▣ H:30cm (1ft) S:30cm (1ft)    *Stks*: Widely available
'Ruffles': Fully double fls on stiff stems, in many shades.
✕▣ H:60cm (2ft) S:45cm (1½ft)    *Stks*: DB, SS, TB

---

## SPECIALIST SUPPLIERS

**DB**    Samuel Dobie & Son Ltd., Upper Dee Mills,
Llangollen, Clwyd, LL20 8SD. Tel: (0978) 860119.

**GP**    'Garden Pride' (Hurst Gunson Cooper Taber Ltd.),
Witham, Essex, CM8 2DX. Tel: Witham 516600.

**SM**    S. E. Marshall & Co. Ltd., Regal Road, Wisbech,
Cambs., PE13 2RF. Tel: Wisbech 3407.

**SS**    Suttons Seeds Ltd., Hele Road, Torquay, Devon,
TQ2 7QJ. Tel: Torquay (0803) 62011.

**TB**    Thomas Butcher Ltd., 60 Wickham Road, Shirley,
Croydon, Surrey, CR9 8AG. Tel: 01–654 3720.

**TM**    Thompson & Morgan Ltd., London Road, Ipswich,
Suffolk, IP2 0BA.

**WJ**    W. W. Johnson & Son Ltd., Boston, Lincolnshire,
PE21 8AD.

**WU**    W. J. Unwin Ltd., Histon, Cambridge, CB4 4LE.
Tel: Histon (022 023) 2270.

**Important:** 'Garden Pride' and W. W. Johnson seeds are
distributed through local shops and garden centres –
they are not available by mail order. However, in cases of
difficulty the companies will be able to tell you the
nearest stockist.

*For key to symbols, see page 7*

# Border Plants

Flowering plants that are perennial but as a general rule die down to ground level in winter, and completely renew above-ground growth each year, are called herbaceous plants, hardy perennials or hardy border flowers. Whatever name one chooses, they are the backbone of many flower gardens.

By choosing varieties carefully it is possible to have attractive flowers, foliage and seed heads virtually the year round. Many kinds flower for weeks and are also suitable for cutting to arrange in water.

Recent plant breeding work has produced varieties with shorter and stouter stems which stand up against wind and rain without stakes and ties. There are kinds to suit every soil and every situation but careful soil preparation will extend the life of any planting, and will also encourage much better growth and flowers. Avoid planting in soils which have perennial weed roots because such weeds are difficult to remove once the flowers are established.

## Where to grow

The traditional herbaceous border is a long narrow bed or pair of parallel borders backed by neatly clipped hedges, but these need a fairly large garden and absorb much time in keeping them weedfree and tidy. If you plant in this way, plant the bed with a narrow grass path between hedge and border to prevent undue competition between plants and hedge. Arrange the taller plants to the back and low-growing ones to the front of the border.

Island beds, introduced by Alan Bloom, have herbaceous plantings to view from all sides, with taller subjects to the middle. Try to group together plants that flower at different times and have contrasting foliage.

Consider too the strength of growth; try to group the stronger growing, more vigorous types like *Chrysanthemum maximum* and *Geranium* 'Johnson's Blue' together. Then they will not smother slower-growing and slower-spreading plants.

A number of early-flowering plants like delphiniums and lupins will produce a second, later flush of autumn flowers if the dead heads are cut off immediately after flowering and the plants well watered and fed.

Hardy border flowers can of course be mixed in with other flowers and shrubs; bright orange crocosmias look startling against a background of yellow spray chrysanthemums, for instance.

A few groups of spring-flowering daffodils and summer-flowering dahlias, gladioli and lilies will give added colour to flower borders.

Spread figures indicate the planting distances for each

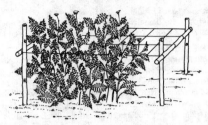

*An effective way to stake border plants if bushy sticks are not available. Large-mesh polythene netting is tied to stakes at about 60cm (2ft) above the ground. It can be raised as the plants grow, and will soon be hidden.*

kind, but allow a little more space around each group of a kind. In all but the smallest flower beds at least three plants of each variety should be planted.

**What to buy**

Large gardens can be inexpensively filled with seed-raised plants of quite a range of varieties. Where you do this it is important to keep raising new seedlings and ruthlessly select out the better quality plants from the point of flower quality and plant habit.

It is safer in smaller gardens where space is precious to buy only the best named varieties which have been selected out over a number of years by experienced herbaceous plant nurserymen and gardeners. Only plant vigorous, strong young plants, free from pests, diseases and perennial weed roots. It is easy to select such stock when seen growing in containers but if dormant root divisions are bought it is advisable to purchase from specialist companies with a reputation for supplying good stock, accurately named.

Cheaper priced plants in small (9cm/3½in) containers with no more than the generic name (e.g. Scabious) are likely to be seed-raised and a poor buy compared with vegetatively propagated named varieties (e.g. *Scabiosa* 'Clive Greaves').

Freshly potted herbaceous plants in containers carry the extra cost of container and compost without the advantages of an established root system. Where the plants are not well rooted in the pots in early spring, plants with roots wrapped in damp peat are usually cheaper and an equally good buy.

A sure sign of a well-rooted container plant is a little root coming through the drainage hole in the base and a little mossy algae growth on the surface. Avoid plants with excessive roots through the drainage hole.

**If you want to know more . . .**

Two useful books are: *Perennial Garden Plants*, by Graham Thomas (J. M. Dent and Sons Ltd.) and *Perennials for your Garden*, by Alan Bloom (Floraprint Ltd.)

21

**Acanthus** (bear's breeches)     LM(M)     ○–◑     \*\*\*
  *spinosus*: Bold, mauve-purple spikes of fls, July–Sept.
  ✂ ⊠ H:1.2m (4ft) S:60cm (2ft)     *Stks*: Widely available

**Achillea** (yarrow)     LM(C)     ○     \*\*\*
  'Gold Plate': Flat, yellow heads, June–Sept. Can be dried.
  ✂ H:1.5m (5ft) S:75cm (2½ft)     *Stks*: BG, KN, SD
  'Moonshine': Silvery lvs. Light yellow fls, June–Aug.
  ✂ ⊠ H:60cm (2ft) S:45cm (1½ft)     *Stks*: Widely available
  *ptarmica* 'The Pearl': White, button-like fls, June–Aug.
  ✂ H:75cm (2½ft) S:60cm (2ft)     *Stks*: Widely available

**Aconitum** (monkshood)     LMH(M,P)     ◑     \*\*\*
  'Bressingham Spire': Tapering violet-blue spires, July–Aug.
  ⊠ H:90cm (3ft) S:60cm (2ft)     *Stks*: Widely available

**Agapanthus** (African lily)     LMH     ○     \*\*
  'Headbourne Hybrids': Blue, trumpet-shaped fls, July–Aug.
  ⊖ ✂ ⊠ H:90cm (3ft) S:75cm (2½ft)     *Stks*: Widely available

**Alchemilla** (lady's mantle)     LMH     ○–◑     \*\*\*
  *mollis*: Sprays of sulphur-yellow fls, June–Aug.
  ≈ ✂ ⊠ H:45cm (1½ft) S:30cm (1ft)     *Stks*: Widely available

**Alstroemeria** (Peruvian lily)     LM(P)     ○     \*\*
  'Ligtu Hybrids': Lily-like fls in pastel shades, June–Aug.
  ✂ ⊠ H:75cm (2½ft) S:30cm (1ft)     *Stks*: BG, KN

**Anaphalis**     LM     ○–◑     \*\*\*
  *triplinervis* 'Summer Snow': Grey lvs, white fls, July–Sept.
  ≈ ✂ ⊠ H:30cm (1ft) S:30cm (1ft)     *Stks*: BC, BG, KN
  *yedoensis*: Silvery lvs. 'Everlasting' white fls, Aug.–Oct.
  ✂ H:75cm (2½ft) S:45cm (1½ft)     *Stks*: BC, BG, KN

**Anchusa**     LM     ○–◑     \*\*\*
  'Loddon Royalist': Brilliant, rich blue fls, May–July.
  H:90cm (3ft) S:60cm (2ft)     *Stks*: Widely available

**Anemone** (Japanese anemone)     LM(M)     ○–◑     \*\*\*
  *hupehensis* 'September Charm': Pink, single fls, Aug.–Oct.
  ⊠ H:60cm (2ft) S:45cm (1½ft)     *Stks*: Widely available
  *japonica* 'Bressingham Glow': Rosy-red fls, Aug.–Oct.
  ⊠ H:45cm (1½ft) S:30cm (1ft)     *Stks*: BG, NN
  *japonica* 'Queen Charlotte': Large, pure pink fls, Aug.–Oct.
  ⊠ H:60cm (2ft) S:45cm (1½ft)     *Stks*: BG, KN, SD
  *japonica* 'White Queen': Large white fls, Aug.–Oct.
  ⊠ H:1.2m (4ft) S:75cm (2½ft)     *Stks*: BG

**Aquilegia** (columbine)     LMH     ○–◑     \*\*\*
  'McKana Hybrids': Spurred fls in many colours, June–Aug.
  ⊠ H:75cm (2½ft) S:45cm (1½ft)     *Stks*: BG, KN, NN

**Armeria** (thrift)     LMH     ○     \*\*\*
  'Bee's Ruby': Round heads of ruby-red fls, June–Aug.
  ⊠ H:38cm (15in) S:30cm (1ft)     *Stks*: Widely available

**Artemisia** (wormwood)     LM     ○     \*\*\*
  *lactiflora*: Plumes of creamy-white fls, Aug.–Oct.
  ⌣ ⊠ H:1.2m (4ft) S:60cm (2ft)     *Stks*: BG, FT, KN

**Aruncus**     LMH(M)     ○–◑     \*\*\*
  *sylvester*: Leafy growth. White plumes of fls, June–July.
  ⊠ H:1.5m (5ft) S:90cm (3ft)     *Stks*: BC, BG, NN

**Asphodelus**     LM(M)     ○–◑     \*\*\*
  *luteus*: Spikes of bright yellow fls, June–Sept.
  H:90cm (3ft) S:60cm (2ft)     *Stks*: Widely available

**Aster** (Michaelmas daisy)  LMH  O–◑  ***
  *amellus frikartii*: Light lavender-blue fls, July–Oct.
  H:90cm (3ft) S:60cm (2ft)  *Stks*: BG

  *amellus frikartii* 'Pink Zenith': Clear pink fls, Aug.–Sept.
  ⊠ H:60cm (2ft) S:45cm (1½ft)  *Stks*: BC, BG

  *novi-belgii* 'Jenny': Double, violet-purple fls, Sept.–Oct.
  ⊠ H:30cm (1ft) S:30cm (1ft)  *Stks*: Widely available

  *novi-belgii* 'Lady in Blue': Semi-double blue fls, Aug.–Oct.
  ⊠ H:25cm (10in) S:23cm (9in)  *Stks*: Widely available

  *novi-belgii* 'Little Pink Beauty': Semi-double, Sept.–Oct.
  ⊠ H:38cm (15in) S:30cm (1ft)  *Stks*: BG, KN

  *novi-belgii* 'Percy Thrower': Deep blue fls, Sept.–Oct.
  H:90cm (3ft) S:45cm (1½ft)  *Stks*: BG, KN

  *novi-belgii* 'Raspberry Ripple': Double red fls, Sept.–Oct.
  H:75cm (2½ft) S:45cm (1½ft)  *Stks*: BG, KN

  *novi-belgii* 'Winston S. Churchill': Ruby fls, Sept.–Oct.
  H:75cm (2½ft) S:45cm (1½ft)  *Stks*: Widely available

**Astilbe**  LMH(M)  O–◑  ***
  'Bressingham Beauty': Long-lasting, rich pink fls, July–Aug.
  ⊠ H:90cm (3ft) S:45cm (1½ft)  *Stks*: Widely available

  'Fanal': Intense deep red plumes of fls, June–Aug.
  ⊠ H:38cm (15in) S:30cm (1ft)  *Stks*: Widely available

  'White Gloria': Dark lvs. Pure white fls, June–July.
  ⊠ H:60cm (2ft) S:45cm (1½ft)  *Stks*: BE, BG

**Astrantia**  LMH(M)  ◑–●  ***
  *major*: Vigorous growth. Pinkish-green fls, June–Aug.
  ✕⊠ H:90cm (3ft) S:60cm (2ft)  *Stks*: Widely available

**Bergenia** (elephant's ears)  LMH  O–◑  ***
  *cordifolia* 'Purpurea': Large lvs. Pink fls, April–May.
  ⏚⊠ H:25cm (10in) S:25cm (10in)  *Stks*: Widely available

**Brunnera**  MH(M)  ◑  ***
  *macrophylla* 'Variegata': Lvs variegated, flowers blue.
  ⊘⊠ H:38cm (15in) S:38cm (15in)  *Stks*: BG, KN, NN

**Caltha** (marsh marigold)  MH(M,P)  O–◑  ***
  *palustris* 'Plena': Double, yellow fls, March–May.
  ⊠ H:25cm (10in) S:20cm (8in)  *Stks*: Widely available

**Campanula**  LMH  O–◑  ***
  *glomerata* 'Superba': Clusters of violet fls, June–July.
  ⊠ H:75cm (2½ft) S:60cm (2ft)  *Stks*: Widely available

  *lactiflora*: Showers of lavender-blue bells, June–Sept.
  H:1m (3½ft) S:60cm (2ft)  *Stks*: Widely available

  *lactiflora* 'Alba': Bell-shaped white fls, June–Aug.
  H:1.2m (4ft) S:60cm (2ft)  *Stks*: BG, NN, SD

  *lactiflora* 'Loddon Anna': Flesh-pink fls, June–Aug.
  H:1.2m (4ft) S:60cm (2ft)  *Stks*: Widely available

  *persicifolia* 'Telham Beauty': Large blue fls, June–Aug.
  H:1m (3½ft) S:60cm (2ft)  *Stks*: BG, KN, NN

**Catananche** (cupid's dart)  LM  O  ***
  *caerulea*: Blue 'cornflowers' on wiry stems, June–Aug.
  ⊠ H:60cm (2ft) S:30cm (1ft)  *Stks*: Widely available

**Centaurea**  LMH  O  ***
  *dealbata* 'John Coutts': Clear pink 'cornflowers', May–Aug.
  H:60cm (2ft) S:45cm (1½ft)  *Stks*: Widely available

  *dealbata* 'Steenbergii': Silvery lvs. Deep rose fls, June–Aug.
  H:75cm (2½ft) S:45cm (1½ft)  *Stks*: BE, BG, FT

*For key to symbols, see page 7*

23

**Chrysanthemum**   LM   ○   ***
*maximum* 'H. Seibert': Large, single fls, July–Sept.
⊠ H:75cm (2½ft) S:45cm (1½ft)   Stks: BG
*maximum* 'Wirral Supreme': Double, white fls, July–Sept.
⊠ H:90cm (3ft) S:45cm (1½ft)   Stks: Widely available

**Cimicifuga**   LM(M)   ◑   ***
*cordifolia*: Slender white spikes of fls, Aug.–Oct.
H:1.2m (4ft) S:45cm (1½ft)   Stks: BG, NN

**Coreopsis** (tickseed)   LM   ○–◑   ***
*verticillata* 'Grandiflora': Starry, yellow fls, July–Sept.
⊠ H:60cm (2ft) S:45cm (1½ft)   Stks: Widely available

**Crocosmia**   LM   ○–◑   ***
'Lucifer': Brilliant, flame-red fls, June–July.
✕⊠ H:1m (3½ft) S:60cm (2ft)   Stks: BG
'Firebird': Richly coloured, flame-orange fls, July–Sept.
✕⊠ H:75cm (2½ft) S:60cm (2ft)   Stks: BG

**Delphinium** see page 88

**Dianthus**   LM(C)   ○   ***
'Doris': Rose-pink double fls, deeper centres, June–Sept.
⌇✕⊠ H:30cm (1ft) S:25cm (10in)   Stks: BG, NN
'Excelsior': Deep, rose-pink double fls, May–July.
⌇✕⊠ H:20cm (8in) S:20cm (8in)   Stks: BG, FT, KN
'Mrs. Sinkins': Double, white fls, June–July.
⌇✕⊠ H:20cm (8in) S:20cm (8in)   Stks: Widely available

**Dicentra** (bleeding heart)   LMH(P)   ○–◑   ***
*eximia*: Ferny lvs. Pinkish fls, April–June.
⊠ H:20cm (8in) S:20cm (8in)   Stks: BG
*eximia* 'Pearl Drops': Glaucous lvs. White fls, May–Oct.
⊠ H:25cm (10in) S:25cm (10in)   Stks: BG
*spectabilis*: Heart-shaped rosy-red fls, May–July.
⊠ H:60cm (2ft) S:45cm (1½ft)   Stks: Widely available
*spectabilis* 'Alba': Light green lvs. White fls, May–July.
⊠ H:45cm (1½ft) S:30cm (1ft)   Stks: BG

**Dictamnus** (burning bush)   LMH(C)   ○   ***
*fraxinella*: Beautiful erect lilac fls, June–Aug.
⊠ H:75cm (2½ft) S:45cm (1½ft)   Stks: BG, NN

**Doronicum** (leopard's bane)   MH(M)   ○–◑   ***
'Miss Mason': Single, yellow fls, April–June.
✕ H:45cm (1½ft) S:30cm (1ft)   Stks: BG, NN, SD
'Spring Beauty': Large, double golden-yellow fls, April–June.
✕ H:45cm (1½ft) S:30cm (1ft)   Stks: Widely available

**Echinacea**   LMH   ○   ***
*purpurea* 'Bressingham': Magenta-purple fls, July–Sept.
⊠ H:90cm (3ft) S:60cm (2ft)   Stks: BE, BG

---

### SOME PLANTS OF ARCHITECTURAL OR DISTINCT APPEARANCE

Acanthus spinosus
Agapanthus 'Headbourne
  Hybrids'
Bergenia cordifolia
  'Purpurea'
Cimicifuga cordifolia
Eryngium alpinum

Hosta (various)
Ligularia clivorum
Macleaya cordata
Miscanthus sinensis
  'Zebrina'
Rogersia pinnata
Stipa gigantea

---

**Echinops** (globe thistle)    LMH    O    \*\*\*
  *ritro*: Grey-green lvs. Steel-blue heads of fls, July–Aug.
  ✕⊠ H:1m (3½ft) S:60cm (2ft)    *Stks*: BG, NN, SD

**Epimedium** (barrenwort)    LMH(M)    ◑    \*\*\*
  *pinnatum colchicum*: Shield-type lvs. Yellow fls, April–May.
  ⌀✿⊠ H:25cm (10in) S:30cm (1ft)    *Stks*: BG, NN
  *rubrum*: Attractive lvs. Reddish, star-like fls, April–May.
  ⌀✿⊠ H:25cm (10in) S:30cm (1ft)    *Stks*: Widely available

**Erigeron**    LMH(M)    O    \*\*\*
  'Foerster's Liebling': Deep Pink, semi-double.
  ⊠ H:38cm (15in) S:30cm (1ft)    *Stks*: Widely available
  'Prosperity': Light-blue, semi-double rayed fls, June–Aug.
  ⊠ H:45cm (1½ft) S:30cm (1ft)    *Stks*: BG, KN
  'Rotes Meer': Semi-double, red, daisy-like fls, June–Aug.
  ⊠ H:45cm (1½ft) S:30cm (1ft)    *Stks*: BG
  'Schwarzes Meer': Lavender fls, yellow centres, June–Aug.
  ⊠ H:60cm (2ft) S:45cm (1½ft)    *Stks*: BG

**Eryngium** (sea holly)    LMH    O    \*\*\*
  *alpinum*: Attractive green lvs. Bright blue fls, June–Aug.
  ✕⊠ H:75cm (2½ft) S:45cm (1½ft)    *Stks*: BC, BG
  *tripartitum*: Branching stems of small blue fls, June–Aug.
  ✕⊠ H:1m (3½ft) S:45cm (1½ft)    *Stks*: Widely available

**Euphorbia** (spurge)    LMH    O–◑    \*\*\*
  *griffithii* 'Fireglow': Orange-red flower heads, April–May.
  ⊠ H:75cm (2½ft) S:45cm (1½ft)    *Stks*: Widely available
  *polychroma*: Beautiful sulphur-yellow fls, April–May.
  ⊠ H:45cm (1½ft) S:30cm (1ft)    *Stks*: Widely available

**Gaillardia**    LMH    O–◑    \*\*\*
  'Croftway Yellow': Large, bright yellow fls, June–Sept.
  H:30cm (1ft) S:30cm (1ft)    *Stks*: BG, FT, SD
  'Mandarin': Beautiful, orange-flame fls, June–Aug.
  H:90cm (3ft) S:45cm (1½ft)    *Stks*: BG

**Geranium**    LMH    O–◑    \*\*\*
  *armenum*: Beautiful, vivid crimson-magenta fls, June–Aug.
  H:90cm (3ft) S:45cm (1½ft)    *Stks*: BG, KN
  *endressii* 'Wargrave Pink': Clear pink fls, June–Sept.
  ✿ H:45cm (1½ft) S:30cm (1ft)    *Stks*: Widely available
  'Johnson's Blue': Cup-shaped, bright blue fls, May–Aug.
  ✿ H:30cm (1ft) S:30cm (1ft)    *Stks*: Widely available
  'Russell Prichard': Intense carmine-red fls, June–Sept.
  ✿ H:20cm (8in) S:20cm (8in)    *Stks*: Widely available
  *sanguineum lancastrense* 'Splendens': Pink fls, June–Sept.
  H:25cm (10in) S:25cm (10in)    *Stks*: Widely available

**Geum** (avens)    LMH    O–◑    \*\*\*
  *borisii*: Tufty growth. Orange fls, June and Aug.–Sept.
  ⊠ H:30cm (1ft) S:25cm (10in)    *Stks*: Widely available
  'Lady Stratheden': Double, yellow fls, June–Aug.
  ⊠ H:60cm (2ft) S:45cm (1½ft)    *Stks*: Widely available
  'Mrs Bradshaw': Attractive double, red fls, June–Aug.
  ⊠ H:60cm (2ft) S:45cm (1½ft)    *Stks*: Widely available

**Gypsophila** (chalk plant)    LMH(C)    O    \*\*\*
  *paniculata* 'Bristol Fairy': Double, white fls, June–Sept.
  ✕⊠ H:90cm (3ft) S:60cm (2ft)    *Stks*: Widely available
  'Rosy Veil': Mounded habit. Double pink fls, June–Sept.
  ✕⊠ H:25cm (10in) S:30cm (1ft)    *Stks*: Widely available

## ORNAMENTAL GRASSES

**Carex**   LMH   O   \*\*\*
*morrowii*'Evergold': Variegated green and yellow lvs.
⌀☒ H:20cm (8in) S:45cm (1½ft)   Stks: BC, BG, KN

**Festuca**   LMH   O–◐   \*\*\*
*glauca*: Very attractive, with blue-grey lvs.
⌀☒ H:25cm (10in) S:45cm (1½ft)   Stks: Widely available

**Hakonechloa**   LMH   O   \*\*\*
*macra*'Albo-aurea': Green and buff variegation.
⌀☒ H:25cm (10in) S:45cm (1½ft)   Stks: BG, KN

**Lasiogrostis**   LMH   O   \*\*\*
*splendens*: Clumpy growth. Buff-shaded plumes.
☒ H:90cm (3ft) S:38cm (15in)   Stks: BG

**Miscanthus**   LMH(M)   O   \*\*\*
*sinensis*'Zebrinus': Green lvs with a broad goldish band.
⌀☒ H:1.2m (4ft) S:45cm (1½ft)   Stks: BG, NN, SD

**Molinia**   LMH   O–◐   \*\*\*
*caerulea*'Variegata': Very neat. Variegated lvs.
⌀☒ H:45cm (1½ft) S:30cm (1ft)   Stks: BC, BG, KN

**Pennisetum**   LM   O   \*\*\*
*alopecuroides*: Poker-like grass heads in autumn.
✕☒ H:90cm (3ft) S:45cm (1½ft)   Stks: BG
*orientale*: Poker-like spires. Blue-grey hairy lvs.
✕☒ H:30cm (1ft) S:30cm (1ft)   Stks: BG

**Stipa**   LMH   O   \*\*\*
*gigantea*: Evergreen lvs. Feathery flower spikes.
✕☒ H:90cm (3ft) S:45cm (1½ft)   Stks: Widely available

---

**Helenium**   LMH   O   \*\*\*
'Coppelia': Warm, coppery-orange fls, July–Aug.
☒ H:90cm (3ft) S:45cm (1½ft)   Stks: BG, KN
'Butterpat': Very attractive. Pure yellow fls, Aug.–Oct.
☒ H:90cm (3ft) S:45cm (1½ft)   Stks: BG, FT, NN

**Helianthus** (perennial sunflower)   LM   O   \*\*\*
*multiflorus*'Loddon Gold': Double, yellow fls, July–Sept.
☒ H:1.5m (5ft) S:90cm (3ft)   Stks: BG, FT, NN

**Heliopsis**   LMH   O   \*\*\*
'Golden Plume': Double yellow fls, June–Sept.
☒ H:1.2m (4ft) S:60cm (2ft)   Stks: BG, KN, NN

**Helleborus**   LMH(M)   ◐–●   \*\*\*
*corsicus*: Delicate, pale apple-green fls, March–April.
☒ H:60cm (2ft) S:45cm (1½ft)   Stks: Widely available
*foetidus*: Dark green lvs. Light green fls, March–May.
☒ H:60cm (2ft) S:45cm (1½ft)   Stks: Widely available
*niger*: Saucer-shaped white fls, Dec.–March.
☒ H:30cm (1ft) S:30cm (1ft)   Stks: Widely available
*orientalis* hybrids: Mixed shades, Feb.–April.
☒ H:20cm (8in) S:20cm (8in)   Stks: Widely available

**Hemerocallis** (day lily)   LMH   O–◐   \*\*\*
'Buzz Bomb': Large, rich, velvety-red trumpet fls, June–Aug.
☒ H:60cm (2ft) S:45cm (1½ft)   Stks: BG
'Hyperion': Pure canary-yellow trumpet fls, June–Aug.
☒ H:1m (3½ft) S:60cm (2ft)   Stks: BG

'Pink Damask': Beautiful pink trumpet fls, June–Aug.
⊠ H:75cm (2½ft) S:45cm (1½ft)    *Stks*: Widely available

**Heuchera**    LM    ○–◑    ***
'Bressingham Hybrids': Sprays in mixed colours, May–July.
☞✕⊠ H:75cm (2½ft) S:60cm (2ft)    *Stks*: BG, FT
'Red Spangles': Crimson-scarlet fls.
☞✕⊠ H:60cm (2ft) S:60cm (2ft)    *Stks*: Widely available

**Heucherella**    LM    ◑    ***
'Bridget Bloom': Beautiful sprays of pink fls, April–May.
⊠ H:45cm (1½ft) S:30cm (1ft)    *Stks*: BC, BG

**Hosta** (plantain lily)    LMH(M)    ◑–●    ***
*fortunei* 'Picta': Lvs cream-yellow, edged green.
∅⊠ H:60cm (2ft) S:45cm (1½ft)    *Stks*: Widely available
*sieboldiana* 'Elegans': Very large, blue-green lvs.
∅⊠ H:90cm (3ft) S:60cm (2ft)    *Stks*: Widely available
'Royal Standard' (●): Green lvs. White fls, Aug.–Oct.
⤵∅⊠ H:90cm (3ft) S:60cm (2ft)    *Stks*: BG, NN
'Thomas Hogg': Broad cream-edged lvs. Mauve fls, June–July.
∅⊠ H:60cm (2ft) S:45cm (1½ft)    *Stks*: Widely available
*undulata* 'Medio Variegata': Variegated, wavy-edged lvs.
∅⊠ H:30cm (1ft) S:30cm (1ft)    *Stks*: Widely available

**Incarvillea**    LMH(P)    ○    ***
*delavayi*: Trumpet-shaped deep pink fls, June–July.
⊠ H:45cm (1½ft) S:30cm (1ft)    *Stks*: Widely available

**Iris**    LMH(C)    ○    ***
*germanica* 'Frost and Flame': White, tangerine beard, June.
⊠ H:1m (3½ft) S:45cm (1½ft)    *Stks*: Widely available
*germanica* 'Party Dress': Pink, tangerine beard, June.
⊠ H:1m (3½ft) S:45cm (1½ft)    *Stks*: Widely available
*germanica* 'Rajah': Orange-yellow, crimson falls, June.
⊠ H:1m (3½ft) S:45cm (1½ft)    *Stks*: BG
*germanica* 'Top Flight': Deep apricot ruffled fls, June.
⊠ H:1m (3½ft) S:45cm (1½ft)    *Stks*: BG, NN
*kaempferi* (M,A): Exquisite blue or purple fls, June–Aug.
⊠ H:75cm (2½ft) S:45cm (1½ft)    *Stks*: BG, FT
*pallida* 'Aurea Variegata': Creamy lvs. Blue fls, June–July.
∅⊠ H:60cm (2ft) S:30cm (1ft)    *Stks*: BG
*pallida* 'Variegata': White variegated lvs. Blue fls, June–July.
∅⊠ H:60cm (2ft) S:30cm (1ft)    *Stks*: BG, NN
*siberica* 'Perry's Blue' (M): Upright. Blue fls, June–July.
⊠ H:90cm (3ft) S:45cm (1½ft)    *Stks*: BG, NN
*stylosa*: Lavender-blue fls, Jan.–March.
⊠ H:30cm (1ft) S:20cm (8in)    *Stks*: Widely available
*unguicularis* see *I. stylosa*

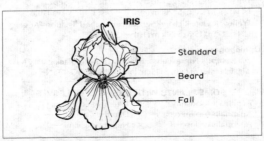

IRIS

Standard

Beard

Fall

**Lamium**   LMH   ◑   ***
*maculatum* 'Beacon Silver': Silvery lvs. Pink fls, May–June.
⊘⌗⊠ H:10cm (4in) S:25cm (10in)   *Stks*: Widely available

**Liatris** (blazing star)   LMH(M)   ○   ***
*callilepis*: Fluffy spikes, bearing lilac-grey fls, July–Sept.
✕⊠ H:90cm (3ft) S:45cm (1½ft)   *Stks*: BG, FT, KN
*callilepis* 'Kobold': Spikes of deep lilac fls, July–Sept.
✕⊠ H:60cm (2ft) S:30cm (1ft)   *Stks*: BG, NN, SD

**Ligularia**   LMH(M)   ○   ***
*clivorum* 'Desdemona': Purplish lvs. Orange fls, July–Sept.
H:1.2m (4ft) S:60cm (2ft)   *Stks*: Widely available

**Limonium** (sea lavender)   LMH   ○   ***
*latifolium* 'Violetta': 'Everlasting' violet fls, July–Sept.
✕⊠ H:60cm (2ft) S:45cm (1½ft)   *Stks*: BC, BG

**Liriope**   LM(P)   ○–◑   ***
*muscari*: Grassy lvs. Violet-mauve spikes, Aug.–Oct.
⊠ H:30cm (1ft) S:23cm (9in)   *Stks*: Widely available

**Lupinus** (lupin)   LM   ○   ***
Russell Hybrids: Superb colour range, June–July.
⊠ H:90cm (3ft) S:45cm (1½ft)   *Stks*: Widely available

**Lychnis**   LMH   ○   ***
*chalcedonica*: Leafy stems with scarlet fls, June–Aug.
H:90cm (3ft) S:45cm (1½ft)   *Stks*: Widely available

**Lythrum**   LMH(M)   ○–◑   ***
*salicaria* 'Firecandle': Spikes of rosy-red fls, July–Sept.
H:90cm (3ft) S:45cm (1½ft)   *Stks*: BG, KN, NN

**Macleaya** (plume poppy)   LM   ○   ***
*cordata*: Attractive foliage. Small white fls, Aug.–Sept.
✕⊠ H:1.2m (4ft) S:45cm (1½ft)   *Stks*: BG, NN

**Meconopsis** (blue poppy)   LM(M)   ◑   ***
*baileyi*: Beautiful blue poppy fls, May–July.
H:90cm (3ft) S:75cm (2½ft)   *Stks*: BG, FT
*betonicifolia* see *M. baileyi*

**Monarda** (bergamot)   LMH(M)   ○–◑   ***
*didyma* 'Croftway Pink': Clear pink fls, June–Aug.
H:90cm (3ft) S:45cm (1½ft)   *Stks*: Widely available
*didyma* 'Cambridge Scarlet': Red fls, July–Sept.
H:90cm (3ft) S:45cm (1½ft)   *Stks*: Widely available

**Nepeta** (catmint)   LMH   ○   ***
*mussinii*: Grey aromatic lvs. Mauve-blue fls, May–Sept.
⊠ H:30cm (1ft) S:30cm (1ft)   *Stks*: Widely available

**Oenothera** (evening primrose)   LM   ○   ***
*missouriensis*: Large canary-yellow fls, June–Sept.
⊠ H:25cm (10in) S:20cm (8in)   *Stks*: Widely available
'Yellow River': Rich yellow, saucer-shaped fls, June–Aug.
⊠ H:38cm (15in) S:30cm (1ft)   *Stks*: BG

**Ophiopogon**   LMH   ◑–●   ***
*planiscapus* 'Nigrescens': Beautiful purple-black grassy lvs.
⊘⌗⊠ H:15cm (6in) S:15cm (6in)   *Stks*: BG, FT, NN

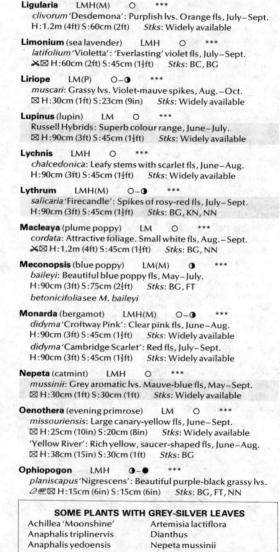

---

### SOME PLANTS WITH GREY-SILVER LEAVES

| | |
|---|---|
| Achillea 'Moonshine' | Artemisia lactiflora |
| Anaphalis triplinervis | Dianthus |
| Anaphalis yedoensis | Nepeta mussinii |

---

**Paeonia** (peony)    LMH(M)    ○–◑    ***
   'Bowl of Beauty': Pink with cream anemone centre, June–July.
   ✄ H:90cm (3ft) S:60cm (2ft)    *Stks*: Widely available
   'Rosea Superba': Double, bright pink fls, May.
   ✄ H:75cm (2½ft) S:45cm (1½ft)    *Stks*: BG, KN
   'Rubra Plena': Double, deep crimson fls, May.
   ✄ H:75cm (2½ft) S:45cm (1½ft)    *Stks*: BG, KN, NN
   'Sarah Bernhardt': Large, apple-blossom pink fls, June.
   ✄ H:90cm (3ft) S:60cm (2ft)    *Stks*: Widely available
   *mlokosewitschii*: Cup-shaped, single yellow fls, April.
   ✄⊠ H:75cm (2½ft) S:45cm (1½ft)    *Stks*: BG, KN

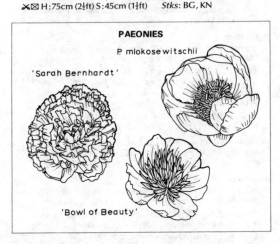

**PAEONIES**

P. mlokosewitschii

'Sarah Bernhardt'

'Bowl of Beauty'

**Papaver** (poppy)    LMH    ○    ***
   'Marcus Perry': Superb orange-scarlet fls, May–July.
   H:75cm (2½ft) S:45cm (1½ft)    *Stks*: Widely available
   'Mrs Perry': Delicate, salmon-pink fls, May–July.
   H90cm (3ft) S:45cm (1½ft)    *Stks*: BG, FT, KN
   'Perry's White': Beautiful white fls, May–July.
   H:90cm (3ft) S:45cm (1½ft)    *Stks*: Widely available

**Penstemon**    LMH    ○    **
   *barbatus*: Spires of tubular rose-red fls, June–Sept.
   H:90cm (3ft) S:38cm (15in)    *Stks*: BC, BG, NN

**Phlox**    MH(M)    ○–◑    ***
   'Prince of Orange': Orange-salmon fls, July–Sept.
   ⊠ H:90cm (3ft) S:38cm (15in)    *Stks*: BG, FT, KN
   'Prospero': Delicate pale lilac heads of fls, July–Sept.
   ⊠ H:90cm (3ft) S:38cm (15in)    *Stks*: BG
   'Sandringham': Pink with a darker centre, July–Sept.
   ⊠ H:75cm (2½ft) S:30cm (1ft)    *Stks*: BG, KN, NN
   'Starfire': Beautiful deep red fls, July–Sept.
   ⊠ H:90cm (3ft) S:38cm (15in)    *Stks*: Widely available
   'Vintage Wine': Large trusses of purple-red fls, July–Sept.
   ⊠ H:75cm (2½ft) S:30cm (1ft)    *Stks*: Widely available
   'White Admiral': Shapely, pure white fls, July–Sept.
   ⊠ H:75cm (2½ft) S:30cm (1ft)    *Stks*: Widely available

**Physostegia** (obedient plant)    LMH(M)    ○–◑    ***
   *virginiana* 'Vivid': Short spikes of deep rose fls, Aug.–Oct.
   ⊠ H:60cm (2ft) S:45cm (1½ft)    *Stks*: Widely available

**Polemonium**  LM  ○  \*\*\*
 'Blue Pearl': Saucer-shaped, bright blue fls, May–June.
 ⊠ H:25cm (10in) S:30cm (1ft)  Stks: BG
 *foliosissimum*: Clusters of lavender-blue fls, May–Aug.
 H:75cm (2½ft) S:45cm (1½ft)  Stks: BG, KN

**Polygonum**  LMH  ○–◑  \*\*\*
 *affine* 'Darjeeling Red': Deep pink spikes, June–Sept.
 ℮⊠ H:25cm (10in) S:38cm (15in)  Stks: BC, BG, NN
 *affine* 'Donald Lowndes': Mat-forming. Pink, June–Sept.
 ℮⊠ H:25cm (10in) S:45cm (1½ft)  Stks: Widely available
 *bistorta* 'Superbum' (M): Bold, clear pink spikes, May–Aug.
 ✕⊠ H:90cm (3ft) S:45cm (1½ft)  Stks: Widely available

**Potentilla**  LMH  ○  \*\*\*
 'Gibson's Scarlet': Single, brilliant red fls, June–Aug.
 ⊠ H:30cm (1ft) S:38cm (15in)  Stks: Widely available
 *nepalensis* 'Miss Willmott': Single, rose-pink fls, June–Sept.
 ⊠ H:30cm (1ft) S:38cm (15in)  Stks: BG, FT
 'William Rollisson': Bright, orange-flame fls, June–Aug.
 ⊠ H:38cm (15in) S:38cm (15in)  Stks: BG
 'Yellow Queen': Attractive, pure yellow fls, June–Aug.
 ⊠ H:30cm (1ft) S:38cm (15in)  Stks: BG, KN

**Pulmonaria** (lungwort)  LMH(M)  ◑  \*\*\*
 *angustifolia* 'Azurea': Heads of deep blue fls, March–May.
 ℮⊠ H:20cm (8in) S:45cm (1½ft)  Stks: Widely available

**Pyrethrum**  LM  ○  \*\*\*
 'Brenda': Delicate, single, deep pink fls, May–July.
 ⊠ H:75cm (2½ft) S:45cm (1½ft)  Stks: Widely available
 'Bressingham Red': Attractive, single red fls, May–July.
 ⊠ H:75cm (2½ft) S:45cm (1½ft)  Stks: BG, KN
 'E. M. Robinson': Single, light pink fls, May–July.
 ⊠ H:75cm (2½ft) S:45cm (1½ft)  Stks: Widely available

**Ranunculus**  LMH(M,P)  ○–◑  \*\*\*
 *aconitifolius* 'Plenus': White, button-like fls, May–July.
 ⊠ H:45cm (1½ft) S:38cm (15in)  Stks: BG, NN

**Rodgersia**  LMH(M)  ◑  \*\*\*
 *pinnata* 'Irish Bronze': Bronze lvs. Pink fls, July–Aug.
 ∅⊠ H:90cm (3ft) S:38cm (15in)  Stks: BG

**Rudbeckia**  LMH  ○  \*\*\*
 *deamii*: Golden-yellow fls, dark centres, July–Sept.
 H:90cm (3ft) S:38cm (15in)  Stks: BG
 'Goldquelle': Double, chrome-yellow fls, Aug.–Oct.
 H:90cm (3ft) S:45cm (1½ft)  Stks: Widely available
 'Goldsturm': Golden fls with black centres, July–Sept.
 ⊠ H:75cm (2½ft) S:38cm (15in)  Stks: BG, FT, NN

**Salvia**  LMH  ○  \*\*\*
 *superba*: Spikes of violet-purple fls, July–Sept.
 ⊠ H:90cm (3ft) S:38cm (15in)  Stks: Widely available
 *superba* 'East Friesland': Violet-purple spikes, July–Sept.
 ⊠ H:45cm (1½ft) S:45cm (1½ft)  Stks: BG, KN, NN
 *superba* 'May Night': Violet-purple spikes, May–Sept.
 ⊠ H:45cm (1½ft) S:45cm (1½ft)  Stks: BG, NN

**Scabiosa** (scabious)  LMH  ○  \*\*\*
 'Clive Greaves': Mid-blue 'pincushion' fls, June–Sept.
 ⊠ H:75cm (2½ft) S:38cm (15in)  Stks: Widely available

**Schizostylis** (Kaffir lily)   LMH(M,P)   **◑**   ***
*coccinea* 'Major': Spikes of large red fls, Oct.–Nov.
✄ H:75cm (2½ft) S:45cm (1½ft)   Stks: BC, BG, NN

**Sedum**   LMH   ○   ***
*spectabile* 'Autumn Joy': Heads of salmon-pink fls, Aug.–Oct.
⊠ H:60cm (2ft) S:30cm (1ft)   Stks: Widely available
*spectabile* 'Brilliant': Glistening deep-pink fls, Aug.–Oct.
⊠ H:38cm (15in) S:30cm (1ft)   Stks: Widely available
'Ruby Glow': Glistening, rose-red fls, July–Aug.
⊠ H:25cm (10in) S:45cm (1½ft)   Stks: Widely available

**Sidalcea**   LMH   ○   ***
'Rose Queen': Graceful rose-pink spikes, June–Aug.
⊠ H:1.2m (4ft) S:38cm (15in)   Stks: Widely available

**Solidago** (golden rod)   LMH   ○–◑   ***
'Goldenmosa': Sprays of golden-yellow fls, Aug.–Sept.
⊠ H:75cm (2½ft) S:38cm (15in)   Stks: BG, FT, NN
'Lemore': Branching heads of soft primrose fls, Aug.–Sept.
⊠ H:75cm (2½ft) S:38cm (15in)   Stks: BG, NN, SD

**Tradescantia**   LMH   ○–◑   ***
*virginiana* 'Isis': Deep blue three-petalled fls, June–Sept.
⊠ H:45cm (1½ft) S:45cm (1½ft)   Stks: BG, FT
*virginiana* 'Osprey': Three-petalled white fls, June–Sept.
⊠ H:45cm (1½ft) S:38cm (15in)   Stks: Widely available
*virginiana* 'Purewell Giant': Orchid-purple fls, June–Sept.
⊠ H:45cm (1½ft) S:45cm (1½ft)   Stks: BG

**Trollius** (globe flower)   MH(M)   ○–◑   ***
*ledebouri* 'Golden Queen': Large orange fls, June–Aug.
⊠ H:90cm (3ft) S:38cm (15in)   Stks: BG, NN

**Verbascum** (mullein)   LMH   ○   ***
'Gainsborough': Spikes of light yellow fls, June–Aug.
H:1.2m (4ft) S:38cm (15in)   Stks: Widely available

**Veronica** (speedwell)   LMH   ○   ***
*incana* 'Wendy': Greyish lvs. Blue spikes, June–Aug.
⊠ H:45cm (1½ft) S:38cm (15in)   Stks: BG, FT, SD
*teucrium* 'Crater Lake Blue': Deep blue spikes, June–Aug.
⊠ H:30cm (1ft) S:38cm (15in)   Stks: BC, BG, KN
*virginica* 'Alba': Slender spikes of white fls, Aug.–Sept.
⊠ H:1.5m (5ft) S:38cm (15in)   Stks: Widely available

---

## SPECIALIST SUPPLIERS

**BC**   Beth Chatto, White Barn House, Elmstead Market,
Colchester, Essex, CO7 7DB. Tel: Wivenhoe 2007.

**BE**   Bees Ltd., Sealand, Chester, CH1 6BA.
Tel: Saughall (0244) 880501.

**BG**   Bressingham Gardens, Diss, Norfolk, IP22 2AB.
Tel: Bressingham (037 988) 464.

**FT**   F. Toynbee Ltd., Barnham, Bognor Regis, West
Sussex, PO22 0BH. Tel: Yapton (0243) 552121.

**KN**   Kelways, The Royal Nurseries, Langport, Somerset,
TA10 9SL. Tel: Langport (0458) 250521.

**NN**   Notcutts Nurseries Ltd., Woodbridge, Suffolk, IP12
4AF. Tel: Woodbridge 3344.

**SD**   Sunningdale Nurseries Ltd., Windlesham, Surrey.
Tel: Ascot 20496.

---

# Bulbs

One of the miracles of life is the efficiency of bulbs. Just plant them in the garden and many will come up year after year, producing masses of flower with little, if any, cultural attention. The outdoor flowering season stretches from aconites in January round to November nerines.

*To plant bulbs in grass it is best to cut a figure H in the turf, then undercut each half. Once loosened, fold the turf back and plant the bulbs with a trowel.*

All garden soils are suitable for the majority of kinds and they need little feeding, staking, or spraying.

Quite a number can be planted in grass, under trees and in rockeries to 'naturalize', that is grow quite naturally season after season without any cultural treatment. The varieties most suitable for naturalizing are clearly indicated in the following pages.

**Where to grow**

Many of the spring-flowering kinds are suited to formal spring bedding displays. Tulips grow well with wallflowers or forget-me-nots, and the low-growing varieties with polyanthus and arabis.

Crocuses form a good edging and daffodils are excellent for cutting. Under deciduous trees an attractive combination is ivy underplanted with daffodils.

A lot of the autumn-planted spring-flowering bulbs grow well in pots. If they are allowed to develop a good strong root system and 5cm (2in) or more of shoot first, many can then be forced into early flowering.

In the garden they are better grouped; at least five and perferably ten or more of each variety should be planted for good effect. The same applies to summer-flowering lilies and gladioli, and while lilies are also excellent to grow in tubs and pots, gladioli are better in the garden, planted deep enough to reduce the need to stake.

## Choosing and buying

The larger the bulb the bigger the flowers and the more flowers it will produce as a general rule. Most bulbs start as quite small, even non-flowering, specimens, but grow larger each season.

Small to medium size (14–15cm circumference) hyacinths are a good buy for bedding. The bulbs and the flower heads get larger after a year's growth in the garden, but just as important is the fact that the smaller flower heads are not so likely to fall over in heavy rain.

Some hyacinths are specially 'prepared' to promote early flowering. This involves lifting the bulbs as soon as possible after the leaves die down and giving special hot and cold periods to advance flower development. Prepared treatment is not completed before mid-August so hyacinths sold as prepared before the third week of August are unlikely to flower until after Christmas.

Small gladiolus corms will produce smaller flower spikes and flower a little later than large corms of the same variety. Big lily bulbs will produce much larger flower heads and are well worth the extra money.

If narcissi are bought in bulk, for naturalizing in grass for example, it is worth cutting one or two bulbs in half to check that embryo flowers have formed in each bulb. Large trumpet daffodils will as a general rule have larger bulbs than small trumpet and pheasant's eye types. Don't, therefore, select all large bulbs if serving yourself from a mixture.

British-grown narcissus bulbs bought by weight are likely to have more flowers per given weight than Dutch, which are likely to produce slightly larger flowers.

Absence of outer brown skin from tulip bulbs is no serious loss and skinless bulbs will grow satisfactorily.

Hardy cyclamen are better bought as growing plants. Dry corms will need to be surrounded by damp peat and the skins kept damp to encourage root and shoot growth.

All the small bulbs and tubers sold in autumn are better planted as soon as possible. Left in shops they dry out and re-establishment is erratic. This is especially the case with aconites, miniature daffodils, snowdrops and small fritillarias. Lily bulbs are also better planted as soon as possible and the hardy types will flower best if transplanted in the autumn or very early spring.

Test the firmness of all bulbs and corms at their *base* before purchase. Any with soft bases are best passed over. Don't damage the base with your thumbnail.

## If you want to know more . . .

For further reading *The Bulb Book*, by Frederic Doerflinger (published by David and Charles) can be recommended. If your interest lies with gladioli, it is worth joining the British Gladiolus Society. The Secretary is Mrs. M. Rowley, 10 Sandbach Road, Thurlwood, Rode Heath, Stoke-on-Trent, ST7 3RN.

**Acidanthera** Bulb LMH ○ *
> *murielae*: Large white fls, purple-blotched, Sept.
> ⏀✕ H:90cm (3ft) S:25cm (10in) *Stks*: Widely available

**Allium** Bulb LM ○ ***
> *aflatuense*: Large purple-lilac fl heads, May–June.
> ✕ H:75cm (2½ft) S:25cm (10in) *Stks*: Widely available
> *albopilosum*: Large, round, silvery-lilac fl heads, June.
> ✕ H:60cm (2ft) S:23cm (9in) *Stks*: Widely available
> *giganteum*: Spectacular, violet, ball-shaped fl heads, July.
> H:1.2m (4ft) S:30cm (1ft) *Stks*: Widely available
> *moly*: Loose heads of yellow, star-shaped fls, June.
> ✕ ⁹⁹ △ H:25cm (10in) S:20cm (8in) *Stks*: Widely available

**Anemone** (windflower) Corm LMH ○–◑ ***
> 'De Caen': Single fls, year-round according to planting.
> ✕ ⏁ H:23cm (9in) S:10cm (4in) *Stks*: Widely available
> 'St. Brigid': Mixture of double and semi-double fls, Jan.–Dec.
> ✕ ⏁ H:23cm (9in) S:10cm (4in) *Stks*: Widely available
> *blanda* (mixed): Daisy fls, in blue, pink, white. Feb.–April.
> △ H:15cm (6in) S:10cm (4in) *Stks*: Widely available

**Camassia** Bulb LMH ○–◑ ***
> *esculenta*: Graceful spikes of blue fls, June–July.
> ✕ ⁹⁹ △ H:75cm (2½ft) S:18cm (7in) *Stks*: Widely available

**Chionodoxa** (glory of the snow) Bulb LMH ○–◑ ***
> *luciliae*: Vivid blue starry fls with white eyes, March.
> △ H:15cm (6in) S:10cm (4in) *Stks*: Widely available

**Colchicum** (autumn crocus) Bulb LMH ○–◑ ***
> *autumnale*: Huge, lavender-coloured 'crocuses', Aug.–Sept.
> ⁹⁹ △ H:20cm (8in) S:23cm (9in) *Stks*: Widely available

**Crinum** Bulb LM ○ **
> × *powellii*: Rosy-pink or white lily-like fls, July–Sept.
> ⏀✕ H:90cm (3ft) S:45cm (1½ft) *Stks*: Widely available

**Crocus** (large-flowered) Corm LMH ○–◑ ***
> 'Large Yellow': Bold, large, yellow fls, Feb.–March.
> ⁹⁹ H:13cm (5in) S:10cm (4in) *Stks*: Widely available
> 'Vanguard': Silvery-lilac fls, violet on outside, Feb.–March.
> ⁹⁹ ⊖ H:13cm (5in) S:10cm (4in) *Stks*: Widely available
> *purpureus grandiflorus*: Striking deep purple, Feb.–March.
> ⁹⁹ ⊖ H:13cm (5in) S:10cm (4in) *Stks*: Widely available

**Crocus** (small-flowered) Corm LMH ○–◑ ***
> *chrysanthus* 'Blue Pearl': Soft, delicate blue fls, Feb.
> △ H:7.5cm (3in) S:5cm (2in) *Stks*: Widely available
> *chrysanthus* 'Snow Bunting': White fls, yellow centres, Feb.
> △ H:7.5cm (3in) S:5cm (2in) *Stks*: Widely available
> *chrysanthus* 'Zwanenburg Bronze': Yellow and bronze, Feb.
> △ H:7.5cm (3in) S:5cm (2in) *Stks*: Widely available

**Cyclamen** Corm LMH ◑–● **/***
> *europaeum*: Small, fragrant, rosy-pink fls, July–Sept.
> ⏀△ H:10cm (4in) S:13cm (5in) *Stks*: Widely available
> *coum*: Small, pink to white fls, Jan.–March.
> ⁹⁹ △ H:7.5cm (3in) S:13cm (5in) *Stks*: Widely available
> *neapolitanum*: Marbled lvs. Mauve to pink fls, Aug.–Nov.
> ⁹⁹ △ H:7.5cm (3in) S:13cm (5in) *Stks*: Widely available
> *repandum* (**): Marbled lvs. Scented, pink fls, April.
> ⏀△ H:15cm (6in) S:18cm (7in) *Stks*: Widely available
> *hederaefolium* see *C. neapolitanum*

**Eranthis** (winter aconite) Tuber    LM(P)    ◑    ***
  *hyemalis*: Yellow fls, set in a green ruff, Feb.–March.
  ♒△ H:7.5cm (3in) S:7.5cm (3in)    *Stks*: Widely available

**Fritillaria** Bulb    LMH    O–◑    ***
  *imperialis*: Large, yellow, bronze or orange bells, April.
  H:90cm (3ft)    *Stks*: Widely available
  *meleagris*: Small bells. Various colours, April–May.
  ♒ H:30cm (1ft) S:15cm (6in)    *Stks*: Widely available

**Galanthus** (snowdrop) Bulb    LMH    O–◑    ***
  *nivalis*: The popular single snowdrop, Jan.–Feb.
  ♒△ H:10cm (4in) S:10cm (4in)    *Stks*: Widely available
  *nivalis* 'Flore-plena': A beautiful double form, Jan.–Feb.
  ♒△ H:10cm (4in) S:10cm (4in)    *Stks*: Widely available
  *nivalis* 'S. Arnott': A vigorous form. White fls, Jan.–Feb.
  ♒ H:13cm (5in) S:13cm (5in)    *Stks*: Widely available

**Galtonia** Bulb    LMH    O–◑    ***
  *candicans*: Resembles a giant white hyacinth, July–Sept.
  H:1m (3½ft) S:25cm (10in)    *Stks*: Widely available

**Gladioli** (large-flowered) Corm    LMH    O    **
  'Flower Song': Frilled, golden-yellow fls, July–Sept.
  ✂ H:90cm (3ft) S:23cm (9in)    *Stks*: Widely available
  'Green Woodpecker': Yellowish-green, July–Sept.
  ✂ H:1m (3½ft) S:23cm (9in)    *Stks*: Widely available
  'Peter Pears': Deep peach, red throat, July–Sept.
  ✂ H:1m (3½ft) S:23cm (9in)    *Stks*: Widely available

**Gladioli** (Butterfly type) Corm    LMH    O    **
  'Confetti': Deep pink with a yellow throat, July–Aug.
  ✂ H:90cm (3ft) S:23cm (9in)    *Stks*: CH
  'Melodie': Pink, with orange and scarlet blotches, July–Aug.
  ✂ H:90cm (3ft) S:23cm (9in)    *Stks*: CH

**Gladioli** (Primulinus type) Corm    LMH    O    **
  'Columbine': Clear pink, white throat marks, July–Aug.
  ✂ H:90cm (3ft) S:15cm (6in)    *Stks*: Widely available
  'Robin': Purple, with reddish-purple throat, July–Aug.
  ✂ H:60cm (2ft) S:15cm (6in)    *Stks*: Widely available

**Gladioli** (Miniature type) Corm    LMH    O    **
  'Bluebird': Bright blue, with a white throat, July–Aug.
  ✂ H:60cm (2ft) S:15cm (6in)    *Stks*: CH
  'Foxfire': Ruffled, scarlet-orange fls, July–Aug.
  ✂ H:60cm (2ft) S:15cm (6in)    *Stks*: CH

**Gladioli** (species) Corm    LM    O    ***
  *byzantinus*: Graceful, dainty spikes of purple-red fls, June.
  ✂♒ H:60cm (2ft) S:15cm (6in)    *Stks*: Widely available

**Hyacinthus** (hyacinth) Bulb    LMH    O–◑    ***
  'Blue Jacket': Rich blue fls, April–May.
  ⅃⊖ H:25cm (10in) S:13cm (5in)    *Stks*: Widely available
  'City of Haarlem': Soft primrose-yellow fls, April–May.
  ⅃ H:25cm (10in) S:13cm (5in)    *Stks*: Widely available
  'Lady Derby': Beautiful rose-pink fls, April–May.
  ⅃⊖ H:25cm (10in) S:13cm (5in)    *Stks*: Widely available
  'L'Innocence': An outstanding pure white, April–May.
  ⅃⊖ H:25cm (10in) S:13cm (5in)    *Stks*: Widely available
  'Ostara': Deep blue fls on large spikes, April–May.
  ⅃⊖ H:25cm (10in) S:13cm (5in)    *Stks*: Widely available
  'Pink Pearl': Carmine-pink fls, April–May. Sturdy growth.
  ⅃⊖ H:25cm (10in) S:13cm (5in)    *Stks*: Widely available

*For key to symbols, see page 7*    35

**Iris** Bulb  LMH  ○  ***
  *danfordiae*: Bright lemon fls on dwarf plants, Feb.–March.
  ꓿△ H:13cm (5in) S:7.5cm (3in)  *Stks*: Widely available
  *reticulata*: Purple-blue, marked yellow, Feb.–March.
  ꓿△ H:15cm (6in) S:7.5cm (3in)  *Stks*: Widely available
  Dutch type: Blue, yellow, white fls, late May–early June.
  ✕ H:45cm (1½ft) S:15cm (6in)  *Stks*: Widely available
  Spanish type: Similar to the Dutch, but a little later.
  ✕꓿ H:45cm (1½ft) S:15cm (6in)  *Stks*: Widely available
  English type: Largest fls of all, June–July.
  ✕ H:60cm (2ft) S:15cm (6in)  *Stks*: Widely available

**Lilium** (lily) Bulb  LMH(A*,P)  ○–◑  ***
  *auratum*: White with yellow stripes, brown spots, Aug.–Sept.
  ꓿✕ H:1.5m (5ft) S:30cm (1ft)  *Stks*: Widely available
  *candicum* (○): The pure white Madonna lily, June–July.
  ꓿✕ H:1.3m (4½ft) S:30cm (1ft)  *Stks*: Widely available
  'Destiny' (Mid-century): Yellow, brown spots, June–July.
  ✕⊖ H:90cm (3ft) S:30cm (1ft)  *Stks*: Widely available
  'Enchantment' (Mid-century): Orange-red fls, June–July.
  ✕⊖ H:90cm (3ft) S:30cm (1ft)  *Stks*: Widely available
  *henryi*: Orange-yellow, spotted brown fls, Aug.
  ꓿✕ H:1.5m (5ft) S:45cm (1½ft)  *Stks*: Widely available
  Mid-century Hybrids: Range of beautiful colours, June–July.
  ✕⊖ H:90cm (3ft) S:30cm (1ft)  *Stks*: Widely available
  'Paprika' (Mid-century Group): Deep crimson, June–July.
  ✕⊖ H:60cm (2ft) S:30cm (1ft)  *Stks*: Widely available
  'Pink Pearl': Large trumpets in shades of pink, July.
  ꓿✕ H:1.5m (5ft) S:45cm (1½ft)  *Stks*: Widely available
  'Pink Perfection': Impressive long, pink trumpets, July.
  ꓿✕ H:1.5m (5ft) S:45cm (1½ft)  *Stks*: Widely available
  *regale*: White, trumpet-shaped fls, pink in bud, July.
  ꓿✕ H:90cm (3ft) S:30cm (1ft)  *Stks*: Widely available
  *regale* 'Royal Gold': Glowing gold fls, July.
  ꓿✕ H:1.2m (4ft) S:45cm (1½ft)  *Stks*: Widely available
  *speciosum melpomene*: Spotted ruby-crimson, Aug.–Sept.
  ꓿✕⊖ H:1.2m (4ft) S:30cm (1ft)  *Stks*: DJ
  *speciosum roseum*: White, heavily spotted pink, Aug.–Sept.
  ꓿✕⊖ H:1.2m (4ft) S:30cm (1ft)  *Stks*: WB
  *speciosum rubrum*: Carmine-red on white, Aug.–Sept.
  ꓿✕✕ H:1.2m (4ft) S:30cm (1ft)  *Stks*: Widely available
  *tigrinum*: Deep orange-red fls, with black spots, July–Aug.
  ✕ H:1.2m (4ft) S:45cm (1½ft)  *Stks*: Widely available
  *The following lilies are lime-tolerant: *L. regale, L. henryi, L. tigrinum*, and *L. candidum*.

**Muscari** (grape hyacinth) Bulb  LMH  ○–◑  ***
  *armeniacum*: Tight clusters of colbalt-blue fls, April–May.
  △ H:20cm (8in) S:10cm (4in)  *Stks*: Widely available

**Narcissus** Bulb  LMH  ○–◑  ***
  **Trumpet** (*flowering March–April*)
  'Dutch Master': Huge yellow perianth and trumpet. Sturdy.
  ❀❀⊖ H:45cm (1½ft) S:20cm (8in)  *Stks*: Widely available
  'Golden Harvest': Good size, and glowing gold colour.
  ✕❀❀⊖ H:45cm (1½ft) S:20cm (8in)  *Stks*: Widely available
  'Mount Hood': White with ivory trumpet, turning white.
  ⊖ H:45cm (1½ft) S:20cm (8in)  *Stks*: Widely available.
  'Spellbinder': Green, sulphur-yellow trumpet tipped lemon.
  ◑ H:38cm (15in) S:15cm (6in)  *Stks*: Widely available

**Large-cupped** (*flowering mid-April*)
'Binkie': Opens sulphur-yellow, changing to white.
H:38cm (15in) S:15cm (6in)     Stks: Widely available
'Carlton': Soft yellow fls, prolific and very free flowering.
✕☺☻ H:45cm (1½ft) S:20cm (8in)     Stks: Widely available
'Duke of Windsor': White perianth, apricot ruffled cup.
H:45cm (1½ft) S:20cm (8in)     Stks: Widely available
'Fortune': Broad yellow perianth, glowing orange crown.
✕ H:45cm (1½ft) S:20cm (8in)     Stks: Widely available
'Ice Follies': Cream and primrose, turning white.
✕☻ H:38cm (15in) S:15cm (6in)     Stks: Widely available
'Queensland': White perianth and pleasing pink frilled cup.
H:38cm (15in) S:15cm (6in)     Stks: DJ

**Small-cupped** (*flowering April*)
'Actaea': White perianth with tiny yellow eye edged red.
☺✕☺ H:45cm (1½ft) S:20cm (8in)     Stks: Widely available
'Barrett Browning': White perianth, flat, ruffled, flame crown.
✕ H:45cm (1½ft) S:20cm (8in)     Stks: Widely available
'Birma': Yellow perianth, deep orange-red goblet cups.
H:45cm (1½ft) S:20cm (8in)     Stks: Widely available
'Pheasant's Eye': Pure white perianth, tiny eye edged red.
☺✕☺ H:38cm (15in) S:15cm (6in)     Stks: Widely available
'Verger': Large white perianth, lemon crown edged orange.
H:45cm (1½ft) S:20cm (8in)     Stks: Widely available

**Double** (*flowering end of April*)
'Flower Drift': White petals interspersed with orange ones.
H:45cm (1½ft) S:20cm (8in)     Stks: Widely available
'Golden Ducat': Large, mid-yellow fls of very good formation.
H:45cm (1½ft) S:20cm (8in)     Stks: DJ
'Texas': Yellow with vivid orange segments.
H:38cm (15in) S:15cm (6in)     Stks: Widely available
'White Lion': White perianth, creamy fully-double centre.
H:45cm (1½ft) S:20cm (8in)     Stks: Widely available

**Multi-flowered** (*flowering April–May*)
'Cheerfulness': Heads of creamy-white fls, orange centres.
☺✕ H:45cm (1½ft) S:20cm (8in)     Stks: Widely available
'Geranium': Clusters of white fls with bright orange cups.
☺✕☻ H:45cm (1½ft) S:20cm (8in)     Stks: Widely available

**Cyclamineus hybrids**
'February Gold': Yellow with deep yellow trumpet, March.
☺☺△☻ H:25cm (10in) S:10cm (4in)     Stks: Widely available
'Peeping Tom': Deep yellow with narrow trumpet, March.
☺☺ H:30cm (1ft) S:10cm (4in)     Stks: Widely available
'Tête-à-Tête': Lemon-yellow, small orange cup, end of Feb.
☺☺△☻ H:20cm (8in) S:10cm (4in)     Stks: Widely available

**Triandus varieties**
'Albus': Clusters of two or three creamy-white fls, March.
△ H:15cm (6in) S:7.5cm (3in)     Stks: Widely available
'Silver Chimes': Nodding white and primrose fls, May.
☺☺ H:30cm (1ft) S:10cm (4in)     Stks: Widely available
'Thalia': Three or more white fls on sturdy stems, April–May.
☺☺ H:38cm (15in) S:10cm (4in)     Stks: VT

**Nerine** Bulb     LM     O     **

bowdenii: Large, spiky, pink fls, Sept.–Nov.
H:60cm (2ft) S:15cm (6in)     Stks: Widely available

**Ornithogalum** Bulb   LMH   O–●   ***
  *nutans*: White and pale green star-shaped fls, April–May.
  ♀♀ H:30cm (1ft) S:15cm (6in)   *Stks*: Widely available

**Puschkinia** (striped squill) Bulb   LM(P)   O–◑   ***
  *libanotica*: Whitish scilla-like fls, blue stripes, March–April.
  △ H:10cm (4in) S:5cm (2in)   *Stks*: Widely available

**Scilla** (squill) Bulb   LMH   O–●   ***
  *non-scripta* (O–●): Large garden bluebell, April–May.
  ♀♀ △ H:18cm (7in) S:10cm (4in)   *Stks*: Widely available
  *siberica* (O–◑): Bright blue, bell-shaped fls, March–April.
  ♀♀ △ H:15cm (6in) S:10cm (4in)   *Stks*: Widely available

**Tulipa** (tulip) Bulb   LMH   O–◑   ***
  **Early Double** (*flowering late April*)
  'Marechal Niel': Yellow tinted soft orange fls.
  H:30cm (1ft) S:15cm (6in)   *Stks*: DJ
  'Peach Blossom': Rosy-pink fls. Stout stems.
  ☻ H:30cm (1ft) S:15cm (6in)   *Stks*: Widely available
  'Vuurbaak': Flame-red and perfect shape, on stout stems.
  H:30cm (1ft) S:15cm (6in)   *Stks*: Widely available

  **Early Single** (*flowering mid-April*)
  'Bellona': Pure golden-yellow heads on strong stems.
  ♪☻ H:38cm (15in) S:15cm (6in)   *Stks*: Widely available
  'Brilliant Star': Exceptionally bright scarlet.
  ☻ H:20cm (10in) S:15cm (6in)   *Stks*: Widely available
  'Prince of Austria': Rich orange-scarlet fls. Strong stems.
  ♪☻ H:30cm (1ft) S:15cm (6in)   *Stks*: Widely available

  **Triumph** (*flowering April–May*)
  'Apricot Beauty': Salmon-pink with cream lustre.
  H:38cm (15in) S:15cm (6in)   *Stks*: Widely available
  'First Lady': Reddish-violet flushed purple. Sturdy stems.
  H:50cm (20in) S:15cm (6in)   *Stks*: Widely available
  'Garden Party': White fls with carmine-pink edged petals.
  H:38cm (15in) S:15cm (6in)   *Stks*: Widely available

  **Lily-flowered** (*flowering early May*)
  'China Pink': Tall flowers, pure satin pink on graceful stems.
  ✕ H:50cm (20in) S:15cm (6in)   *Stks*: Widely available
  'West Point': Deep yellow with shapely recurving petals.
  ✕ H:50cm (20in) S:15cm (6in)   *Stks*: Widely available
  'White Triumphator': Elegant pure white fls on tall stems.
  ✕ H:65cm (26in) S:15cm (6in)   *Stks*: Widely available

  **Cottage and Darwin** (*flowering May*)
  'Clara Butt': Shapely salmon-pink fls on strong stems.
  ✕ H:60cm (2ft) S:15cm (6in)   *Stks*: Widely available
  'Golden Age': Buttercup-yellow fls, on strong stems.
  ☻ H:60cm (2ft) S:15cm (6in)   *Stks*: DJ
  'Halcro': Huge carmine-red fls with dark lustre.
  H:75cm (2½ft) S:15cm (6in)   *Stks*: Widely available
  'Renown': Soft carmine rose fls, lighter at petal edge.
  H:75cm (2½ft) S:15cm (6in)   *Stks*: WB

  **Darwin Hybrid** (*flowering April–May*)
  'Apeldoorn': Exceptionally bright orange-scarlet. Very large.
  ✕ H:60cm (2ft) S:15cm (6in)   *Stks*: Widely available
  'Golden Apeldoorn': Rounded, golden fls with a black base.
  H:60cm (2ft) S:15cm (6in)   *Stks*: Widely available

'Gudoshnik': Hugh fls, dark yellow flushed and striped red.
H:60cm (2ft) S:15cm (6in)   *Stks*: Widely available

'Holland's Glory': Orange-red, well-shaped fls.
✕ H:60cm (2ft) S:15cm (6in)   *Stks*: Widely available

'Yellow Dover': Clear buttercup yellow, shapely fls.
✕ H:60cm (2ft) S:15cm (6in)   *Stks*: DJ

**Parrot and Fringed** (*flowering mid-May*)

'Blue Parrot': Bright violet flushed blue, on tall stems.
H:60cm (2ft) S:15cm (6in)   *Stks*: DJ

'Burgundy Lace': Fringed tulip with wine-red fls.
H:60cm (2ft) S:15cm (6in)   *Stks*: Widely available

'Fantasy': Soft rose striped red and crested green.
H:60cm (2ft) S:15cm (6in)   *Stks*: Widely available

'Swan Wings': Fringed, white with black anthers.
✕ H:60cm (2ft) S:15cm (6in)   *Stks*: DJ

'Texas Gold': Large yellow fls tinged red and crested green.
H:60cm (2ft) S:15cm (6in)   *Stks*: WB

**Tulipa praestans** (*flowering April*)

'Fusilier': Up to five orange-scarlet fls on each stem.
△ H:25cm (10in) S:15cm (6in)   *Stks*: Widely available

**Tulipa fosteriana hybrids** (*flowering late March–April*)

'Princeps': Bright vivid scarlet fls on sturdy stems.
H:25cm (10in) S:15cm (6in)   *Stks*: Widely available

'Madam Lefeber' see 'Red Emperor'

'Red Emperor': Very large fls, bright scarlet.
H:38cm (15in) S:15cm (6in)   *Stks*: Widely available

**Tulipa greigii hybrids** (*flowering April*)

'Cape Cod': Bronze-yellow fls, with insides tinged scarlet.
H:20cm (8in) S:15cm (6in)   *Stks*: Widely available

'Plaisir': Creamy-white with vermilion stripes and shading.
◔ H:20cm (8in) S:15cm (6in)   *Stks*: Widely available

'Red Riding Hood': Vivid scarlet fls with black centres.
△ ◔ H:20cm (8in) S:15cm (6in)   *Stks*: Widely available

**Tulipa kaufmanniana hybrids** (*flowering March*)

'Heart's Delight': Carmine-red fls edged white, rose inside.
H:23cm (9in) S:15cm (6in)   *Stks*: Widely available

'Shakespeare': Blend of salmon, apricot and orange shades.
△ H:15cm (6in) S:15cm (6in)   *Stks*: Widely available

'Stresa': Very bright yellow with scarlet markings.
H:23cm (9in) S:15cm (6in)   *Stks*: Widely available

'The First': White tinted carmine-red on reverse. Very early.
H:20cm (8in) S:15cm (6in)   *Stks*: Widely available

---

## SPECIALIST SUPPLIERS

**CH**  Cramphorn Ltd., Cuton Mill, Springfield, Chelmsford, Essex, CM2 6PD. Tel: Chelmsford 466221.

**DJ**  P. de Jager & Sons Ltd., The Nurseries, Marden, Kent, TN12 9BP. Tel: Maidstone (0622) 831235.

**VT**  Van Tubergen Ltd., P.O. Box 156, Kingston-upon-Thames, Surrey, KT2 6AN.

**WB**  Walter Blom & Son Ltd., Coombelands Nurseries, Leavesden, Watford, Herts. WD2 7BH. Tel: Garston 72071.

# Rock Garden Plants

Most alpines are hardy, undemanding of space and time, and generally easy to grow. They thrive in any well-drained garden soil that has peat or well-rotted compost incorporated to retain moisture. But best results can be expected from a mixture of two parts good garden soil, two parts peat or well-rotted leaves, and one part sharp sand or grit. Animal manure and fertilizers should be avoided as they can lead to excessive growth, which is quite out of character for this group of plants.

A number of rock plants require an acid or peaty soil, and some of these require a north-facing position or some shade. These plants are likely to do best in a raised peat bed, edged with peat blocks or inverted heather turves, and containing a mixture of at least two parts moss peat to one part good lime-free soil and one part of sand or grit.

Most rock plants prefer a position in full sun, but some will tolerate shade and these should be chosen where shade is likely to be a problem. Plants with grey, felty and hairy leaves are better with some form of overhead protection from excessive wet in winter, and a sheet of glass supported on two bricks serves the purpose well.

## Where to grow

Although a large rock garden built on a bank is an ideal site, it does need to be *constructed*. It is not just a matter of scattering reject lumps of concrete over a hump, like currants on a bun – a natural-looking outcrop should be the ultimate aim. Remember, however, that a large area can take up much time weeding, dividing, replanting and trimming, so start modestly and see how it goes.

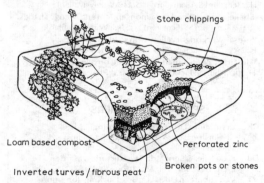

Stone chippings

Loam based compost

Perforated zinc

Inverted turves / fibrous peat

Broken pots or stones

*Stone sinks make ideal miniature gardens. Good drainage is essential, but a layer of peat or inverted turves will help the soil retain sufficient moisture and prevent the compost being washed away. Stone chippings can be placed on the surface to enhance its appearance and retain moisture.*

A small raised bed is perfectly adequate for a small collection of rock plants, and some species are suitable for growing in the crevices of dry stone walls or between crazy-paving.

Consider growing some of the choicest kinds in a cold-frame or alpine greenhouse (one plant to a pot), in equal parts loam, peat and sand.

Sink gardens can be delightful if planted with compact subjects. Old stone sinks can be expensive and it is cheaper to convert a glazed sink. First wash it clean, and then paint over it when dry with a builder's glue such as Polybond or Unibond; when this is tacky slap on a doughy mixture of one part cement, one part fine sand, and one part fine peat.

A charming effect can also be achieved by planting a strawberry pot with a small collection of houseleeks (sempervivums), for example.

### Choosing and buying

Selecting species that bloom at different times makes it possible to ensure interest at all seasons.

Many of the more popular rock plants are widely available from nurseries and garden centres, but for particular varieties and some of the less common species, it may be necessary to buy from a nursery specializing in alpines.

Many small bulbs and dwarf conifers are also suitable for a rock garden, and these, together with stockists, will be found in the relevant chapters.

Most alpines are sold in pots. Look for pots with the top covered with healthy growing plant. Avoid any that have toppled over and look either dried out, too wet, or pot-bound. Buy plants that are clearly named with fresh clean labels.

### If you want to know more . . .

Anyone interested in learning more about alpines should consider joining the Alpine Garden Society. The Secretary's address is Lye End Link, St. John's, Woking, Surrey.

A useful reference book is *The Ingwersen Manual of Alpine Plants*, by Will Ingwersen.

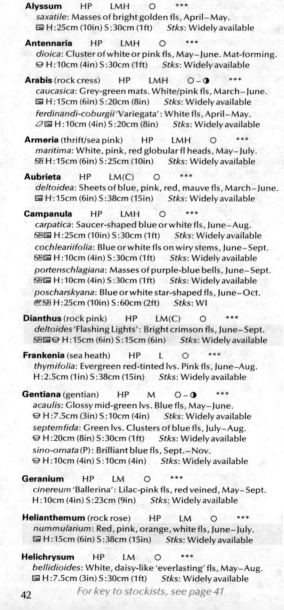

**Achillea** (yarrow)    HP    LMH    O    ***
*tomentosa*: Flat heads of yellow fls, July–Sept.
H:15cm (6in) S:30cm (1ft)    *Stks*: Widely available

**Ajuga** (bugle)    HP    LMH    O–●    ***
*reptans*: 'Burgundy Glow': Bronze lvs. Blue fls, May–June.
H:10cm (4in) S:30cm (1ft)    *Stks*: Widely available

**Alyssum**    HP    LMH    O    ***
*saxatile*: Masses of bright golden fls, April–May.
H:25cm (10in) S:30cm (1ft)    *Stks*: Widely available

**Antennaria**    HP    LMH    O    ***
*dioica*: Cluster of white or pink fls, May–June. Mat-forming.
H:10cm (4in) S:30cm (1ft)    *Stks*: Widely available

**Arabis** (rock cress)    HP    LMH    O–◐    ***
*caucasica*: Grey-green mats. White/pink fls, March–June.
H:15cm (6in) S:20cm (8in)    *Stks*: Widely available
*ferdinandi-coburgii* 'Variegata': White fls, April–May.
H:10cm (4in) S:20cm (8in)    *Stks*: Widely available

**Armeria** (thrift/sea pink)    HP    LMH    O    ***
*maritima*: White, pink, red globular fl heads, May–July.
H:15cm (6in) S:25cm (10in)    *Stks*: Widely available

**Aubrieta**    HP    LM(C)    O    ***
*deltoidea*: Sheets of blue, pink, red, mauve fls, March–June.
H:15cm (6in) S:38cm (15in)    *Stks*: Widely available

**Campanula**    HP    LMH    O    ***
*carpatica*: Saucer-shaped blue or white fls, June–Aug.
H:25cm (10in) S:30cm (1ft)    *Stks*: Widely available
*cochleariifolia*: Blue or white fls on wiry stems, June–Sept.
H:10cm (4in) S:30cm (1ft)    *Stks*: Widely available
*portenschlagiana*: Masses of purple-blue bells, June–Sept.
H:10cm (4in) S:30cm (1ft)    *Stks*: Widely available
*poscharskyana*: Blue or white star-shaped fls, June–Oct.
H:25cm (10in) S:60cm (2ft)    *Stks*: WI

**Dianthus** (rock pink)    HP    LM(C)    O    ***
*deltoides* 'Flashing Lights': Bright crimson fls, June–Sept.
H:15cm (6in) S:15cm (6in)    *Stks*: Widely available

**Frankenia** (sea heath)    HP    L    O    ***
*thymifolia*: Evergreen red-tinted lvs. Pink fls, June–Aug.
H:2.5cm (1in) S:38cm (15in)    *Stks*: Widely available

**Gentiana** (gentian)    HP    M    O–◐    ***
*acaulis*: Glossy mid-green lvs. Blue fls, May–June.
H:7.5cm (3in) S:10cm (4in)    *Stks*: Widely available
*septemfida*: Green lvs. Clusters of blue fls, July–Aug.
H:20cm (8in) S:30cm (1ft)    *Stks*: Widely available
*sino-ornata* (P): Brilliant blue fls, Sept.–Nov.
H:10cm (4in) S:10cm (4in)    *Stks*: Widely available

**Geranium**    HP    LM    O    ***
*cinereum* 'Ballerina': Lilac-pink fls, red veined, May–Sept.
H:10cm (4in) S:23cm (9in)    *Stks*: Widely available

**Helianthemum** (rock rose)    HP    LM    O    ***
*nummularium*: Red, pink, orange, white fls, June–July.
H:15cm (6in) S:38cm (15in)    *Stks*: Widely available

**Helichrysum**    HP    LM    O    ***
*bellidioides*: White, daisy-like 'everlasting' fls, May–Aug.
H:7.5cm (3in) S:30cm (1ft)    *Stks*: Widely available

**Hepatica**   HP   LM(C)   ○ – ◑   ***
*nobilis*: Partially evergreen. Large blue fls, Feb.–April.
H:7.5cm (3in) S:30cm (1ft)   *Stks*: Widely available

**Iberis** (perennial candytuft)   HP   LMH   ○   ***
*sempervirens*: Masses of white fls, May–June. Evergreen.
⊟ H:15cm (6in) S:20cm (8in)   *Stks*: Widely available

**Leontopodium** (Edelweiss)   HP   LM   ○   ***
*alpinum*: Grey flannel-like fls with woolly bracts, June–July.
⊠ H:15cm (6in) S:15cm (6in)   *Stks*: Widely available

**Lewisia**   HP   LM   ○   ***
Hybrids: White, red, yellow, pink, apricot fls, May–Aug.
⊟⊖ H:15cm (6in) S:20cm (8in)   *Stks*: Widely available

**Lithospermum** (gromwell)   HP   LM(P)   ○   ***
*diffusum* 'Grace Ward': Dark lvs. Intense blue fls, June–Oct.
⊟ H:10cm (4in) S:25cm (10in)   *Stks*: Widely available

**Mimulus** (monkey flower)   HP   LMH(M)   ○ – ◑   ***
× *burnettii*: Orange-yellow fls, yellow throats, June–Aug.
H:25cm (10in) S:23cm (9in)   *Stks*: Widely available

**Phlox**   HP   LMH   ○ – ◑   ***
*douglasii*: Bright red, pink, or white fls, May–June.
⊟ H:7.5cm (3in) S:45cm (1½ft)   *Stks*: Widely available
*subulata*: Masses of pink, red, white, or blue fls, April–May.
⊟ H:15cm (6in) S:30cm (1ft)   *Stks*: Widely available

**Primula**   HP   MH(M)   ◑   ***
*rosea* 'Delight': Intense deep pink heads, March–May.
H:15cm (6in) S:15cm (6in)   *Stks*: BG

**Pulsatilla** (pasque flower)   HP   LMH   ○   ***
*vulgaris*: White, purple, or pink fls, April–May.
H:20cm (8in) S:15cm (6in)   *Stks*: Widely available

**Raoulia**   HP   M   ○   **
*australis*: Silvery-grey mat. Tiny yellow fls, April–May.
⊖ H:12mm (½in) S:30cm (1ft)   *Stks*: Widely available

**Rhodohypoxis**   HP   LM(P)   ○   ***
*baurii*: White, pink to red fls above lvs, June–Sept.
⊖ H:7.5cm (3in) S:15cm (6in)   *Stks*: WI

**Saxifraga**   HP   LM(C)   ○ – ●   ***
*aizoon* 'Lutea' (○): Pale green rosettes. Lemon fls, May–June.
⊖ H:15cm (6in) S:15cm (6in)   *Stks*: Widely available
*aizoon* 'Rosea' (○): Sprays of pink fls, May–June.
⊖ H:15cm (6in) S:15cm (6in)   *Stks*: Widely available
*fortunei* (●): Showers of white fls over lobed lvs, Oct.–Nov.
H:30cm (1ft) S:30cm (1ft)   *Stks*: Widely available
*paniculata*: see *S. aizoon*

**Sedum** (stonecrop)   HP   LMH   ○   ***
*spathulifolium* 'Purpureum': Purple lvs. Golden fls, June.
⊟⊖ H:7.5cm (3in) S:23cm (9in)   *Stks*: Widely available

**Sempervivum** (houseleek)   HP   LM   ○   ***
*arachnoideum*: 'Cobwebbed' rosettes. Pink fls, June–July.
⊟⊖ H:10cm (4in) S:23cm (9in)   *Stks*: Widely available
'Othello': Large ruby-red rosettes. Pink fls, June-July.
⊟ H:20cm (8in) S:30cm (1ft)   *Stks*: BG

**Thymus** (thyme)   HP   LM(C)   ○   ***
*serpyllum* 'Coccineus': Aromatic lvs. Crimson fls, May–July.
⌖⊟⊠ H:5cm (2in) S:60cm (2ft)   *Stks*: Widely available

*For key to symbols, see page 7*

# Trees

We should all be looking for opportunities to plant any kind of tree. Evergreen trees give year-round effect but the deciduous kinds have the attraction of richly coloured new growth in spring, a moving canopy of foliage in summer, and lovely autumn shades before leaves fall.

Care should be taken to choose the best tree for each situation. Having said that, I see no harm in planting a fast-growing kind for rapid effect with the plan to cut it back or down once it has outgrown the space available. There are several really large trees in the following list, like beech, oak and lime, that are too big for the average garden. We do have the opportunity, however, to plant these for the benefit of ourselves and future generations in school and other playing fields, public greens and open spaces.

Naturally trees will grow bigger and faster in fertile soils, smaller and more slowly in poor soils. The heights listed here are a guide to likely height in 20 years under average garden conditions.

### Where to grow

A group of trees like *Populus candicans* 'Aurora' makes a good shelter belt to protect exposed gardens. The flowering crabs (*Malus*) provide attractive flowers and fruits, and cultivars like *M.* 'Golden Hornet' also act as pollinators to eating apples.

There are many different trees to use as attractive single specimens, and the weeping forms are often smaller and more suited to the small modern garden. Willows are a good choice for wet soils but the golden weeping willow makes a very large tree quite quickly and should only be planted in large gardens. Where space is limited use the compact *Salix caprea* 'Pendula'.

Use the attractive flowering and berry-producing kinds to give height and an extra dimension to shrub borders.

Try to keep the soil cultivated for several feet around newly planted trees. Competition from grass can severely check growth in the first two or three years following transplanting. All newly planted trees will need canes or stakes for support until very well rooted.

Weeping trees will need the top lead shoot tied upright to a tall cane until the required height of trunk is achieved.

### What to buy

Select stout, straight-stemmed specimens. Good trees will have produced strong young shoots of 45cm (1½ft) to 1m (3½ft) during the immediate past season. Bare root trees should never have the roots exposed to hard frost or be allowed to dry. It is better if the roots are well

## HOW TO PLANT A BARE-ROOT TREE

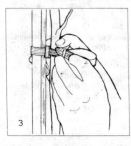

**1.** *Use a batten to ensure the soil will be level with the old soil mark on the trunk.*

**2.** *Insert a stout stake on the windward side before firming the soil around the roots.*

**3.** *Always use a tree tie to secure the stem to the top of the stake. Use adjustable ties.*

branched with a fair amount of fibrous root.

Avoid trees with just a few roots which are thick, thongy and cut back very short when lifted. Some root damage is inevitable when trees are lifted and as long as the damaged root ends are pruned off neatly and cleanly, new roots will soon form. The best time to transplant deciduous trees lifted from the open ground is late October or during November. They can, however, be transplanted any time from October to late March provided the soil is neither too wet nor too frozen.

When selecting trees with roots wrapped in peat the heavier specimens are usually the best buy.

Container-*grown* trees can be planted the year round as long as the soil is neither too wet nor frozen. It is very important to look for trees with plenty of strong *new* growth. A little small weed growth and algae on the surface of the pot, and a few roots through the base, is a good sign and indicates plants well rooted in their containers. These specimens should transplant well. If when you lift the tree by the stem it starts to leave the container, it has only recently been potted.

Container trees that have stood on sale for many months, have little new growth and have had much of the surface compost hosed out of the container, are not usually a good buy.

### If you want to know more . . .

Two useful publications are *Hilliers' Manual of Trees and Shrubs* (David and Charles), and *Trees for Your Garden*, by Roy Lancaster (Floraprint).

**Acer** (maple) (D)   LMH   ○   \*\*\*
*davidii*: Green and white striped bark. Yellow lvs in autumn.
🌢▣♠ H:6m+ (20ft+) S:3m+ (10ft+)   *Stks*: HW, SD
*negundo* 'Elegans': Bright yellow margins to lvs.
∅ H:6m+ (20ft+) S:4m+ (13ft+)   *Stks*: HW, NN, RN
*negundo* 'Variegata': Broad lvs with irregular white edges.
∅ H:6m+ (20ft+) S:4m+ (13ft+)   *Stks*: Widely available
*platanoides* 'Crimson King': Deep purplish-crimson lvs.
∅🌢 H:10.5m+ (35ft+) S:4.5m+ (15ft+)   *Stks*: Wdly avail.
*platanoides* 'Drummondii': Marginal white band to the lvs.
∅ H:10.5m+ (35ft+) S:4.5m+ (15ft+)   *Stks*: Wdly avail.
*pseudoplatanus* 'Brilliantissimum': Shrimp-pink young lvs.
∅♠ H:6m+ (20ft+) S:4m+ (13ft+)   *Stks*: Widely available
*pseudoplatanus* 'Worleei': Yellow lvs spring to July.
∅ H:11m+ (36ft+) S:5m+ (16ft+)   *Stks*: Widely available

**Aesculus** (horse chestnut) (D)   LMH   ○   \*\*\*
× *carnea* 'Briotii': Large clusters of deep pink fls. No conkers.
♠ H:7.5m+ (25ft+) S:4.5m (15ft)   *Stks*: Widely available

**Alnus** (alder) (D)   MH(M)   ○   \*\*\*
*cordata*: Shiny green lvs. Interesting catkins and fruit.
🗲 H:15m+ (50ft+) S:7m+ (23ft+)   *Stks*: Widely available
*glutinosa* 'Aurea': Golden lvs in spring, fading to green.
∅ H:12m+ (40ft+) S:6m+ (20ft+)   *Stks*: HN, NN

**Betula** (birch) (D)   LMH   ○–◑   \*\*\*
*pendula*: Sharply-cut, diamond-shaped lvs. Silver bark.
🌢▣ H:11m+ (36ft+) S:4.5m+ (15ft+)   *Stks*: Wdly avail.
*pendula* 'Tristis': Beautiful slender pendulous branches.
▣⊤ H:7.5m+ (25ft+) S:3m+ (10ft+)   *Stks*: Wdly avail.
*pendula* 'Youngii': Small, weeping, dome-shaped tree.
🌢▣⊤ H:6m+ (20ft+) S:3m+ (10ft+)   *Stks*: Wdly avail.

**Carpinus** (hornbeam) (D)   MH(C)   ○   \*\*\*
*betulus* 'Fastigiata': Erect, columnar tree. Broadens with age.
♠ H:6m+ (20ft+) S:3m+ (10ft+)   *Stks*: Widely available

**Catalpa** (Indian bean tree) (D)   LM(C)   ○   \*\*
*bignonioides* 'Aurea': Large, soft, velvety, yellow lvs.
∅♠ H:4.5m+ (15ft+) S:4.5m+ (15ft+)   *Stks*: Widely avail.

**Cotoneaster** (E)   LMH   ○   \*\*\*
'Hybridus Pendulus': Small, weeping tree. Red fruits.
🗲♠⊤ H:1.8m (6ft) S:1.8m (6ft)   *Stks*: Widely available
*salicifolius* 'Autumn Fire': Pendulous habit. Red fruits.
🗲 H:6m+ (20ft+) S:4.5m+ (15ft+)   *Stks*: Widely available

**Crataegus** (thorn) (D)   LMH   ○–◑   \*\*\*
*crus-galli*: White fls, June, followed by red haws.
🗲♠ H:5m+ (16ft+) S:6m+ (20ft+)   *Stks*: Widely available
*oxyacantha* 'Coccinea Plena' ('Paul's Scarlet'): Double red fls.
H:4.5m+ (15ft+) S:4.5m+ (15ft+)   *Stks*: Widely available

**Eucalyptus** (gum) (E)   MH   ○   \*
*gunnii*: Young lvs rounded and glaucous blue.
✕▣ H:15m+ (50ft+) S:4m+ (13ft+)   *Stks*: Widely available
*niphophila*: Large, leathery, grey-green lvs. Slow-growing.
▣♠ H:6m+ (20ft+) S:6m+ (20ft+)   *Stks*: HW, SN

**Fagus** (beech) (D)   LMH(C)   ○   \*\*\*
*sylvatica*: Noble tree of large proportions. Good autumn lvs.
🌢 H:11m+ (36ft+) S:7m+ (23ft+)   *Stks*: Widely available

*sylvatica* 'Pendula': Spectacular, large, weeping tree.
🦜 T H:11m+ (36ft+) S:7m+ (23ft+)  *Stks*: Widely available

*sylvatica* 'Purpurea': Pale red lvs, becoming dark purple.
⊘ H:11m+ (36ft+) S:7m+ (23ft+)  *Stks*: Widely available

**Fraxinus** (ash) (D)  LMH  ○  ***
*excelsior* 'Jaspidea': Golden-yellow young shoots. Vigorous.
🦜 ⑥ H:9m+ (30ft+) S:5m+ (16ft+)  *Stks*: HW, NN, SN

*excelsior* 'Pendula': Attractive, pendulous branches.
T H:8m+ (26ft+) S:5m+ (16ft+)  *Stks*: Widely available

**Gleditsia** (honey locust) (D)  LMH  ○–◑  ***
*triacanthos* 'Sunburst': Bright yellow young lvs.
⊘ H:7.5m+ (25ft+) S:4.5m+ (15ft+)  *Stks*: Widely available

**Juglans** (walnut) (D)  LMH  ○  ***
*regia*: Long pinnate lvs set in an attractive round head.
H:8m+ (26ft+) S:6m+ (20ft+)  *Stks*: Widely available

**Koelreuteria** (golden-rain tree) (D)  LMH  ○  ***
*paniculata*: Yellow fls. Bladder-like fruits.
🦜 ♠ H:6m+ (20ft+) S:4m+ (13ft+)  *Stks*: Widely available

**Laburnum** (golden rain) (D)  LMH  ○–◑  ***
× *watereri* 'Vossii': Long branches of yellow fls, June.
♠ H:8m+ (26ft+) S:3m+ (10ft+)  *Stks*: Widely available

**Liquidambar** (sweet gum) (D)  MH(A)  ○  ***
*styraciflua*: Maple-like lvs, spectacular colour in autumn.
🦜 H:6m+ (20ft+) S:3.5m+ (12ft+)  *Stks*: Widely available

**Liriodendron** (tulip tree) (D)  LMH  ○  ***
*tulipifera*: Greenish tulip-shaped fls in June and July.
🦜 H:11m+ (36ft+) S:9m+ (30ft+)  *Stks*: Widely available

**Magnolia** (E and D)  LMH  ○  **
*grandiflora* (E): Fragrant, creamy-white fls. Best against wall.
🌑 H:6m+ (20ft+) S:5m+ (16ft+)  *Stks*: Widely available

*kobus* (D): Slightly fragrant white fls borne in April.
H:6m+ (20ft+) S:3.5m+ (12ft+)  *Stks*: HW, NN, RN

**Malus** (flowering crabs) (D)  LMH  ○  ***
*floribunda*: Pinkish-red fls in spring. Yellow and red fruits.
🌑🗶 ♠ H:3m+ (10ft+) S:3m+ (10ft+)  *Stks*: Widely avail.

'Golden Hornet': White fls in May. Bright yellow fruits.
🗶 ♠ H:4.5m+ (15ft+) S:3m+ (10ft+)  *Stks*: Widely available

'John Downie': White fls in May. Red, conical fruits.
🗶 ♠ H:7.5m+ (25ft+) S:4.5m+ (15ft+)  *Stks*: Widely avail.

'Profusion': Single, red fls in May. Rich purple young lvs.
🌑⊘🗶 ♠ H:4.5m+ (15ft+) S:3m+ (10ft+)  *Stks*: Wdly avail.

'Red Jade': White and pink fls. Red fruits.
🗶 ♠ T H:6m+ (20ft+) S:4m+ (13ft+)  *Stks*: Widely avail.

× *robusta*: Beautiful yellow or cherry-red fruits.
🗶 ♠ H:8m+ (26ft+) S:5m+ (16ft+)  *Stks*: HW, NN, SN

'Royalty': Rich purple lvs. Pink fls. Red-purple fruits.
⊘🗶 ♠ H:4.5m+ (15ft+) S:3m+ (10ft+)  *Stks*: Widely avail.

*tschonoskii*: Single, white, pink-tinted fls. Upright growth.
🦜 ♠ H:9m+ (30ft+) S:3m+ (10ft+)  *Stks*: Widely available

'Van Eseltine': Semi-double pink fls. Erect habit. Small fruit.
🌑🗶 ♠ H:6m+ (20ft+) S:3m+ (10ft+)  *Stks*: HW, NN

**Morus** (mulberry) (D)  LM  ○  ***
*nigra*: Heart-shaped lvs. Beautiful black-red fruits.
🗶 ♠ H:4.5m+ (15ft+) S:3m+ (10ft+)  *Stks*: Widely available

*For key to symbols, see page 7*  47

**Nothofagus** (D)    LMH(A)    O    **
  *antarctica*: Small, rounded, heart-shaped dark green lvs.
  H:11m+ (36ft+) S:7m+ (23ft+)    *Stks*: HW, NN

**Nyssa** (tupelo) (D)    LMH(A, M)    O    ***
  *sylvatica*: Lvs become rich scarlet, orange and yellow.
  ❧ H:6m+ (20ft+) S:3m+ (10ft+)    *Stks*: HW, RN, SD

**Platanus** (D)    LMH(A)    O    **
  × *hispanica* (London plane): Maple-like lvs. Peeling bark.
  🖻 H:9m+ (30ft+) S:4.5m+ (15ft+)    *Stks*: Widely available

**Populus** (poplar) (D)    MH(M)    O    ***
  *alba* 'Raket': Glossy grey lvs – white beneath.
  H:10.5m+ (35ft+) S:4.5m+ (15ft+)    *Stks*: HN, HW, SN
  × *candicans* 'Aurora': Heart-shaped lvs, variegated white.
  ∅ H:10.5m+ (35ft+) S:4.5m+ (15ft+)    *Stks*: Wdly avail.
  *nigra* 'Italica' (Lombardy poplar): Large, columnar, erect tree.
  H:10.5m+ (35ft+) S:3m+ (10ft+)    *Stks*: Widely available

**Prunus** (cherry trees) (D)    LMH    O    ***
  'Amanogawa': Shell-pink fls, April–May. Very erect growth.
  🌿● H:4.5m+ (15ft+) S:1m+ (3½ft+)    *Stks*: Widely available
  *cerasifera* 'Pissardii': Dark red young lvs, turning purple.
  ∅● H:6m+ (20ft+) S:5m+ (16ft+)    *Stks*: Widely available
  'Kanzan': Double, pink fls in April–May. 45° angle branches.
  ● H:7.5m+ (25ft+) S:6m+ (20ft+)    *Stks*: Widely available
  'Kiku-shidare Sakura': Weeping cherry. Rose-pink fls, April.
  ●⊤ H:4.5m+ (15ft+) S:4.5+ (15ft+)    *Stks*: Widely available
  *padus*: Almond-scented white fls, hanging in sprays, May.
  🌿● H:7.5m+ (25ft+) S:4.5m+ (15ft+)    *Stks*: Widely avail.
  *serrulata pubescens*: White or pink fls, late April–May.
  ● H:4.5m+ (15ft+) S:4.5m+ (15ft+)    *Stks*: SN
  'Shirotae': Snow-white, semi-double fls, late April.
  🌿● H:6m+ (20ft+) S:9m+ (30ft+)    *Stks*: Widely available
  'Tai Haku': Large, dazzling white fls in April.
  ● H:10.5m+ (35ft+) S:6m+ (20ft+)    *Stks*: Widely available
  *subhirtella* 'Autumnalis': Pale-blush fls, Nov.–March.
  ● H:7.5m+ (25ft+) S:7.5m+ (25ft+)    *Stks*: Widely available
  *triloba*: Rosette-like peach-pink fls, March–April.
  ● H:10.5m+ (35ft+) S:7.5m+ (25ft+)    *Stks*: Widely avail.

**Pyrus** (pear) (D)    LMH    O    ***
  *salicifolia* 'Pendula': Beautiful, silvery-grey lvs.
  ⊤ H:6m+ (20ft+) S:3.5m+ (12ft+)    *Stks*: Widely available

**Quercus** (oak) (D)    MH    O    ***
  *robur*: Large tree with a broad dome-shaped head.
  ❧ H:12m+ (40ft+) S:10.5m+ (35ft+)    *Stks*: Widely available
  *rubra*: Lobed lvs, crimson to deep red-brown in autumn.
  ❧ H:10.5m+ (35ft+) S:7m+ (23ft+)    *Stks*: Widely available

---

### SOME TREES FOR COASTAL PLANTING

| | |
|---|---|
| Crataegus crus-galli | Salix 'Basfordiana' |
| Crataegus oxyacantha | Salix caprea |
| Eucalyptus gunnii | Salix × chrysocoma |
| Eucalyptus niphophila | Salix matsudana |
| Fraxinus excelsior | Salix purpurea |
| Morus nigra | Sorbus aria |
| Populus alba | Sorbus aucuparia |

**Rhus** (sumach) (D)    LMH    ○    ***
 *typhina* 'Laciniata': Cut-leaved. Conical crimson fruit.
 Ⓓ ❧ H:3m+ (10ft+) S:4.5m+ (15ft+)    *Stks*: Widely available

**Robinia** (false acacia) (D)    LMH    ○    ***
 *pseudoacacia* 'Frisia': Rich yellow lvs, spring to autumn.
 Ⓓ H:6m+ (20ft+) S:3m+ (10ft+)    *Stks*: Widely available

**Salix** (willow) (D)    MH(M)    ○    ***
 'Basfordiana': Long, narrow lvs. Red twigs in winter.
 Ⓑ H:7.5m+ (25ft+) S:4.5m+ (15ft+)    *Stks*: HW
 *caprea* 'Pendula': Umbrella-like tree; pendulous branches.
 ❀ ⊤ H:4m (13ft) S:3m (10ft)    *Stks*: Widely available
 × *chrysocoma*: Pendent, yellow stems on a weeping tree.
 Ⓑ ⊤ H:12m+ (40ft+) S:7.5m+ (25ft+)    *Stks*: Widely avail.
 *matsudana* 'Tortuosa': Branches and twigs much contorted.
 Ⓑ H:7.5m+ (25ft+) S:4.5m+ (15ft+)    *Stks*: Widely available
 *purpurea* 'Pendula': Pendulous; shoots often purplish.
 ❀ ⊤ H:3m+ (10ft+) S:3m+ (10ft+)    *Stks*: Widely available

**Sorbus** (D)    MH    ○    ***
 *aria* 'Lutescens': Upper surfaces of lvs creamy-white.
 ❀ H:4.5m+ (15ft+) S:3m+ (10ft+)    *Stks*: Widely available
 *aucuparia* 'Aspleniifolia': Finely divided fern-like lvs.
 ✄ ❀ H:4.5m+ (15ft+) S:3m+ (10ft+)    *Stks*: Widely available
 *aucuparia* 'Sheerwater Seedling': Upright. Orange-red fruits.
 ✄ ❀ H:6m+ (20ft+) S:3m+ (10ft+)    *Stks*: Widely available
 *discolor*: Sharply-pointed leaflets. Yellowish-pink fruits.
 ❧ ✄ ❀ H:4.5m+ (15ft+) S:3m+ (10ft+)    *Stks*: Wdly avail.
 'Joseph Rock': Excellent autumn colour; yellow fruits.
 ❧ ✄ ❀ H:4.5m+ (15ft+) S:3m+ (10ft+)    *Stks*: Wdly avail.

**Tilia** (lime) (D)    LMH    ○    ***
 *cordata*: Glossy green heart-shaped leathery lvs.
 ⚘ H:9m+ (30ft+) S:4.5m+ (15ft+)    *Stks*: Widely available
 × *euchlora*: Ovate, shiny, dark green lvs. Aphid-free.
 H:9m+ (30ft+) S:4.5m+ (15ft+)    *Stks*: Widely available

**Ulmus** (elm) (D)    LMH    ○    ***
 *glabra* 'Camperdownii': Compact, pendulous, neat.
 ❀ ⊤ H:7.5m+ (25ft+) S:4.5m+ (15ft+)    *Stks*: NN, RR
 × *hollandica* 'Wredei': Lvs suffused yellow. Upright growth.
 Ⓓ H:7.5m+ (25ft+) S:4.5m+ (15ft+)    *Stks*: NN

---

## SPECIALIST SUPPLIERS

**HN**   Highfield Nurseries, Whitminster, Gloucester, GL2 7PL. Tel: Gloucester (0252) 740266.

**HW**   Hillier Nurseries Ltd., Ampfield House, Ampfield, Romsey, Hants, SO5 9PA. Tel: Braishfield 68733.

**NN**   Notcutts Nurseries Ltd., Ipswich Road, Woodbridge, Suffolk, IP12 4AF. Tel: Woodbridge (03943) 3344.

**RN**   L. R. Russell Ltd., Richmond Nurseries, Windlesham, Surrey, GU20 6LL. Tel: Ascot 21411.

**RR**   R. V. Roger Ltd., The Nurseries, Pickering, North Yorkshire, YO18 7HG. Tel: Pickering (0751) 72226.

**SD**   Sunningdale Nurseries Ltd., Windlesham, Surrey. Tel: Ascot 20496.

**SN**   Scotts Nurseries (Merriott) Ltd., Merriott, Somerset, TA16 5PL. Tel: Crewkerne (0460) 72306.

---

*For key to symbols, see page 7*

# Conifers

The evergreens often referred to in common language as cupressus are all cone bearing and because of this are called conifers. They serve many purposes in the garden but you need to choose carefully to satisfy each one.

A number ideally suited to screening and hedging are listed on pages 70–71, though others suitable for this purpose are included here. All of the *Chamaecyparis lawsoniana* varieties can be used for screens but they do not take kindly to cutting back hard.

Many of the attractively coloured forms make superb specimens and others provide added height in the garden and associate well with heathers. There are numerous low-growing and spreading kinds, some can even replace grass, while others are ideal for clothing banks and hiding manhole covers. The stronger-growing prostrate kinds are excellent for weed-smothering ground cover. Several upright slow-growing kinds make good specimens for tub culture and the upright yews and junipers can be planted to give a colonnade effect.

## Where to grow

There are different types to suit all soils and as a general rule the junipers are toughest and withstand both poor soils and cold, exposed situations. Golden-leaved varieties will thrive and produce a better colour in full sun.

Choose yew for alkaline (chalky) soils, but *Chamaecyparis* will grow better in free-draining but moist acid soils. Adding plenty of peat before planting and seeing that they are watered and fed well in summer will give the best growth for all types.

Speed of growth and ultimate size vary tremendously with different kinds. The heights and spreads given for each one are likely averages after 20 years of growth. Naturally the growth rates will be slower in poor soil and faster in a fertile, carefully tended garden.

It is difficult to draw a clear line to separate the slow-growing and dwarf from the tall varieties and inevitably there is some blurring of categories.

Beware of very young plants – usually little more than rooted cuttings – being sold as dwarf when in fact they are fast-growing and ultimately very tall varieties. This guide will help you sort out the tall-growing kinds as long as they are named correctly.

While such plants can be used as temporary fillers it is usually better to start out with the right type.

## What to buy

Container-grown plants are the best without doubt. The absence of root damage also allows transplanting at any time of year, as long as the soil is neither frozen nor waterlogged.

Conifers grown in fields and lifted for sale will be cheaper but need great care. They are most likely to move successfully in September and October or March and April. A large soil-ball containing as much root as possible is held in place with a sheet of sacking or polythene tied tightly around the trunk.

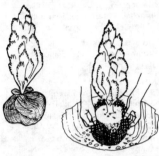

Conifers are often sold as 'balled' plants. If the root-ball is covered with a plastic material this should be removed before planting, but a hessian or sacking covering can be left in place as it will eventually rot.

Sacking can be left in place to rot but all plastic must be removed. Should the soil crumble away when wraps are removed from 'balled' conifers, pack wet peat around the roots in its place when filling soil back into the hole.

Purchase only balled specimens that have been plunged in damp peat or soil to keep them moist. Check to see that each plant has a large and firm root-ball.

Avoid all conifers which have browned lower branches (a little browning occurs in the *centre* of most well-established plants and this is quite normal). Any plants with light, dull-coloured leaves and signs of un-natural yellowing should also be avoided.

Aphids produce a white, waxy secretion on the leaves and the tiny red spider mite can cause defoliation, especially on piceas. Avoid purchasing plants showing these symptoms. Should you have plants that are subsequently attacked, spray with malathion. Watch out especially in May and June and in hot dry weather, and spray at the first sighting.

Younger, smaller plants will be cheaper than older and larger specimens. Young, fast-growing specimens of the taller kinds are a good buy. The young plants quickly develop a strong root system after planting. Larger specimens will need careful staking and watering, both overhead and to the root-ball, for several months until well established. A thin, long, whippy tip growth in summer is a good sign of strong healthy growth on the taller kinds.

Larger sizes of the dwarf and slow-growing kinds do provide excellent value for money. Where else can you buy several years for a few extra pounds?

**If you want to know more . . .**
A well-illustrated and informative book is *Conifers for your Garden*, by Adrian Bloom (Floraprint).

## TALL VARIETIES

**Abies** (fir) (E)  LMH  ○  ***
*grandis*: Shiny, bright green lvs, silvery bands beneath.
H:15m+ (50ft+) S:9m+ (30ft+)  *Stks*: HW
*koreana*: Dark green lvs, silvery undersides. Purple cones.
H:4.5m (15ft) S:3m (10ft)  *Stks*: Widely available

**Araucaria** (monkey puzzle tree) (E)  LMH(M)  ○  ***
*araucana*: Radiating branches. Lvs arranged in spirals.
♣ H:7.5m+ (25ft+) S:4.5m+ (15ft+)  *Stks*: HW, SN

**Calocedrus** (syn. Libocedrus) (E)  LMH  ○  ***
*decurrens*: Upright columns of rich green foliage.
H:13.5m (45ft) S:3m (10ft)  *Stks*: HW

**Cedrus** (cedar) (E)  LMH  ○  ***
*atlantica* 'Glauca': Beautiful blue-green foliage.
♣ H:15m+ (50ft+) S:4.5m+ (15ft+)  *Stks*: HW, SN
*atlantica* 'Glauca Pendula': Glaucous, weeping foliage.
♣ T H:6m+ (20ft+) S:2.4m+ (8ft+)  *Stks*: HW, WN
*deodara*: Young blue-grey lvs, darkening with age.
♣ H:12m+ (40ft+) S:4.5m+ (15ft+)  *Stks*: HW, SN
*deodara* 'Aurea' (**): Bright golden-yellow foliage in spring.
♣ H:9m+ (30ft+) S:3m+ (10ft+)  *Stks*: HW, WN
*libani* (cedar of Lebanon): Majestic, horizontal branches.
H:12m+ (40ft+) S:7.5m+ (25ft+)  *Stks*: HW, SN

**Chamaecyparis** (E)  LMH(P)  ○  ***
*lawsoniana* 'Allumii': Upright, conical shape. Blue-grey lvs.
H:6m+ (20ft+) S:1.5m+ (5ft+)  *Stks*: Widely available
*lawsoniana* 'Columnaris Glauca': Slender, upright conifer.
H:4.5m+ (15ft+) S:60cm+ (2ft+)  *Stks*: HW, SN
*lawsoniana* 'Ellwoodii': Frothy sprays, grey-green foliage.
H:3m (10ft) S:60cm (2ft)  *Stks*: Widely available
*lawsoniana* 'Ellwood's Gold': Tips of lvs tinged yellow.
H:2.7m (9ft) S:45cm (1½ft)  *Stks*: Widely available
*lawsoniana* 'Erecta' see *C.l.* 'Erecta Viridis'
*lawsoniana* 'Erecta Viridis': Cigar-shaped. Light green lvs.
H:9m+ (30ft+) S:1.5m+ (5ft+)  *Stks*: HW, SD
*lawsoniana* 'Fletcheri': Blue-green, densely-packed foliage.
H:6m+ (20ft+) S:1.8m+ (6ft+)  *Stks*: Widely available
*lawsoniana* 'Lanei': Conical. Brightest yellow foliage.
H:6m+ (20ft+) S:1.8m+ (6ft+)  *Stks*: Widely available
*lawsoniana* 'Pembury Blue': Light, silvery-blue foliage.
H:7.5m+ (25ft+) S:1.8m+ (6ft+)  *Stks*: BG, HW
*lawsoniana* 'Stardust': Yellow foliage. Bronze at tips.
H:6m (20ft) S:1.5m (5ft)  *Stks*: HW, SN
*lawsoniana* 'White Spot': Dark green foliage flecked white.
H:7.5m (25ft) S:1.5m (5ft)  *Stks*: HW
*nootkatensis* 'Lutea': Conical. Young foliage is yellow.
♣ H: 6m+ (20ft+) S:1.5m+ (5ft+)  *Stks*: HW
*nootkatensis* 'Pendula': Branches in graceful streamers.
T H:6m+ (20ft+) S:1.5m+ (5ft+)  *Stks*: HW

**Cryptomeria** (E)  LMH  ○  ***
*japonica* 'Elegans': Lvs light then blue-green, later coppery.
❦ H:4.5m+ (15ft+) S:3m+ (10ft+)  *Stks*: Widely available

**Cupressus** (E)  LMH  ○  **
*macrocarpa* 'Goldcrest': Feathery, bright yellow foliage.
♣ H:7.5m+ (25ft+) S:1.2m+ (4ft+)  *Stks*: HW, SN

**Gingko** (maidenhair tree) (D)   LMH   O   **

   *biloba*: Lvs shaped like maidenhair fern leaflets.
   🍂 ∅ ♦ H:9m+ (30ft+) S:3m+ (10ft+)   Stks: Wdly avail.

**Juniperus** (juniper) (E)   LMH   O   ***

   *chinensis* 'Pyramidalis': Conical. Prickly, silver-blue lvs.
   H:2.4m (8ft) S:1.2m (4ft)   Stks: Widely available
   *communis* 'Hibernica': Columnar habit. Rich green lvs.
   H:3m+ (10ft+) S:1.5m+ (5ft+)   Stks: Widely available
   *scopulorum* 'Blue Heaven': Bright, silver-blue foliage.
   H:2.4m (8ft) S:1.2m (4ft)   Stks: BG, HW
   *scopulorum* 'Skyrocket': Pencil-shape. Grey-blue foliage.
   H:3.5m (12ft) S:30cm (1ft)   Stks: Widely available

**Larix** (larch) (D)   LMH   O   ***

   *decidua*: Graceful conifer, with light green foliage.
   🍂 H:15m+ (50ft+) S:6m+ (20ft+)   Stks: HW, SN

**Metasequoia** (dawn redwood) (D)   LMH   O   ***

   *glyptostroboides*: Bright, larch-green foliage.
   🍂 H:12m+ (40ft+) S:3m+ (10ft+)   Stks: Widely available

**Picea** (spruce) (E)   LMH   O   ***

   *brewerana* (O–●): A most spectacular weeping conifer.
   🌲 H:7.5m+ (25ft+) S:3m+ (10ft+)   Stks: Widely available
   *omorika*: Tall, most attractive 'Christmas tree'.
   H:13.5+ (45ft+) S:3m+ (10ft+)   Stks: HW, SN
   *orientalis* 'Aurea': Dark green lvs, young shoots rich yellow.
   H:12m+ (40ft+) S:3m+ (10ft+)   Stks: BG, HW
   *pungens* 'Hoopsii': Vivid, glaucous blue foliage.
   ♦ H:7.5m+ (25ft+) S:3m+ (10ft+)   Stks: Widely available
   *pungens* 'Koster': Foliage intensely silver-blue.
   ♦ H:7.5m+ (25ft+) S:3m+ (10ft+)   Stks: Widely available

**Pinus** (pine) (E)   LMH   O   ***

   *nigra*: Makes a large tree. Dark green lvs. Good windbreak.
   H:10.5m+ (35ft+) S:4.5m+ (15ft+)   Stks: HW, SN
   *sylvestris* (Scots pine): Tall, spreading habit. Reddish bark.
   H:10.5m+ (35ft+) S:4.5m+ (15ft+)   Stks: HW, SN
   *sylvestris* 'Watereri': Slow-growing. Conical, then rounded.
   ♦ H:4.5m+ (15ft+) S:3m+ (10ft+)   Stks: Widely available

**Taxodium** (swamp cypress) (D)   LMH(M, A)   O   ***

   *distichum*: Fresh green lvs, turning bronze in autumn.
   🍂 H:10.5m+ (35ft+) S:4.5m+ (15ft+)   Stks: HW, SN

**Taxus** (E)   LMH(C)   O   ***

   *baccata*: Beautiful dark green lvs. The common yew.
   H:4.5m+ (15ft+) S:4.5m+ (15ft+)   Stks: Widely available
   *baccata* 'Fastigiata': Closely packed lvs, erect habit.
   H:4.5m+ (15ft+) S:1.8m+ (6ft+)   Stks: Widely available
   *baccata* 'Fastigiata Aurea' see Taxus baccata 'Fastigiata
   Aureomarginata'.
   *baccata* 'Fastigiata Aureomarginata': Beautiful golden lvs.
   H:4.5m+ (15ft+) S:1.8m+ (6ft+)   Stks: HW, SN

**Thuya** (Thuja) (E)   LMH   O   ***

   *occidentalis* 'Smaragd': Pyramidal. Emerald-green foliage.
   H:2.4m (8ft) S:1m (3¼)   Stks:: BG
   *plicata*: Green lvs. Attractive pineapple scent.
   H:12m (40ft) S:4m (13ft)   Stks: HW, SN
   *plicata* 'Zebrina': Green foliage, banded creamy-yellow.
   H:10.5m+ (35ft+) S:3.5m+ (12ft+)   Stks: HW

## DWARF VARIETIES

**Abies** (fir) (E)  LMH  ○  ***
  *balsamea* 'Hudsonia': Semi-globular. Dark green lvs.
  △ H:30cm (1ft) S:25cm (10in)  *Stks*: Widely available

**Chamaecyparis** (E)  LMH(P)  ○  ***
  *lawsoniana* 'Minima Aurea': Bright yellow lvs year-round.
  △ ⊖ H:45cm (1½ft) S:30cm (1ft)  *Stks*: Widely available
  *lawsoniana* 'Minima Glauca': Rounded shape. Sea-green lvs.
  △ H:60cm (2ft) S:45cm (1½ft)  *Stks*: Widely available
  *lawsoniana* 'Nana Albospica': Light green lvs splashed cream.
  H:75cm (2½ft) S:45cm (1½ft)  *Stks*: BG, WN
  *lawsoniana* 'Pygmaea Argentea': Lvs splashed silvery-white.
  H:45cm (1½ft) S:30cm (1ft)  *Stks*: Widely available
  *lawsoniana* 'Tamariscifolia': Dome-shaped. Bright green.
  H:1.5m (5ft) S:3m (10ft)  *Stks*: BG, HW
  *obtusa* 'Nana Gracilis': Curled, rounded sprays of dark lvs.
  △ ⊖ H:75cm (2½ft) S:60cm (2ft)  *Stks*: Widely available
  *obtusa* 'Nana Lutea': Twisting sprays of yellow to green lvs.
  △ H:45cm (1½ft) S:30cm (1ft)  *Stks*: BG, WN
  *pisifera* 'Boulevard': Intense, silver-blue foliage.
  H:1.8m (6ft) S:90cm (3ft)  *Stks*: Widely available
  *pisifera* 'Filifera Aurea': Golden, thread-like foliage.
  H:75cm (2½ft) S:75cm (2½ft)  *Stks*: Widely available
  *pisifera* 'Nana': Bun-shaped plant. Rich green foliage.
  △ ⊖ H:20cm (8in) S:30cm (1ft)  *Stks*: Widely available
  *pisifera* 'Plumosa Aurea Nana': Bright yellow, feathery lvs.
  H:1.5m (5ft) S:60cm (2ft)  *Stks*: Widely available
  *pisifera* 'Plumosa Rogersii' (**): Pyramidal bush. Gold lvs.
  △ H:45cm (1½ft) S:30cm (1ft)  *Stks*: SN, WN
  *pisifera* 'Squarrosa Sulphurea': Silvery/bluish feathery lvs.
  H:1.8m (6ft) S:60cm (2ft)  *Stks*: BG, HW
  *thyoides* 'Andleyensis': Pillar-shaped. Lvs bronzed in winter.
  H:90cm (3ft) S:23cm (9in)  *Stks*: BG, HW

**Juniperus** (juniper) (E)  LMH(C)  ○–◑  ***
  *chinensis* 'Aurea' (○): Beautiful, bright gold foliage.
  H:3m (10ft) S:90cm (3ft)  *Stks*: Widely available
  *chinensis* 'Kuriwao Gold': Upright growth. Yellow foliage.
  H:1.3m (4½ft) S:1m (3½ft)  *Stks*: BG
  *communis* 'Compressa': Column-shaped, compact.
  △ ⊖ H:45cm (1½ft) S:25cm (10in)  *Stks*: Widely available
  *communis* 'Depressa Aurea' (○): Lvs bright yellow in spring.
  △ ⊠ H:15cm (6in) S:1.2m (4ft)  *Stks*: Widely available
  *communis* 'Repanda': Prostrate. Dark green prickly lvs.
  ⊠ H:15cm (6in) S:1.8m (6ft)  *Stks*: Widely available
  *conferta*: Attractive, bright green prickly lvs.
  △ ⊠ H:30cm (1ft) S:3m (10ft)  *Stks*: BG, WN
  *horizontalis* 'Blue Moon' (○): Silvery-blue foliage in summer.
  ⊠ H:15cm (6in) S:90cm (3ft)  *Stks*: BG, HW
  *horizontalis* 'Glauca': Ground-hugging. Steel-blue foliage.
  ⊠ H:15cm (6in) S:1.5m (5ft)  *Stks*: Widely available
  x *media* 'Hetzii': Vigorous grey-green foliage. Branches at 45°.
  ⊠ H:1.5m (5ft) S:1.8m (6ft)  *Stks*: HW, SD
  x *media* 'Mint Julep': Mint-green lvs, the year-round.
  ⊠ H:90cm (3ft) S:1.5m (5ft)  *Stks*: Widely available
  x *media* 'Old Gold' (○): Semi-prostrate; old-gold lvs.
  ⊠ H:1.5m (5ft) S:1.5m (5ft)  *Stks*: Widely available
  x *media* 'Pfitzerana Aurea' (○): Semi-prostrate; golden lvs.
  ⊠ H:1m (3½ft) S:1.5m (5ft)  *Stks*: HW

*For key to stockists, see page 55*

*procumbens* 'Nana': Bright, apple-green foliage.
H:18cm (7in) S:1.5m (5ft)   *Stks*: Widely available

*sabina* 'Tamariscifolia': Bluish-green lvs. Covers manholes.
H:38cm (15in) S:1m (3½ft)   *Stks*: Widely available

*squamata* 'Blue Carpet' (O): Sheets of intense silver-blue lvs.
H:30cm (1ft) S:2m (6½ft)   *Stks*: Widely available

*squamata* 'Blue Star' (O): Compact habit. Steel-blue foliage.
H:30cm (1ft) S:45cm (1½ft)   *Stks*: Widely available

*squamata* 'Meyeri': Steel-blue lvs. Responds to clipping.
H:1.8m (6ft) S:75cm (2½ft)   *Stks*: HW

*virginiana* 'Grey Owl': Semi-prostrate. Grey-blue foliage.
H:30cm (1ft) S:1.5m (5ft)   *Stks*: BG, HW

**Picea** (spruce) (E)   LMH   O   \*\*\*
*abies* 'Nidiformis': Horizontal tiered branches. Green lvs.
H:1m (3½ft) S:60cm (2ft)   *Stks*: Widely available

*glauca albertina* 'Conica': Bright green tips in spring.
H:1m (3½ft) S:60cm (2ft)   *Stks*: Widely available

*pungens* 'Globosa': Rounded, silver-blue foliage. Compact.
H:60cm (2ft) S:60cm (2ft)   *Stks*: Widely available

**Pinus** (pine) (E)   LMH   O   \*\*\*
*mugo* 'Gnom': Compact, forming a dense dark green mound.
H:1m (3½ft) S:90cm (3ft)   *Stks*: Widely available

*mugo pumilio*: Dark green lvs. Attractive buds in winter.
H:1.5m (5ft) S:1.8m (6ft)   *Stks*: HW

*strobus* 'Nana': Compact. Thin, silver-blue-green foliage.
H:60cm (2ft) S:90cm (3ft)   *Stks*: Widely available

**Taxus** (yew) (E)   LMH(C)   O–●   \*\*\*
*baccata* 'Repandens': Deep green lvs. Low-spreading plant.
H:45cm (1½ft) S:1m (3½ft)   *Stks*: BG, HW

*baccata* 'Semperaurea': Low-growing. Rich, golden foliage.
H:1.2m (4ft) S:1.5m (5ft)   *Stks*: Widely available

*baccata* 'Standishii': Golden lvs. Upright, slow-growing form.
H:1.2m (4ft) S:30cm (1ft)   *Stks*: Widely available

**Thuya** (Thuja) (E)   LMH   O   \*\*\*
*occidentalis* 'Lutea Nana': Golden foliage. Pyramidal habit.
H:1.8m (6ft) S:1.5m (5ft)   *Stks*: BG

*occidentalis* 'Rheingold': Lvs old gold to copper in winter.
H:1.2m (4ft) S:90cm (3ft)   *Stks*: Widely available

*orientalis* 'Aurea Nana': Lvs yellow. Globular shape.
H:75cm (2½ft) S:60cm (2ft)   *Stks*: Widely available

*orientalis* 'Conspicua': Upright shape. Golden-yellow lvs.
H:1.5m (5ft) S:45cm (1½ft)   *Stks*: Widely available

*orientalis* 'Elegantissima': Columnar. Yellow lvs in summer.
H:1.2m (4ft) S:30cm (1ft)   *Stks*: Widely available

*plicata* 'Stoneham Gold': Deep, golden-yellow tipped lvs.
H:75cm (2½ft) S:60cm (2ft)   *Stks*: Widely available

---

## SPECIALIST SUPPLIERS

**BG**  Bressingham Gardens, Diss, Norfolk, IP22 2AB.
Tel: Bressingham (037 988) 464.

**HW**  Hillier Nurseries Ltd., Ampfield House, Ampfield,
Romsey, Hants, SO5 9PA. Tel: Braishfield 68733.

**SD**  Sunningdale Nurseries Ltd, Windlesham, Surrey.
Tel: Ascot 20496.

**SN**  Scotts Nurseries (Merriott) Ltd., Merriott,
Somerset, TA16 5PL. Tel: Crewkerne (0460) 72306.

**WN**  The Wansdyke Nursery, Hillworth Road, Devizes,
Wilts, SN10 5HD. Tel: (0380) 3008.

# Shrubs, Climbers and Hedges

The backbone to most gardens is formed of shrubs, both deciduous and evergreen. They clothe the outer perimeter, divide the garden into pleasant views, stand as attractive specimens, and provide ground cover.

We often speak of year-round colour in the garden, and nothing provides this better than shrubs. They give us attractive coloured bark, variegated evergreen foliage, fruits and even flowers in mid-winter.

There are many attractive spring-flowering kinds and several with richly coloured young shoots and foliage. A number of the summer-flowering kinds are fragrant and in autumn yet others provide more flowers and lots have attractively coloured leaves at this time.

## Where to grow

Most shrubs grow very quickly and while new gardens look very sparsely planted, in three or four years what looked like wide spacing will seem right.

There is no harm in planting the cheaper fast-growing kinds like forsythias, philadelphus, deutzias and buddleias quite close for nearly instant effect. Be prepared to prune them back, however, and remove altogether if slower-growing and more valuable varieties need the space.

Where the soil is thoroughly dug over and peat or well-rotted garden compost mixed in, most shrubs can be grown in almost all garden soils. However, very chalky soils and very acid ones are best planted with kinds that thrive in each respective condition.

A number are suitable to grow in tubs but be sure to keep these very well watered, especially in hot, sunny weather. Evergreens can dry out in cold winter winds as well as sun, so always keep an eye on the moisture of compost in plant containers.

## What to buy

The cheapest will be no more than year-old rooted cuttings in small pots and polythene sleeve packs. As long as you can wait the year or two for these to establish and you are sure they are correctly named and not a vigorously growing, easily-rooted poor type, then they give value for money. Plant from October to March.

Avoid polythene sleeve packed shrubs if they are very lightweight, have shrivelled stems, dead or dying and mouldy leaves, or have pale yellow, etiolated shoots.

Small pot-grown plants should be growing vigorously and have no old and dying lower leaves.

Several years will be saved by buying larger plants,

## PLANTING A CONTAINER-GROWN SHRUB

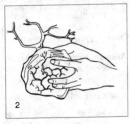

**1.** *Lift a container-grown plant by the stem. If well-rooted it should not be loose.*

**2.** *A large root through the base of the container suggests that the plant is starved.*

**3.** *Before returning and firming the soil, slit and carefully remove the container.*

which will naturally cost a little more. If the shrubs have been lifted from the field and have bare roots wrapped in peat or straw to keep them damp in transit, then prune the branches back by at least a third, several weeks after planting, in early spring.

Container-grown plants will suffer no root disturbance and are a much better buy. Good container plants can be lifted by the stem and will not come out of the compost. Plants which do start to come out have been freshly potted are are no easier to transplant successfully than field-lifted bare-root specimens.

Avoid big, top-heavy plants in small pots, with bare leafless stems lower down the plant. Do not buy plants that are poorly anchored and flop from side to side in the compost. Good buys will have no sign of pests or diseases.

A number of plants such as clematis, pyracanthas, brooms, and most evergreens, do not grow well if the soil around the roots is loosened or removed when they are transplanted. Container-grown plants avoid this problem and they can be moved at any time of year when the ground is suitable.

Where evergreens have to be moved from open soil, March and April or September and October is the time to do it. Soil is kept in place with sacking or polythene sheet tied tightly around the roots (see Conifers, page 51).

**if you want to know more ...**
Several of the specialist tree and shrub mail order companies produce excellent catalogues with much useful information. A standard reference work is *Hilliers' Manual of Trees and Shrubs.*

**Acer** (maple) (D)    LMH    O─◑    **
  *palmatum* 'Atropurpureum': Lobed, bronzy-crimson lvs.
  ∅ H:4.5m (15ft) S:3.5m (12ft)    *Stks*: Widely available
  *palmatum* 'Dissectum Atropurpureum': Divided, purple lvs.
  ∅ H:1.8m (6ft) S:1.8m (6ft)    *Stks*: Widely available

**Amelanchier** (snowy mespilus) (D)    LMH    O─◑    ***
  *lamarckii*: Profusion of white fls, April. Coppery young lvs.
  ❦ H:3.5m (12ft) S:3m (10ft)    *Stks*: HW, NN, SN

**Aralia sieboldii** see *Fatsia japonica*

**Aucuba** (E)    LMH    O─●    ***
  *japonica* 'Variegata': Shiny dark green lvs, speckled yellow.
  ∅ ❧ H:1.5m (5ft) S:1.5m (5ft)    *Stks*: Widely available

**Azalea** see page 67

**Berberis** (barberry)    (D or E)    LMH    O─◑    ***
  *darwinii* (E): Yellow fls. Bluish-purple berries.
  H:2.4m (8ft) S:2.4m (8ft)    *Stks*: Widely available
  *linearifolia* (E): Spikes of bright orange-red fls, April.
  H:1.8m (6ft) S:1.2m (4ft)    *Stks*: HW, RN
  *linearifolia* 'Orange King' (E): Orange and apricot fls, April.
  H:1.8m (6ft) S:1.2m (4ft)    *Stks*: Widely available
  × *ottawensis* 'Purpurea' (D): Attractive, rich copper lvs.
  ∅ ❦ H:2.4m (8ft) S:1.5m (5ft)    *Stks*: Widely available
  × *stenophylla* (E): Arching sprays of yellow fls, April.
  H:3m (10ft) S:3m (10ft)    *Stks*: Widely available
  *thunbergii* (D): Yellow fls. Bright red fruits.
  ❦ ❧ H:1.5m (5ft) S:1.5m (5ft)    *Stks*: Widely available
  *thunbergii* 'Atropurpurea Nana' (D): Rich copper lvs.
  ∅ ❧ H:45cm (1½ft) S:45cm (1½ft)    *Stks*: Widely available
  *thunbergii* 'Aurea' (D): Bright yellow lvs, turning green.
  ∅ ❦ H:60cm (2ft) S:1m (3½ft)    *Stks*: Widely available
  *thunbergii* 'Rose Glow' (D): Purple lvs, streaked pink.
  ∅ ❧ H:60cm (2ft) S:1m (3½ft)    *Stks*: Widely available

**Buddleia** (butterfly bush) (D or E)    LMH    O    ***
  *alternifolia* (D): Arching sprays of lilac fls, June.
  ❂ H:3.5m (12ft) S:3m (10ft)    *Stks*: Widely available
  *davidii* 'Black Knight' (D): Deep violet trusses, July–Oct.
  ❂ H:2.4m (8ft) S:2.4m (8ft)    *Stks*: Widely available
  *davidii* 'Empire Blue' (D): Rich violet-blue fls, orange eye.
  ❂ H:2.4m (8ft) S:2.4m (8ft)    *Stks*: Widely available
  *davidii* 'Harlequin' (D): Red-purple fls, July–Oct. Variegated.
  ❂∅ H:2.1m (7ft) S:2.1m (7ft)    *Stks*: Widely available
  *davidii* 'Royal Red' (D): Reddish-purple fls, July–Oct.
  ❂ H:2.4m (8ft) S:2.4m (8ft)    *Stks*: Widely available
  *globosa* (E): Orange, ball-shaped fl heads, June.
  ❂ H:3m (10ft) S:3m (10ft)    *Stks*: Widely available

**Callicarpa** (D)    LMH    O    **
  *bodinieri giraldii*: Mauve-pink fls, Aug. Violet berries.
  ❦ ❧ H:1.8m (6ft) S:1.5m (5ft)    *Stks*: Widely available

**Calluna** see page 66

**Camellia** (E)    LMH(P)    ◑    **/***
  *japonica* 'Adolphe Audusson' (**): Red fls, March–May.
  H:1.8m (6ft) S:1.8m (6ft)    *Stks*: Widely available
  *japonica* 'Apollo' (**): Red fls, blotched white, March–May.
  H:1.8m (6ft) S:1.8m (6ft)    *Stks*: HW, SD, SN

*japonica* 'Elegans' (\*\*): Deep pink fls, March–May.
H:1.8m (6ft) S:1.8m (6ft)   *Stks*: Widely available

× *williamsii* 'Donation' (\*\*\*): Pink fls, March–May.
H:1.8m (6ft) S:1.8m (6ft)   *Stks*: Widely available

× *williamsii* 'J.C. Williams' (\*\*\*): Single pink fls, March–May.
H:1.8m (6ft) S:1.8m (6ft)   *Stks*: HW, NN, SN

**Caryopteris** (blue spiraea) (D)   LMH(C)   ○   \*\*\*
× *clandonensis* 'Arthur Simmonds': Violet-blue fls, Aug.–Sept.
H:90cm (3ft) S:90cm (3ft)   *Stks*: Widely available

**Ceanothus** (E or D)   LM   ○–◑   \*\*
'A.T. Johnson' (E): Rich blue fls, spring and autumn.
H:1.8m (6ft) S:1.5m (5ft)   *Stks*: HW
'Gloire de Versailles' (D): Blue fls, summer and autumn.
H:1.8m (6ft) S:1.8m (6ft)   *Stks*: Widely available

**Ceratostigma** (hardy plumbago) (D)   LMH   ○   \*\*
*willmottianum*: Very rich blue fls, July–Sept.
❧ H:90cm (3ft) S:90cm (3ft)   *Stks*: Widely available

**Chaenomeles** (flowering quince) (D)   LMH   ○–●   \*\*\*
*speciosa* (syn. *Cydonia speciosa*): Red fls in spring.
❀ H:1.2m (4ft) S:1.8m (6ft)   *Stks*: Widely available
*speciosa* 'Nivalis': Large, pure white fls, late spring.
❀ H:1.2m (4ft) S:1.8m (6ft)   *Stks*: Widely available
× *superba* 'Nicoline': Large, scarlet-red fls in spring.
❀ H:1.8m (6ft) S:1.8m (6ft)   *Stks*: Widely available
× *superba* 'Pink Lady': Clear, rose-pink fls, spring.
❀ H:1.8m (6ft) S:1.8m (6ft)   *Stks*: Widely available

**Chimonathus** (winter sweet) (D)   LMH(C)   ○–●   \*\*
*praecox* (syn. *C. fragrans*): Waxy, yellow fls, Dec.–Feb.
❧ H:3m (10ft) S:2.4m (8ft)   *Stks*: Widely available

**Choisya** (Mexican orange blossom) (E)   LMH   ○   \*\*
*ternata*: White fls, May–June. Orange-scented lvs if bruised.
❧ H:1.8m (6ft) S:2.4m (8ft)   *Stks*: Widely available

**Cistus** (rock rose) (E)   LM(C)   ○   \*\*
'Silver Pink': Masses of silver-pink single fls, June–July.
H:60cm (2ft) S:90cm (3ft)   *Stks*: Widely available

**Cornus** (dogwood) (D)   LMH(M)   ○–◑   \*\*\*
*alba*: Young stems are a rich red in winter.
❧ ⊞ H:1.8m (6ft) S:1.5m (5ft)   *Stks*: Widely available
*alba* 'Elegantissima': Lvs margined and mottled white/green.
∅ ❧ H:1.8m (6ft) S:1.5m (5ft)   *Stks*: Widely available
*alba* 'Sibirica': Brilliant crimson winter stems.
❧ ⊞ H:1.8m (6ft) S:1.2m (4ft)   *Stks*: Widely available
*stolonifera* 'Flaviramea': Young shoots yellow to olive-green.
⊞ H:1.8m (6ft) S:1.8m (6ft)   *Stks*: Widely available

**Cortaderia** (pampas grass) (E)   LM   ○   \*\*
*argentea* see *C. selloana*
*selloana* (syn. *C. argentea*): Long and silvery grass plumes.
H:2.1m (7ft) S:1.5m (5ft)   *Stks*: Widely available
*selloana* 'Pumila': A compact form. Silvery plumes.
H:1.2m (4ft) S:90cm (3ft)   *Stks*: Widely available

**Corylus** (hazel) (D)   LMH   ○–◑   \*\*\*
*avellana* 'Contorta': Twisted stems and yellow catkins.
⊞ H:6m (20ft) S:4.5m (15ft)   *Stks*: Widely available
*maxima* 'Purpurea': Reddish-purple, attractive foliage.
∅ H:3m (10ft) S:2.4m (8ft)   *Stks*: Widely available

**Cotinus** (smoke tree) (D)    LMH    O–●    ***
   *coggygria* 'Royal Purple': Wine-purple lvs, red in autumn.
   ⌀❧ H:2.1m (7ft) S:2.1m (7ft)    *Stks*: Widely available

**Cotoneaster** (D or E)    LMH    O–●    ***
   *conspicuus* 'Decorus' (E): Low-growing shrub for banks.
   ⌗ H:75cm (2½ft) S:90cm (3ft)    *Stks*: Widely available
   'Exburiensis' (E): Apricot-yellow fruits; spreading habit.
   ⌗ H:3m (10ft) S:2.4m (8ft)    *Stks*: Widely available
   *franchetii sterniana* (E): Lvs green above, silver below.
   ⌗ H:2.1m (7ft) S:2.1m (7ft)    *Stks*: Widely available
   *horizontalis* (D): Attractive branches in a herring-bone style.
   ⌗ H:1.2m (4ft) S:2.1m (7ft)    *Stks*: Widely available
   *horizontalis* 'Variegatus' (D): Cream lvs, suffused red.
   ⌀⌗ H:90cm (3ft) S:1.5m (5ft)    *Stks*: Widely available
   'Valkenburg' (D): Prostrate growth. Good autumn colour.
   ❧⌷ H:30cm (1ft) S:90cm (3ft)    *Stks*: HW

**Cydonia speciosa** see *Chaenomeles speciosa*

**Cytisus** (broom) (D)    LMH    O    ***
   'Burkwoodii': Cerise fls, edged yellow, May–June.
   H:2.1m (7ft) S:1.8m (6ft)    *Stks*: Widely available
   × *kewensis*: Spectacular cream fls borne in May.
   ⌷ H:45cm (1½ft) S:1.2m (4ft)    *Stks*: Widely available
   'Killiney Red': Rich red fls, May–June.
   H:1.8m (6ft) S:1.5m (5ft)    *Stks*: HW, NN
   × *praecox*: Masses of scented cream fls borne in May.
   ⌴ H:1.5m (5ft) S:1.5m (5ft)    *Stks*: Widely available
   × *praecox* 'All Gold': Arching sprays of yellow fls, May.
   H:1.5m (5ft) S:1.5m (5ft)    *Stks*: Widely available
   *scoparius* 'Andreanus': Yellow fls marked crimson, May.
   H:2.1m (7ft) S:1.8m (6ft)    *Stks*: Widely available
   *scoparius* 'Golden Sunlight': Rich yellow fls, June.
   H:2.1m (7ft) S:1.8m (6ft)    *Stks*: Widely available

**Daboecia** see page 66

**Daphne** (mezereon) (D or E)    LM    O–◑    **/***
   *mezereum* (D) (***): Purplish fls on bare stems, Feb.–March.
   ⌴⌗ H:90cm (3ft) S:45cm (1½ft)    *Stks*: Widely available
   *odora* 'Aureo-marginata' (E) (**): Purple fls, March–April.
   ⌴ H:90cm (3ft) S:90cm (3ft)    *Stks*: Widely available

**Deutzia** (D)    LMH    O–◑    ***
   'Mont Rose': Clusters of dainty mauvish-pink fls, June–July.
   H:1.5m (5ft) S:1.5m (5ft)    *Stks*: Widely available

**Elaeagnus** (E)    LMH    O–●    ***
   × *ebbingei*: Fragrant, silvery-white fls, Aug.–Sept.
   ⌴ H:2.4m (8ft) S:2.4m (8ft)    *Stks*: Widely available
   × *ebbingei* 'Gilt Edge': Beautiful lvs margined gold.
   ⌀ H:2.4m (8ft) S:2.4m (8ft)    *Stks*: Widely available
   *pungens* 'Maculata': Striking lvs, splashed yellow and gold.
   ⌀ H:2.4m (8ft) S:2.4m (8ft)    *Stks*: Widely available

**Erica** see page 66

**Escallonia** (E)    LM    O–◑    **
   'Apple Blossom': Pink and white fls, July–Aug.
   H:1.8m (6ft) S:1.2m (4ft)    *Stks*: Widely available
   'Crimson Spire': Bright crimson fls, July–Aug.
   H:2.1m (7ft) S:1.5m (5ft)    *Stks*: Widely available

**...onymus** (E)   LMH   O─●   ***
*fortunei radicans* 'Emerald 'n' Gold': Yellow and green lvs.
∅☘ H:30cm (1ft) S:45cm (1½ft)   *Stks*: Widely available
*fortunei radicans* 'Silver Queen': Creamy and green lvs.
∅☘ H:30cm (1ft) S:60cm (2ft)   *Stks*: Widely available
*japonicus* 'Ovatus Aureus': Lvs suffused creamy-yellow.
∅ H:2.4m (8ft) S:1.5m (5ft)   *Stks*: HW

**Fatsia** (E)   LM   ◑─●   **
*japonica*: Large, palmate lvs. Milky-white fls, Oct.–Nov.
∅ H:2.1m (7ft) S:1.5m (5ft)   *Stks*: Widely available

**Forsythia** (D)   LMH   O─◑   ***
× *intermedia* 'Spectabilis': Bright-yellow fls, March–April.
H:2.1m (7ft) S:1.5m (5ft)   *Stks*: Widely available

**Fuchsia** (D)   LMH   O─◑   **
*magellanica* 'Versicolor': Grey-green lvs tinted white.
∅ H:90cm (3ft) S:75cm (2½ft)   *Stks*: Widely available
'Mrs Popple': Large fls. Scarlet sepals/violet petals, July–Sept.
H:90cm (3ft) S:75cm (2½ft)   *Stks*: Widely available
'Riccartonii': Long, narrow, scarlet and purple fls, July–Aug.
H:1.2m (4ft) S:90cm (3ft)   *Stks*: Widely available

**Garrya** (E)   LMH   O─●   **
*elliptica*: Greyish-green catkins (best on males), Jan.–Feb.
H:1.8m (6ft) S:1.5m (5ft)   *Stks*: Widely available

**Genista** (E)   LM   O   ***
*hispanica*: Prickly lvs, with yellow fls, May–June.
☘ H:90cm (3ft) S:90cm (3ft)   *Stks*: Widely available
*lydia*: Masses of golden-yellow fls, May–June.
☘ H:45cm (1½ft) S:45cm (1½ft)   *Stks*: Widely available

**Hamamelis** (D)   LMH(P)   O─◑   ***
*mollis* 'Pallida': Sulphur-yellow fls, Dec.–March.
☙☘ H:3m (10ft) S:2.4m (8ft)   *Stks*: Widely available

**Hebe** (E)   LMH   O─◑   **
'Autumn Glory': Small, violet fl heads, June–Oct.
H:75cm (2½ft) S:75cm (2½ft)   *Stks*: Widely available
'Carl Teschner': Violet fls with white throats, June–July.
☘ H:30cm (1ft) S:75cm (2½ft)   *Stks*: Widely available
*pinguifolia* 'Pagei': Glacous grey lvs. White fls, May.
☘ H:23cm (9in) S:60cm (2ft)   *Stks*: Widely available

**Hibiscus** (D)   LMH   O   **
*syriacus* 'Blue Bird': Violet-blue fls, dark eyes, Aug.–Oct.
H:1.8m (6ft) S:1.5m (5ft)   *Stks*: Widely available
*syriacus* 'Woodbridge': Rose-pink fls, Aug.–Oct.
H:1.8m (6ft) S:1.5m (5ft)   *Stks*: Widely available

**Hydrangea** (D)   LMH(P)   O─◑   **/***
*macrophylla* (mop-head type): Large heads of fls, July–Sept.
H:1.5m (5ft) S:1.5m (5ft)   *Stks*: Widely available
*macrophylla* 'Blue Wave': Pink or blue fls, July–Sept.
H:1.5m (5ft) S:1.5m (5ft)   *Stks*: Widely available
*paniculata* 'Grandiflora': Huge sprays of white fls, Aug.–Sept.
H:3m (10ft) S:3m (10ft)   *Stks*: Widely available

**Hypericum** (St. John's wort) (E)   LM   O─◒   ***
*calycinum* (rose of Sharon): Large, pale yellow fls, June–Sept.
☘ H:30cm (1ft) Spreads widely.   *Stks*: Widely available
'Hidcote': Semi-evergreen. Golden-yellow fls, July–Oct.
H:45cm (1½ft) Spreads widely.   *Stks*: Widely available

**Ilex** (holly) (E)    LMH    O─●    ***
  × *altaclarensis* 'Golden King': Golden edged lvs. Berried.
  ⊘ ✿ H:6m (20ft) S:3m (10ft)    *Stks*: Widely available
  *aquifolium* 'Pyramidalis': Spiny and spineless lvs. Berried.
  ✿ H:6m (20ft) S:3m (10ft)    *Stks*: Widely available
  *aquifolium* 'Silver Queen': Silvery edges to lvs. No berries.
  ⊘ H:4.5m (15ft) S:2.4m (8ft)    *Stks*: Widely available

**Kalmia** (calico bush) (E)    LMH(A)    ◐    ***
  *latifolia*: Clusters of five-sided pink fls, June.
  H:2.1m (7ft) S:2.1m (7ft)    *Stks*: Widely available

**Kerria** (Jew's mallow) (D)    LMH    O─●    ***
  *japonica* 'Plenifolia': Double, bright yellow fls, April–May.
  H:1.5m (5ft) S:1.5m (5ft)    *Stks*: Widely available

**Kolkwitzia** (D)    LMH    O    ***
  *amabilis* 'Pink Cloud': Pink, foxglove-like fls, May–June.
  H:2.4m (8ft) S:2.1m (7ft)    *Stks*: Widely available

**Laurus** (E)    LMH    O─●    **
  *nobilis* (bay): Lvs used for flavouring. Can be clipped to shape.
  H:4.5m (15ft) S:4.5m (15ft)    *Stks*: Widely available

**Lavandula** (lavender)    LMH    O─◐    ***
  *spica* 'Hidcote': Grey-green lvs. Deep violet fls, July.
  ⌣ H:60cm (2ft) S:60cm (2ft)    *Stks*: Widely available
  'Vera': Soft blue spires of fls, July–Sept.
  ⌣ H:1m (3½ft) S:60cm (2ft)    *Stks*: Widely available

**Ligustrum** (privet) (E)    LMH    O─●    ***
  *ovalifolium* 'Aureum': Glossy green and yellow lvs.
  H:3.5m (12ft) S:3m (10ft)    *Stks*: Widely available

**Magnolia** (D)    LMH(A)    O    ***
  × *soulangiana*: White fls stained rose-purple, May.
  H:3.5m (12ft) S:3m (10ft)    *Stks*: Widely available
  × *soulangiana* 'Lennei': Rose-purple fls, April–May.
  H:3.5m (12ft) S:3m (10ft)    *Stks*: Widely available
  *stellata*: Semi-double narrow-petalled white fls, March–April.
  H:2.4m (8ft) S:1.8m (6ft)    *Stks*: Widely available
  *stellata*: 'Rosea': Semi-double, pale pink, March–April.
  H:2.4m (8ft) S:1.8m (6ft)    *Stks*: Widely available

---

### SOME SHRUBS FOR INDUSTRIAL AREAS

| | |
|---|---|
| Aucuba japonica | Hypericum |
| Berberis | Ilex |
| Buddleia davidii | Kerria japonica |
| Chaenomeles | Ligustrum ovalifolium |
| Cistus | Mahonia |
| Cornus alba | Pernettya mucronata |
| Cornus stolonifera | Philadelphus |
| Cotoneaster | Prunus laurocerasus |
| Cytisus | Pyracantha |
| Deutzia | Ribes sanguineum |
| Elaeagnus | Salix alba |
| Euonymus fortunei | Senecio greyi |
| Euonymus japonicus | Skimmia japonica |
| Fatsia japonica | Symphoricarpos × doorenbosii |
| Forsythia × intermedia | Syringa vulgaris |
| Hebe armstrongii | Viburnum |
| Hebe pinguifolia | Vinca |
| Hydrangea macrophylla | Weigela florida |

---

*For key to stockists, see page 70*

**Mahonia** (Oregon grape) (E)    LMH    O–●    ***
   *aquifolium*: Yellow fls, April. Blue-black berries.
   ✻ H:1.2m (4ft) S:1.5m (5ft)   *Stks*: Widely available
   'Charity': Large trusses, fragrant yellow fls, Dec.–Feb.
   ⚘ H:1.8m (6ft) S:1.8m (6ft)   *Stks*: Widely available
   *japonica*: Large pinnate lvs. Fragrant yellow fls, Dec.–Feb.
   ⚘ H:1.8m (6ft) S:1.8m (6ft)   *Stks*: Widely available

**Osmanthus** (E)    LMH    O–●    **
   *delavayi*: Clusters of jasmine-scented white fls, April.
   ⚘ H:1.8m (6ft) S:1.8m (6ft)   *Stks*: Widely available

**Pernettya** (prickly heath) (E)    LMH(A)    O–●    ***
   *mucronata* 'Bell's Seedling': Bright cherry-red berries.
   ✻ H:90cm (3ft) S:90cm (3ft)   *Stks*: Widely available

**Philadelphus** (mock orange) (D)    LMH(C)    O–◑    ***
   'Beauclerk': Single white fls, blotched red, June–July.
   ⚘ H:1.8m (6ft) S:1.5m (5ft)   *Stks*: Widely available
   *coronarius* 'Aureus': Young lvs bright yellow, turning green.
   ⚘⊘ H:1.8m (6ft) S:1.8m (6ft)   *Stks*: Widely available
   'Virginal': Double, white fls, highly fragrant, June–July.
   ⚘ H:2.4m+ (8ft+) S:1.8m (6ft)   *Stks*: Widely available

**Photinia** (E)    LM(C)    O    **
   × *fraseri* 'Red Robin': Attractive, rich red young lvs.
   ⊘ ✻ H:3m (10ft) S:2.4m (8ft)   *Stks*: Widely available

**Pieris** (E)    LM(P)    O    **
   *formosa forrestii*: White fls, April–May. Young shoots red.
   ⚘⊘ H:2.4m (8ft) S:2.4m (8ft)   *Stks*: Widely available
   *formosa forrestii* 'Wakehurst': As above, but lvs more vivid.
   ⚘⊘ H:3m (10ft) S:3m (10ft)   *Stks*: Widely available

**Potentilla** (D)    LMH    O–◑    ***
   *dahurica* 'Manchu': White fls, June–Sept. Greyish lvs.
   H:45cm (1½ft) S:1m (3½ft)   *Stks*: SN
   'Elizabeth': Large, rich, canary-yellow fls, May–Oct.
   H:90cm (3ft) S:1.2m (4ft)   *Stks*: Widely available
   'Goldfinger': Large, deep-yellow fls, June–Sept.
   H:1.2m (4ft) S:1m (3½ft)   *Stks*: HW, RN
   'Red Ace': Bright vermilion-flame fls, May–Nov.
   H:60cm (2ft) S:1m (3½ft)   *Stks*: Widely available

---

### SOME SHRUBS FOR COASTAL PLANTING

| | |
|---|---|
| Choisya ternata | Ilex aquifolium |
| Cotoneaster | Lavandula spica |
| Cytisus | Lavandula 'Vera' |
| Elaeagnus | Pyracantha |
| Escallonia | Rosmarinus officinalis |
| Euonymus fortunei | Salix alba |
| Euonymus japonicus | Salix lanata |
| Fatsia japonica | Salix melanostachys |
| Fuchsia magellanica | Salix × smithiana |
| Fuchsia 'Mrs Popple' | Santolina chamaecyparissus |
| Fuchsia 'Riccartonii' | Senecio greyi |
| Garrya elliptica | Spartium junceum |
| Genista hispanica | Spiraea × arguta |
| Genista lydia | Spiraea × bumalda |
| Hebe | Tamarix pentandra |
| Hydrangea macrophylla | Viburnum tinus |
| Ilex × altaclarensis | Viburnum rhytidophyllum |

---

**Prunus** (D or E)   LMH   O–◐   ***
   × *cistena* (D): White fls in April. Coppery lvs.
   ⊘ H:90cm (3ft) S:60cm (2ft)   *Stks*: Widely available
   *laurocerasus* 'Otto Luyken' (E): White 'candle' fls, April.
   🌺 H:75cm (2½ft) S:1.2m (4ft)   *Stks*: Widely available

**Pyracantha** (firethorn) (E)   LMH   O–◐   ***
   'Orange Glow': Creamy-white fls, June. Orange berries.
   ⚘ H:3.5m (12ft) S:2.4m (8ft)   *Stks*: Widely available
   'Soleil d'Or': Rather lax habit. Attractive yellow berries.
   ⚘ H:2.4m (8ft) S:1.8m (6ft)   *Stks*: HW, NN, SD

**Rhododendron** see page 67

**Ribes** (flowering currant) (D)   LMH   O–◐   ***
   *odoratum*: Beautiful, golden-yellow fls, borne in April.
   🌱 H:1.5m (5ft) S:1.5m (5ft)   *Stks*: HW, NN
   *sanguineum* 'King Edward VII': Intense crimson fls, April.
   H:1.8m (6ft) S:1.2m (4ft)   *Stks*: Widely available

**Rosmarinus** (rosemary) (E)   LM   O   **
   *officinalis*: Spires of blue fls, May. Greyish-green lvs.
   H:1.2m (4ft) S:1.2m (4ft)   *Stks*: Widely available
   *officinalis* 'Miss Jessop's Variety': Light mauve fls, May.
   H:1.5m (5ft) S:90cm (3ft)   *Stks*: Widely available

**Rubus** (D)   LMH   O–●   ***
   × *tridel* 'Benenden': White, saucer-shaped fls, May.
   H:1.8m (6ft) S:2.1m (7ft)   *Stks*: Widely available

**Salix** (willow) (D)   LMH(M)   O–◐   ***
   *alba* 'Chermesina': Beautiful orange stems in winter.
   ▣ H:6m (20ft) S:4.5m (15ft)   *Stks*: Widely available
   *alba* 'Vitellina': Distinctive, bright golden-yellow shoots.
   ▣ H:6m (20ft) S:4.5m (15ft)   *Stks*: Widely available
   *lanata*: Beautiful catkins and silvery, woolly lvs.
   H:60cm (2ft) S:1.2m (4ft)   *Stks*: Widely available
   *melanostachys*: Distinctive and attractive black catkins.
   H:1.5m (5ft) S:1.2m (4ft)   *Stks*: HW
   × *smithiana*: Large, attractive catkins in the spring.
   H:6m (20ft) S:4.5m (15ft)   *Stks*: SN

**Salvia** (sage) (E)   LM   O   ***
   *officinalis* 'Purpurascens': Attractive lvs, suffused purple.
   ⊘ H:60cm (2ft) S:60cm (2ft)   *Stks*: Widely available
   *officinalis* 'Tricolor': Lvs splashed creamy-white and purple.
   ⊘ H:60cm (2ft) S:60cm (2ft)   *Stks*: HW, SN

**Santolina** (cotton lavender) (E)   LMH   O   ***
   *chamaecyparissus*: Finely cut silvery lvs. Yellow fls, July.
   H:60cm (2ft) S:60cm (2ft)   *Stks*: Widely available

**Senecio** (E)   LMH   O   ***
   *greyi*: Yellow fls, June–July. Felted, grey-white lvs.
   H:90cm (3ft) S:90cm (3ft)   *Stks*: Widely available

**Skimmia** (E)   LM(A)   ◐–●   ***
   *japonica* 'Foremanii': Brilliant red berries (needs male).
   ⚘ H:90cm (3ft) S:90cm (3ft)   *Stks*: Widely available
   *japonica* 'Rubella': Red buds in winter. White fls. Male.
   🌱 H:90cm (3ft) S:90cm (3ft)   *Stks*: Widely available

**Spartium** (Spanish broom) (D)   LM   O   ***
   *junceum*: Mass of golden-yellow pea-like fls, July–Aug.
   H:2.4m (8ft) S:1.8m (6ft)   *Stks*: Widely available

**Spiraea** (D)   LMH   O–●   ***
 × *arguta*: Slender, arching sprays of white fls, April–May.
 H:1.2m (4ft) S:1.2m (4ft)   *Stks*: Widely available
 × *bumalda* 'Anthony Waterer': Crimson fl heads, June–Sept.
 H:90cm (3ft) S:90cm (3ft)   *Stks*: Widely available
 × *bumalda* 'Goldflame': Coppery shoots, variegated lvs.
 ∅ H:75cm (2½ft) S:75cm (2½ft)   *Stks*: Widely available

**Symphoricarpos** (snowberry) (D)   LMH   ●   ***
 × *doorenbosii* 'Mother of Pearl': White marble-like berries.
 ✿ H:1.5m (5ft) S:1.5m (5ft)   *Stks*: Widely available

**Syringa** (lilac) (D)   LMH   O–◑   ***
 × *josiflexa* 'Bellicent': Clear, rose-pink fls, June.
 ✿ H:3m (10ft) S:3m (10ft)   *Stks*: Widely available
 *palibiniana* see *S. velutina*
 *vulgaris* 'Charles Joly': Dark purplish-red fls, May–June.
 ✿✕ H:4.5m (15ft) S:3.5m (12ft)   *Stks*: Widely available
 *vulgaris* 'Katherine Havemeyer': Purple-lavender fls, June.
 ✿✕ H:4.5m (15ft) S:3.5m (12ft)   *Stks*: Widely available
 *vulgaris* 'Madame Lemoine': Double, white fls, May–June.
 ✿✕ H:4.5m (15ft) S:3.5m (12ft)   *Stks*: Widely available
 *velutina*: Pale lilac-pink, single fls, May–June.
 ✿ H:1.5m (5ft) S:1.5m (5ft)   *Stks*: Widely available

**Tamarix** (tamarisk) (D)   LM   O   ***
 *pentandra*: Bright pink fls, on slender stems, Aug.
 H:3.5m (12ft) S:3.5m (12ft)   *Stks*: Widely available

**Viburnum** (D or E)   LMH(C)   O–●   ***
 × *bodnantense* 'Deben' (D): White heads of fls, Oct.–April.
 ✿ H:2.7m (9ft) S:2.7m (9ft)   *Stks*: Widely available
 × *bodnantense* 'Dawn' (D): Fragrant, pinkish fls, Oct.–April.
 ✿ H:2.7m (9ft) S:2.7m (9ft)   *Stks*: Widely available
 *carlesii* 'Aurora' (D): Fragrant pink fls, April–May.
 ✿ H:1.5m (5ft) S:1.5m (5ft)   *Stks*: Widely available
 *opulus* 'Compactum' (D): White fls, May–June. Free-fruiting.
 ✿ H:1.5m (5ft) S:1.5m (5ft)   *Stks*: Widely available
 *plicatum* 'Lanarth' (D): Masses of white fls, May–June.
 H:2.4m (8ft) S:3m (10ft)   *Stks*: Widely available
 *tinus* (laurustinus) (E): Pink buds and white fls, Dec.–April.
 H:2.1m (7ft) S:1.8m (6ft)   *Stks*: Widely available
 *rhytidophyllum* (E): Creamy-white fls, May. Attractive lvs.
 ∅ ✿ H:3m (10ft) S:3m (10ft)   *Stks*: Widely available

**Vinca** (periwinkle) (E)   LMH   O–●   ***
 *major* 'Variegata': Green lvs, margined creamy-white. Blue fls.
 ∅ ✿ H:23cm (9in) S:90cm (3ft)   *Stks*: Widely available
 *minor*: Attractive, bright blue fls, April–June.
 ✿ H:15cm (6in) S:1m (3½ft)   *Stks*: Widely available

**Weigela** (D)   LMH   O–●   ***
 *florida* 'Foliis Purpureis': Deep pink fls, purple-flushed lvs.
 ∅ H:1.8m (6ft) S:1.8m (6ft)   *Stks*: Widely available
 *florida* 'Variegata': Lvs edged creamy-white. Pink fls, June.
 ∅ H:1.2m (4ft) S:1.2m (4ft)   *Stks*: Widely available
 *florida* 'Bristol Ruby': Sparkling ruby-red fls, May–June.
 H:1.8m (6ft) S:1.8m (6ft)   *Stks*: Widely available

**Yucca** (E)   LM   O   **
 *filamentosa*: Spiky lvs. Creamy-white fls, July–Aug.
 H:75cm (2½ft) S:90cm (3ft)   *Stks*: Widely available

*For key to symbols, see page 7*

# Shrubs for Acid Soils

The majority of soils contain chalk or lime and this restricts the supply of some trace elements such as iron to several groups of acid-loving plants, including azaleas and rhododendrons. There are simple soil test kits (available from most garden centres) that can be used to indicate the acidity or alkalinity of the soil. A sure sign of excessively alkaline (chalky) soils is foliage turning yellowish, especially between leaf veins. Watering with a solution of 'sequestered' iron (available from all good garden retailers) will quickly bring the leaves back to a healthy green colour. Sequestrene is best applied to the soil in spring when the plants are growing quickly and the trace elements can be absorbed rapidly.

While annual watering with such chemicals will help these plants to thrive, it is better to provide acid soil conditions from the outset. This can be achieved by the generous addition of peat and/or well-rotted leaves to the planting site and regular peat mulches.

Applying flowers of sulphur at 100–150g per sq m (4–6oz per sq yd) and mixing this well into the soil before planting will also reduce the alkalinity.

When introducing peat for acid-loving (ericaceous) plants, try to build it up and plant slightly above surrounding chalky soil, to reduce the chance of alkaline water seeping in from the sides.

**Azalea** see *Rhododendron*

**Calluna** (Scottish heather) (E)  LM(P)  O  ***
 *vulgaris* 'Golden Feather': Golden-yellow foliage.
  H:45cm (1½ft) S:45cm (1½ft)  *Stks*: Widely available
 *vulgaris* 'H.E. Beale': Double, rose fls, Aug.–Nov.
  H:60cm (2ft) S:45cm (1½ft)  *Stks*: Widely available
 *vulgaris* 'My Dream': Attractive white fls, Sept.–Oct.
  H:60cm (2ft) S:45cm (1½ft)  *Stks*: RN
 *vulgaris* 'Robert Chapman': Bronze, gold, red, yellow lvs.
  H:25cm (10in) S:25cm (10in)  *Stks*: Widely available
 *vulgaris* 'Silver Queen': Silvery-grey lvs. Mauve fls, Sept.
  H:25cm (10in) S:25cm (10in)  *Stks*: HN, HW, RN

**Daboecia** (Irish heath) (E)  LM(P)  O  ***
 *cantabrica* 'Atropurpurea': Large red-purple fls, June–Oct.
  H:60cm (2ft) S:45cm (1½ft)  *Stks*: Widely available

**Erica** (heath) (E)  LM(P)  O  ***
 *carnea* 'Myretoun Ruby': Large ruby-red fls, Feb.–April.
  H:25cm (10in) S:30cm (1ft)  *Stks*: HN, HW, NN
 *carnea* 'Springwood White': White heather. Fls, Feb.–April.
  H:25cm (10in) S:60cm (2ft)  *Stks*: Widely available
 *carnea* 'Vivellii': Rich carmine fls, Feb.–March. Bronze lvs.
  H:25cm (10in) S:30cm (1ft)  *Stks*: Widely available
 *cinerea* 'C. D. Eason': Glowing, deep pink fls, July–Sept.
  H:30cm (1ft) S:30cm (1ft)  *Stks*: Widely available
 *cinerea* 'Velvet Knight': Blackish-purple fls, June–Sept.
  H:30cm (1ft) S:30cm (1ft)  *Stks*: HW, RR, SN

× *darleyensis* 'Darley Dale': Pale pink fls, Nov.–March.
✖🌿 H:45cm (1½ft) S:45cm (1½ft)    *Stks*: Widely available

× *darleyensis* 'Silberschmelze': White fls, Nov.–April.
✖🌿 H:45cm (1½ft) S:45cm (1½ft)    *Stks*: Widely available

× *darleyensis* 'Silver Beads' see × *d.* 'Silberschmelze'

*vagans* 'Lyonesse': Pure white fls, Aug.–Oct.
🌿 H:45cm (1½ft) S:45cm (1½ft)    *Stks*: Widely available

*vagans* 'Mrs. D. F. Maxwell': Deep cerise fls, Aug.–Oct.
🌿 H:45cm (1½ft) S:45cm (1½ft)    *Stks*: Widely available

## Rhododendron    LM(P)    ◑    ***

### DWARF/ALPINE VARIETIES (evergreen)

*impeditum*: Dome-like habit. Purplish-blue fls, April–May.
△ H:30cm (1ft) S:45cm (1½ft)    *Stks*: Widely available

'Blue Tit': Funnel-shaped, lavender-blue fls, April.
H:90cm (3ft) S:90cm (3ft)    *Stks*: Widely available

'Chikor': Small lvs. Clusters of yellow fls, May.
H:60cm (2ft) S:60cm (2ft)    *Stks*: HN, HW, RN

'Elizabeth': Dark red, trumpet-shaped fls, April.
H:75cm (2½ft) S:60cm (2ft)    *Stks*: Widely available

'Praecox': Dark green lvs. Rosy-purple fls, Feb.–March.
H:1m (3½ft) S:75cm (2½ft)    *Stks*: Widely available

### TALL HYBRIDS (evergreen)

'Britannia': Rounded bush. Glowing crimson-scarlet fls, May.
H:1.8m (6ft) S:2.4m (8ft)    *Stks*: Widely available

'Cynthia': Rose-carmine fls, blackish-crimson markings, May.
H:4.5m (15ft) S:3m (10ft)    *Stks*: Widely available

'Gomer Waterer': White flushed mauve, yellow throat, May.
H:3m (10ft) S:2.4m (8ft)    *Stks*: Widely available

'Pink Pearl': Deep lilac-pink fls, crimson-brown ray, May.
H:4.5m (15ft) S:3m (10ft)    *Stks*: Widely available

'Purple Splendour': Purplish-blue fls, black ray, May–June.
H:2.1m (7ft) S:1.8m (6ft)    *Stks*: Widely available

'Sappho': Pure white fls, with purple blotch, May.
H:4.5m (15ft) S:3m (10ft)    *Stks*: Widely available

### AZALEAS (deciduous)

'Coccinea Speciosa': Long-lasting bright orange-red fls, May.
🌿 H:2.1m (7ft) S:1.8m (6ft)    *Stks*: Widely available

'Nancy Waterer': Golden-yellow fls, with deeper eyes, May.
🌿 H:2.1m (7ft) S:1.8m (6ft)    *Stks*: HW, RN, SN

'Persil': White fls with orange throats, May.
🌿 H:2.1m (7ft) S:1.8m (6ft)    *Stks*: Widely available

'Strawberry Ice': Fls flesh-pink, narrow throat, May.
🌿 H:2.1m (7ft) S:1.8m (6ft)    *Stks*: HW, SD, SN

Mollis azaleas: Many different cultivars and colours, May.
H:1.5m (5ft) S:1.5m (5ft)    *Stks*: Widely available

### AZALEAS (evergreen)

'Christina': Double, rose-pink fls, May. Attractive lvs.
H:75cm (2½ft) S:75cm (2½ft)    *Stks*: HN

'Hino Crimson': Bright crimson fls borne in May.
H:1m (3½ft) S:90cm (3ft)    *Stks*: Widely available

'Mother's Day': Rose-red, semi-double fls, mid-May–June.
H:1.2m (4ft) S:1m (3½ft)    *Stks*: Widely available

'Nico': Large, single, cherry-red fls borne in May.
H:75cm (2½ft) S:75cm (2½ft)    *Stks*: RN

'White Lady': A pure white variety, fls in May.
H:60cm (2ft) S:60cm (2ft)    *Stks*: HN

# Climbers

The high cost of land inevitably causes gardens to become smaller, but careful covering of walls, fences, trellises, sheds and unsightly structures, with climbers will hide them and make the garden feel larger.

## Where to grow

A good volume of soil – at least a cubic metre – is needed to achieve vigorous growth to cover large areas. While many climbers can be grown in pots and tubs the amount of growth achieved is usually in direct proportion to the amount of water and liquid feeding the containers get when the plants are growing strongly.

Self-clinging plants such as ivies (*hedera*), Virginia creeper (*Parthenocissus*), and climbing hydrangea (*Hydrangea petiolaris*) are best for walls. If the wall surface and pointing between bricks is sound they will cause no structural damage.

If there is a strip of soil about 60–90cm (2–3ft) wide along the fence or wall then free-standing plants like pyracanthas can be used. Alternatively construct a plastic or wire support for twining plants like honeysuckle (*Lonicera*), clematis, Russian vine (*Polygonum baldschuanicum*), and vitis.

Large-flowered clematis planted with large-leaved ivies or climbing roses can be very effective.

## What to buy

Several of the climbers resent root disturbance and for this reason it is advisable to buy pot or container-grown plants. Avoid plants that have been in the pots for a long time and obviously look to have exhausted all the goodness in the compost. Such plants may well grow satisfactorily, but will take one or two seasons to recover from the check to growth.

---

**Actinidia** (D)  LMH  O–◑  ***
    *kolomikta*: Heart-shaped lvs, pink or white at their tips.
    ⊘ H:3m (10ft) S:1.8m (6ft)  *Stks*: Widely available

**Clematis** (D)  LMH(C)  O–◑  ***
    *montana*: Small white fls in May. Attractive seed heads.
    H:7.5m (25ft) S:3m+ (10ft+)  *Stks*: Widely available
    *montana rubens*: Bronze-green lvs. Pale pink fls, May.
    H:7.5m (25ft) S:3m+ (10ft+)  *Stks*: Widely available
    *tangutica*: Yellow, bell-shaped fls, Aug.–Sept.
    H:3m (10ft) S:3m (10ft)  *Stks*: Widely available

**Clematis** (large-flowered) (D)  LMH(C)  O–◑  ***
    'Ernest Markham': Single, petunia-red fls, June–Sept.
    H:3.5m (12ft) S:1.2m (4ft)  *Stks*: Widely available
    'Jackmanii Superba': Dark, violet-purple single fls, July–Oct.
    H:4.5m (15ft) S:1.2m (4ft)  *Stks*: Widely available
    'Mrs Cholmondeley': Pale-blue single fls, May–Oct.
    H:3m (10ft) S:1.2m (4ft)  *Stks*: Widely available

'Marie Boisselot': Large, pure white fls, June–Sept.
H:3m (10ft) S:1.2m (4ft)   Stks: HW, NN, RN

'Nelly Moser'(●): Single, pink fls, carmine bar, June–Sept.
H:3.5m (12ft) S:1.2m (4ft)   Stks: Widely available

'The President': Blue-purple single fls, June–Sept.
H:3m (10ft) S:1.2m (4ft)   Stks: Widely available

'Vyvyan Pennell': Double fls, violet-purple, May–July.
H:3m (10ft) S:1.2m (4ft)   Stks: Widely available

**Hedera** (ivy) (E)   LMH   ○–●   **/***
*canariensis* 'Gloire de Marengo' (**): White variegation.
☞ H:4.5m (15ft) S:3m (10ft)   Stks: Widely available

*colchica* 'Dentata Variegata' (***): Lvs margined yellow.
H:6m (20ft) S:3m (10ft)   Stks: Widely available

*colchica* 'Paddy's Pride' (***): Lvs centrally splashed yellow.
H:6m (20ft) S:3m (10ft)   Stks: HW, SN

*helix* 'Goldheart' (***): Small green lvs, splashed yellow.
H:9m (30ft) S:3.5m (12ft)   Stks: Widely available

*helix* 'Hibernica' (***): Large, dark green lvs.
☞ H:9m (30ft) S:3.5m (12ft)   Stks: Widely available

**Humulus** (hop) (D)   LMH   ○   ***
*lupulus* 'Aureus': Attractive, soft yellow lvs.
H:4.5m (15ft) S:1.8m (6ft)   Stks: Widely available

**Hydrangea** (D)   LMH   ○–●   ***
*petiolaris*: White fls, borne in June. Self-clinging.
H:7.5m (25ft) S:3.5m (12ft)   Stks: Widely available

**Jasminum** (jasmine) (D)   LMH   ○   **/***
*nudiflorum* (***): Yellow fls, borne Nov.–Feb. Wall shrub.
H:1.5m (5ft) S:1.2m (4ft)   Stks: Widely available

*officinale* (**): Fragrant white fls, July–Sept.
⚘ H:4.5m (15ft) S:1.5m (5ft)   Stks: Widely available

**Lonicera** (honeysuckle) (D or E)   LMH   ○–◑   ***
*japonica* 'Aureoreticulata' (E): Lvs veined golden-yellow.
H:6m (20ft) S:2.1m (7ft)   Stks: Widely available

*periclymenum* 'Belgica' (D): Red to yellow, May–June.
⚘ H:3m (10ft) S:1.2m (4ft)   Stks: Widely available

*periclymenum* 'Serotina' (D): Red-purple, cream, July–Oct.
⚘ H:3m (10ft) S:1.2m (4ft)   Stks: Widely available

**Parthenocissus** (D)   LMH   ○–●   ***
*tricuspidata* 'Veitchii': Self-clinging. Rich autumn colour.
❧ H:9m (30ft) S:3.5m (12ft)   Stks: Widely available

**Passiflora** (passion flower) (D)   LMH   ○   **
*caerulea*: Large, interesting blue fls, June–Sept.
H:6m (20ft) S:2.4m (8ft)   Stks: Widely available

**Polygonum** (D)   LMH   ○–◑   ***
*baldschuanicum*: Rampant climber, with white fls, July–Sept.
H:7.5m (25ft) S:4.5m (15ft)   Stks: Widely available

**Vitis** (D)   LMH   ○–●   ***
*coignetiae*: Large, handsome lvs, beautiful in autumn.
❧ H:10.5m (35ft) S:6m (20ft)   Stks: Widely available

**Wisteria** (D)   LMH   ○   ***
*floribunda*: Fragrant, violet-blue fls, May–June.
⚘ H:9m (30ft) S:4.5m (15ft)   Stks: HN, SN

*floribunda* 'Macrobotrys': Lilac-blue fls, 75cm (2½ft) long.
⚘ H:9m (30ft) S:4.5m (15ft)   Stks: HW, RN

*For key to symbols, see page 7*

# Hedges

Living plants are the cheapest and longest lasting means of retaining a fence and barrier between properties. They do not blow down in strong wind and do not rot and decay after a few years.

Living plants also look more attractive, act as a baffle to noise, filter and soften strong wind, and trap and reduce dust and dirt. Prickly kinds will also keep out unwanted intruders.

Chosen carefully to suit your purpose, a hedge need not take up a lot of time. Hedge cutting need not be an irksome chore – even very strong-growing plants like green privet need only be cut once a year in May, and then sprayed with a growth retardant (Cutlass, ICI) to make a bushier hedge and save several cuts per year.

## Where to grow

While the boundaries of gardens are the obvious place for hedges, informal screens and low hedges can also be used effectively within every garden. The old idea of low box hedging around the vegetable plot was a good one, as it gives early vegetables protection from cold winds in spring.

The closer you plant, the faster the hedge will fulfil your requirements, but the really fast-growing conifers like × *Cupressocyparis leylandii* will make a dense screen in three to five years at 1.5–1.8m (5–6ft) spacing.

## What to buy

Small, healthy young plants will be cheaper and in well-prepared soil will grow very quickly to catch up with larger more expensive sizes.

Avoid bare-root hedge plants if they have any signs of the roots having been allowed to dry, especially in the case of beech.

---

## SPECIALIST SUPPLIERS

**HN** Highfield Nurseries, Whitminster, Gloucester, GL2 7PL. Tel: Gloucester (0252) 740266.

**HW** Hillier Nurseries Ltd., Ampfield House, Ampfield, Romsey, Hants., SO5 9PA. Tel: Braishfield 68733.

**NN** Notcutts Nurseries Ltd., Ipswich Road, Woodbridge, Suffolk, IP12 4AF. Tel: Woodbridge (03943) 3344.

**RN** L. R. Russell Ltd., Richmond Nurseries, Windlesham, Surrey, GU20 6LL. Tel: Ascot 21411.

**RR** R. V. Roger Ltd., The Nurseries, Pickering, North Yorkshire, YO18 7HG. Tel: Pickering (0751) 72226.

**SD** Sunningdale Nurseries Ltd., Windlesham, Surrey. Tel: Ascot 20496.

**SN** Scotts Nurseries (Merriott) Ltd., Merriott, Somerset, TA16 5PL. Tel: Crewkerne (0460) 72306.

*For key to symbols, see page 7*

**Buxus** (box)   LMH   ○–●   ***
  *sempervirens*: Small, glossy-green scented lvs. Slow-growing.
  H:90cm (3ft) D:45–90cm (1½–3ft)   *Stks*: Widely available
  *sempervirens* 'Suffruticosa': A dwarf form for edging borders.
  H:25cm (10in) D:15cm (6in)   *Stks*: HW, NN

**Carpinus** (hornbeam) (D)   LMH(C)   ○–◑   ***
  *betulus*: Mid-green, oval lvs, brown in winter, like beech.
  H:3m (10ft) D:45–90cm (1½–3ft)   *Stks*: Widely available

**Chamaecyparis** (E)   LMH   ○   ***
  *lawsoniana*: Conifer forming a dense closely-formed screen.
  H:1.5–6m (5–20ft) D:90cm (3ft)   *Stks*: Widely available
  *lawsoniana* 'Kilmacurragh': Dense, dark upright growth.
  H:1.5–6m (5–20ft) D:90cm (3ft)   *Stks*: HW, NN

**Cotoneaster** (E)   LMH   ○–●   ***
  *lacteus*: Oval, leathery lvs. White fls, cluster of red berries.
  ✿ H:2.4m (8ft) D:45–90cm (1½–3ft)   *Stks*: Widely available
  *simonsii*: Semi-evergreen. Large red fruits, close to stem.
  ✿ H:1.8m (6ft) D:45cm (1½ft)   *Stks*: Widely available

**Crataegus** (thorn) (D)   LMH   ○–●   ***
  *monogyna*: White fls, May. Glorious red berries.
  ✿ H:1.5–6m (5–20ft) D:30cm (1ft)   *Stks*: Widely available

×**Cupressocyparis** (E)   LMH   ●   ***
  *leylandii*: Exceptionally fast-growing conifer. Green.
  H:2.4–9m (8–30ft) D:1–1.5m (3–5ft)   *Stks*: Widely available

**Fagus** (beech) (D)   LMH(C)   ●   ***
  *sylvatica*: Useful because dead lvs hang until spring.
  H:1.5–6m (5–20ft) D:30–45cm (1–1½ft)   *Stks*: Widely avail.

**Griselinia** (E)   LM   ○   **
  *littoralis*: Leathery apple-green lvs. May suffer frost damage.
  H:1.5m (5ft) D:60cm (2ft)   *Stks*: Widely available

**Hippophae** (sea buckthorn) (E)   LMH   ○   ***
  *rhamnoides*: Silver-grey lvs. Fierce thorns. Orange berries.
  ✿ H:2.4m (8ft) D:75cm (2½ft)   *Stks*: Widely available

**Ilex** (holly) (E)   LMH   ○–●   ***
  *aquifolium*: Prickly lvs, making a strong, defensive hedge.
  H:3m (10ft) D:60–90cm (2–3ft)   *Stks*: Widely available

**Ligustrum** (privet) (E)   LMH   ○–●   ***
  *ovalifolium*: Green, oval lvs. Tolerates most conditions.
  H:1.5m (5ft) D:45cm (1½ft)   *Stks*: Widely available

**Lonicera** (Shrubby honeysuckle) (E)   LMH   ○–●   ***
  *nitida*: Small, light green lvs. Best kept to 90cm (3ft).
  H:1.2m (4ft) D:45cm (1½ft)   *Stks*: Widely available

**Prunus** (D or E)   LMH   ○–●   ***
  *cerasifera* 'Pissardii' (D): Purple lvs. Very attractive.
  H:3m (10ft) D:45–60cm (1½–2ft)   *Stks*: Widely available
  *laurocerasus* (E): Large, green lvs. Grows well in shade.
  H:3m (10ft) D:75–90cm (2½–3ft)   *Stks*: Widely available

**Taxus** (yew) (E)   LMH   ○–●   ***
  *baccata*: Very dark green lvs. One of the best clipped hedges.
  H:3m (10ft) D:75–90cm (2½–3ft)   *Stks*: Widely available

**Thuya** (thuja) (E)   LMH   ○   ***
  *plicata* 'Atrovirens': Bright green conifer; trims well.
  H:6m (20ft) D:90cm (3ft)   *Stks*: Widely available

# Roses

Roses are the most popular of all garden flowers. They give tremendous value for money and once well established will flower year after year with the minimum of attention. Good healthy roses planted in new soil can thrive for 50 years or more.

## What and when to buy

Roses grown in fields, lifted and the soil removed before sale, can be planted from October to March. Lifted roses are better with damp peat around the roots to prevent drying out and shrivelling.

Container and pot-grown roses can be planted at any time of the year. However, it is better not to plant any roses when the soil is very wet or frozen.

Visit rose fields in flower in summer and place orders for autumn delivery, or select container-grown roses in flower to be sure the flower colour and fragrance is to your liking.

The stronger the young plants and the more branches they have of finger thickness or more, the better they are. Top quality bushes have at least two and preferably three or more strong branches. Good miniatures also have several branches, but little over straw thickness.

When buying rose bushes lifted from fields and sold in polythene, check the weight. The thicker and stronger the plant, the heavier and better it will be. Do not buy plants if they have thin, spindly branches. Avoid plants in polythene with thin cream or white drawn shoots, especially where such shoots show signs of brown and black mould. Avoid plants showing signs of black-spot disease, orange spots of rust disease on the underside of leaves, and white mildewed leaves, flowers or stems.

**ROSE TYPE**

| | |
|---|---|
| 3 m (10 ft.) | |
| 2·4 m (8 ft.) | |
| 1·5 – 1·8 m ( 5 – 6 ft.) | |
| 1·2 – 1·8 m ( 4 – 6 ft.) | |
| 75 – 90 cm ( $2\frac{1}{2}$ – 3 ft.) | |
| 60 – 75 cm ( 2 – $2\frac{1}{2}$ ft.) | |
| 30 – 45 cm ( 1 – $1\frac{1}{2}$ ft) | |

Miniature    Floribunda    Hybrid tea    Shrub

## How to plant

Roses grow well in a wide variety of soils and the average garden soil will give excellent results. Very light, sandy soil and thin, chalky soil will give poor growth.

All soils need digging well and benefit from plenty of well-rotted garden compost, rotted manure or peat.

While roses grow happily in the same soil for very many years, if you lift a well-established rose and put another in its place, the second one is unlikely to grow as well. Where roses are replanted, to avoid this so-called replant disease, always dig out a good heap of old soil and replace with new. Exchanging soil with some from the vegetable plot will suffice.

## Disease resistance and the Rose Analysis

Every year the Royal National Rose Society conducts a 'rose analysis', in which selected members and visitors to their Rose Festival and Northern Show complete a questionnaire. The results of these are analysed for the various rose groups, and a list published annually. Where roses in the following table have been in the top 20 places at the last available analysis, the position has been indicated in brackets after the name.

The other bracketed number following the name, prefixed with 'D' indicates disease resistance:

> D1: very resistant
> D2: good resistance
> D3: fair resistance
> D4: poor resistance

## If you want to know more . . .

Anyone keen on roses should consider joining The Royal National Rose Society. It is based at Chiswell Green Lane, St. Albans, Hertfordshire, AL2 3NR, and over 1,600 varieties are grown in their grounds, making it a good place to select varieties suitable for your garden.

**AND HEIGHTS**

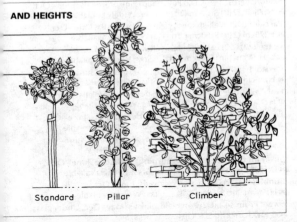

Standard  Pillar  Climber

*Hybrid tea roses provide shapely individual blooms and are ideal for cutting.*

## Hybrid Tea

**'Alec's Red'**: (18) (D2) Light crimson, double fls, June–Oct.
H: 90cm (3ft) S: 60cm (2ft)   *Stks*: Widely available

**'Alexander'**: (20) (D2) Bright orange-vermilion fls, June–Oct.
H: 1m (3½ft) S: 60cm (2ft)   *Stks*: Widely available

**'Alpine Sunset'**: (D2) Peach-pink, flushed yellow, June–Sept.
H: 90cm (3ft) S: 60cm (2ft)   *Stks*: Widely available

**'Belle Blonde'**: (D3) Bright golden-yellow fls, June–Oct.
H: 75cm (2½ft) S: 60cm (2ft)   *Stks*: SR

**'Bettina'**: (D2) Orange with a golden base, June–Oct.
H: 75cm (2½ft) S: 60cm (2ft)   *Stks*: SR, WT

**'Blessings'**: (D2) Large coral-pink attractive fls, June–Oct.
H: 75cm (2½ft) S: 60cm (2ft)   *Stks*: Widely available

**'Blue Moon'**: (D2) Large, rich lilac-blue fls, June–Oct.
H: 75cm (2½ft) S: 60cm (2ft)   *Stks*: Widely available

**'Double Delight'**: (D3) Cream centre, crimson petals, June–Oct.
H: 75cm (2½ft) S: 60cm (2ft)   *Stks*: Widely available

**'Ernest H. Morse'**: (8) (D2) Brilliant red fls, June–Oct.
H: 75cm (2½ft) S: 60cm (2ft)   *Stks*: Widely available

**'Family Circle'**: (D2) Light vermilion fls, May–Dec. under glass.
H: 75cm (2½ft) S: 60cm (2ft)   *Stks*: SR

**'Fragrant Cloud'**: (6) (D2) Geranium red fls, June–Oct.
H: 75cm (2½ft) S: 60cm (2ft)   *Stks*: Widely available

**'Grandpa Dickson'**: (1) (D2) Shapely, lemon fls June–Oct.
H: 75cm (2½ft) S: 60cm (2ft)   *Stks*: Widely available

**'Just Joey'**: (23) (D2) Frilled, coppery-orange fls, June–Oct.
H: 90cm (3ft) S: 60cm (2ft)   *Stks*: Widely available

**'King's Ransom'**: (D2) Rich, pure yellow fls, June–Oct.
H: 75cm (2½ft) S: 60cm (2ft)   *Stks*: Widely available

**'Mischief'**: (22) (D2) Well-shaped, coral-salmon fls, June–Oct.
H: 75cm (2½ft) S: 60cm (2ft)   *Stks*: Widely available

**'National Trust'**: (16) (D2) Full, deep crimson-red fls, June–Oct.
H: 75cm (2½ft) S: 60cm (2ft)   *Stks*: Widely available

**'Pascali'**: (D2) Well-shaped, clear pure white fls, June–Oct.
H: 75cm (2½ft) S: 60cm (2ft)   *Stks*: Widely available

**'Peace'**: (2) (D2) Large golden-yellow, flushed pink, June–Oct.
H: 90cm (3ft) S: 60cm (2ft)   *Stks*: Widely available

**'Piccadilly'**: (7) (D2) Scarlet inside, gold outside, June–Oct.
H: 75cm (2½ft) S: 60cm (2ft)   *Stks*: Widely available

**'Pink Favourite'**: (9) (D1) Shapely, deep rose-pink fls, June–Oct.
H: 75cm (2½ft) S: 60cm (2ft)   *Stks*: Widely available

**'Prima Ballerina'**: (D2) Long-lasting, deep pink fls, June–Oct.
H: 75cm (2½ft) S: 60cm (2ft)   *Stks*: Widely available

**'Rose Gaujard'**: (17) (D2) Deep rose, silver reverse, June–Oct.
H: 75cm (2½ft) S: 60cm (2ft)   *Stks*: JC, JM, RH, WR

**'Silver Jubilee'**: (3) (D2) Delicate pink fls, shaded, June–Oct.
H: 75cm (2½ft) S: 60cm (2ft)   *Stks*: Widely available

**'Sunblest'**: (D2) Good, rich yellow fls, June–Oct.
H: 90cm (3ft) S: 60cm (2ft)   *Stks*: Widely available

**'Sweet Promise'**: (D2) Porcelain-pink fls, May–Dec. Under glass.
H: 75cm (2½ft) S: 60cm (2ft)   *Stks*: SR

'Troika': (12) (D2) Light apricot to orange-yellow fls, June–Oct.
❀ H:75cm (2½ft) S:60cm (2ft)    *Stks*: Widely available

'Wendy Cussons': (5) (D2) Cerise fls flushed scarlet, June–Oct.
❀✖⊙ H:75cm (2½ft) S:60cm (2ft)    *Stks*: Widely available

'Whisky Mac': (D2) Harvest-gold fls, bronze in bud, June–Oct.
❀ H:75cm (2½ft) S:60cm (2ft)    *Stks*: Widely available

*Floribunda (multi-headed) roses are best for a colourful massed display.*

## Floribunda (Multi-headed)

'Allgold': (7) (D1) Small unfading, deep yellow fls, June–Oct.
❀ H:75cm (2½ft) S:60cm (2ft)    *Stks*: Widely available

'Chorus': (D2) Bright, vermilion-red fls, June–Oct.
H:75cm (2½ft) S:60cm (2ft)    *Stks*: CC, SR, WR

'City of Leeds': (4) (D2) Shapely, rich salmon fls, June–Oct.
H:75cm (2½ft) S:60cm (2ft)    *Stks*: Widely available

'Dearest': (D3) Shapely, warm salmon-pink fls, June–Oct.
❀ H:75cm (2½ft) S:60cm (2ft)    *Stks*: Widely available

'Elizabeth of Glamis': (6) (D3) Salmon-pink double fls, June–Oct.
❀✖ H:75cm (2½ft) S:60cm (2ft)    *Stks*: Widely available

'Europeana': (22) (D2–3) Deep crimson fls, June–Oct.
H:75cm (2½ft) S:60cm (2ft)    *Stks*: JC

'Evelyn Fison': (2) (D2) Vivid red with scarlet fls, June–Oct.
H:75cm (2½ft) S:60cm (2ft)    *Stks*: Widely available

'Eye Paint': (20) (D3) Scarlet fls, white eyes, June–Oct.
H:75cm (2½ft) S:60cm (2ft)    *Stks*: FR, JM, RH, WR

'Glenfiddich': (16) (D2) Attractive, amber-gold fls, June–Oct.
✖ H:75cm (2½ft) S:60cm (2ft)    *Stks*: Widely available

'Iceberg': (1) (D2) Attractive, pure white fls, June–Oct.
✖ H:75cm (2½ft) S:60cm (2ft)    *Stks*: Widely available

'Korresia': (18) (D2) Bright yellow, full fls, June–Oct.
❀ H:75cm (2½ft) S:60cm (2ft)    *Stks*: Widely available

'Margaret Merril': (21) (D2) Pearly white. Sturdy. June–Oct.
❀❀ H:90cm (3ft) S:60cm (2ft)    *Stks*: Widely available

'Marlena': (D2) Clusters of crimson-scarlet fls, June–Oct.
H:60cm (2ft) S:45cm (1½ft)    *Stks*: Widely available

'News': (D2) Rich, clear purple fls, golden anthers, June–Oct.
H:75cm (2½ft) S:60cm (2ft)    *Stks*: JM

'Orange Sensation': (D2) Orange and red fls, June–Oct.
❀ H:75cm (2½ft) S:60cm (2ft)    *Stks*: Widely available

'Paddy McGredy': (D3) Deep carmine-pink fls, June–Oct.
H:75cm (2½ft) S:60cm (2ft)    *Stks*: AR, CG, FR, JM

'Pink Parfait': (8) (D2) Pink fls, yellow at base, June–Oct.
❀✖ H:75cm (2½ft) S:60cm (2ft)    *Stks*: AR, JC, RH, WT

'Priscilla Burton': (D2) White and red, silver 'eye', June–Oct.
H:90cm (3ft) S:60cm (2ft)    *Stks*: CC, JM, WR

'Queen Elizabeth': (3) (D2) Pure, glowing pink fls, June–Oct.
✖ H:1.8m (6ft) S:90cm (3ft)    *Stks*: Widely available

'Tip Top': (D4) Warm, salmon fls shaded pink, June–Oct.
H:45cm (1½ft) S:45cm (1½ft)    *Stks*: Widely available

'Topsi': (24) (D3) Glowing orange-scarlet fls, June–Oct.
H:45cm (1½ft) S:45cm (1½ft)    *Stks*: Widely available

## ROSES

### Miniature

'Angela Rippon': (14) (D2) Double, salmon-pink fls, June–Oct.
H:35cm (14in) S:30cm (1ft)     *Stks*: Widely available

'Baby Masquerade': (3) (D2) Yellow, pink, red fls, June–Oct.
H:35cm (14in) S:30cm (1ft)     *Stks*: Widely available

'Darling Flame': (2) (D2) Orange with golden shading, June–Oct.
☺ H:38cm (15in) S:30cm (1ft)     *Stks*: Widely available

'Dresden Doll' (15) (D3) Double, pink fls, June–Oct.
H:35cm (14in) S:30cm (1ft)     *Stks*: CG, JM, RH

'Little Buckaroo': (D2) Red fls with white centres, June–Oct.
H:45cm (1½ft) S:30cm (1ft)     *Stks*: CC, SR, WR, WT

'Mr Bluebird': (D2) Small lavender-blue fls, June–Oct.
H:35cm (14in) S:30cm (1ft)     *Stks*: AR, CC, SR, WR

'Pour Toi': (4) (D2) White, with hint of cream, June–Oct.
☺ H:30cm (1ft) S:30cm (1ft)     *Stks*: Widely available

'Snow Carpet': (D2) Shapely double white fls, June–Oct.
☷ H:25cm (10in) S:90cm (3ft) *Stks*: JM

'Starina': (1) (D2) Bicolor of scarlet and gold, June–Oct.
☺ H:30cm (1ft) S:30cm (1ft)     *Stks*: Widely available

'Sun Blaze': (D2) Luminous scarlet fls, June–Oct.
☺☢ H:30cm (1ft) S:30cm (1ft)     *Stks*: CC, RH, SR

'Yellow Doll': (D2) Attractive, creamy-white fls, June–Oct.
☺ H:30cm (1ft) S:30cm (1ft)     *Stks*: CC, CG, JC, SR

### Climbers

'Compassion': (3) (D2) Pale orange-scarlet fls, June–Oct.
☙☙ H:2.4m+ (8ft+) S:1.8m (6ft)     *Stks*: Widely available

'Copenhagen': (D2) Rich scarlet, June–Oct.
☙ H:3m (10ft) S:1.8m (6ft)     *Stks*: JM

'Ena Harkness, Climbing': (17) (D2) Crimson-scarlet, June–Oct.
☙☙✗ H:2.4m+ (8ft+) S:1.8m (6ft)     *Stks*: Widely available

'Danse du Feu': (5) (D2) Double, orange fls, June–Oct.
H:2.4m (8ft) S:1.8m (6ft)     *Stks*: Widely available

'Golden Showers': (2) (D 2–3) Long, golden buds, June–Oct.
☙✗ H:1.8m (6ft) S:1.5m (5ft)     *Stks*: Widely available

'Guinée': (D2) Large, very dark scarlet fls, June–July.
☙☙ H:4.5m (15ft) S:3m (10ft)     *Stks*: CC, JM, RH

'Handel': (1) (D2) Cream flushed rich rose-pink fls, June–Oct.
✗ H:3m (10ft) S:1.8m (6ft)     *Stks*: Widely available

'Kiftsgate': (D2) Large clusters, creamy-white fls, June–July.
H:6m (20ft) S:4m (13ft)     *Stks*: CC, JM, RH

'Maigold': (6) (D2) Large, bronzy-yellow fls, June.
☙ H:4m (13ft) S:1.8m (6ft)     *Stks*: Widely available

'Mermaid': (12) (D1) Single, primrose-yellow fls, June–Oct.
H:6m (20ft) S:6m (20ft)     *Stks*: Widely available

'Parkdirektor Riggers': (D2) Semi-double, crimson, June–Oct.
H:3.5m (12ft) S:3m (10ft)     *Stks*: CC, JC, JM, WR

'Pink Perpetue': (4) (D2) Pink and carmine fls, June–Oct.
H:2.4m (8ft) S:1.8m (6ft)     *Stks*: Widely available

'Schoolgirl': (8) (D2) Attractive orange-apricot fls, June–Oct.
☙ H:3m (10ft) S:1.8m (6ft)     *Stks*: Widely available

'Swan Lake': (10) (D2) White fls tinged pink, June–Oct.
H:3m (10ft) S:1.8m (6ft)     *Stks*: Widely available

### Ramblers

'Albertine': (7) (D3) Buds opening to a coppery-pink, June.
☙ H:6m (20ft) S:4m+ (13ft+)     *Stks*: Widely available

'New Dawn': (11) (D2) Beautiful fresh pink fls, June–Oct.
☙ H:4.5m (15ft) S:4m (13ft)     *Stks*: Widely available

*Rosa moyesii has attractive single flowers and the bonus of glossy red heps.*

### Shrub roses

'Ballerina': (3) (D2) Apple blossom pink fls, June–Oct.
H:1.2m (4ft) S:1.2m (4ft)   *Stks*: Widely available

'Canary Bird': (5) (D1) Single golden-yellow fls, May–June.
H:1.8–3m (6–10ft) S:1.8m (6ft)   *Stks*: Widely available

'Frau Dagmar Hartopp': (D1) Pink fls, large heps, June–Oct.
H:1.5m (5ft) S:1.2m (4ft)   *Stks*: CC, JM, RH, WR

'Frau Dagmar Hastrup' *see* 'Frau Dagmar Hartopp'

'Fred Loads': (1) (D2) Bright vermilion semi-double, June–Oct.
H:2.1m (7ft) S:1.5m (5ft)   *Stks*: Widely available

'Fountain': (7) (D2) Semi-double, rich blood-red fls, June–Oct.
H:1.8m (6ft) S:1.5m (5ft)   *Stks*: Widely available

'Frühlingsgold': (10) (D1–2) Large, pale yellow fls, May–June.
H:2.1m (7ft) S:1.5m (5ft)   *Stks*: Widely available

'Nevada': (4) (D2) Semi-double creamy-white fls, June and Sept.
H:2.4m (8ft) S:1.5m (5ft)   *Stks*: Widely available

'Penelope': (8) (D2) Creamy-pink fls, in trusses, June–Sept.
H:1.2m (4ft) S:90cm (3ft)   *Stks*: Widely available

*Rosa moyesii* 'Geranium': (18) (D1) Single rich red fls, June.
H:3m (10ft) S:1.8m (6ft)   *Stks*: CC, JC, RH, WR

*Rosa rubrifolia*: (20) (D3) Coppery lvs. Cerise-pink fls, June.
H:2.1m (7ft) S:1.8m (6ft)   *Stks*: CC, JC, RH, WR

---

### SPECIALIST SUPPLIERS

**AR**  Anderson's Rose Nurseries, Cults, Aberdeen, Scotland, AB1 9QT. Tel: (0224) 48881.

**CC**  Cants of Colchester Ltd., The Old Rose Garden, Stanway, Colchester, Essex, CO3 5UP. Tel: Colchester 210176.

**CG**  C. Gregory & Son Ltd., The Rose Gardens, Stapleford, Nottingham, NG9 7JA. Tel: Sandiacre (0602) 395454.

**FR**  Fryer's Roses, Fryer's Nurseries Ltd., Knutsford, Cheshire, WA16 0SX. Tel: Knutsford 2642.

**JC**  James Cocker & Sons, Whitemyres, Lang Stracht, Aberdeen, AB9 2XH. Tel: Aberdeen 33261.

**JM**  John Mattock Ltd., Rose Nurseries, Nuneham Courtenay, Oxford, OX9 9PY. Tel: Nuneham Courtenay 265.

**RH**  R. Harkness & Co. Ltd., The Rose Gardens, Hitchin, Hertfordshire, SG4 0JT. Tel: Hitchin 4027.

**SR**  Meilland Star Roses Ltd., 464 Goff's Lane, Goff's Oak, Waltham Cross, Herts., EN7 5EN. Tel: (070787) 3232.

**WR**  Warley Rose Gardens Ltd., Warley Street, Great Warley, Brentwood, Essex, CM13 3JH. Tel: Brentwood 221966.

**WT**  Wheatcroft Roses Ltd., Landmere Lane, Edwalton, Nottingham, NG12 4DE. Tel: (0602) 216061.

# Dahlias and Chrysanthemums

These traditional summer and autumn flowers are invaluable, filling in gaps in borders, enlivening bedding schemes, creating a mass display, and providing long-lasting flowers for the home.

### Dahlia classifications

Dahlias are classified according to the formation of the flowers. There are ten different groupings given to them by the National Dahlia Society, and these include collerettes, peony-flowered, decoratives, ball types, pompons, cactus and semi-cactus, single-flowered and anemone-flowered. In addition, certain groups are further classified by their sizes into giant, large, medium, small and miniature types. All good dahlia catalogues give full explanation of these groupings.

### Chrysanthemum classifications

Similarly to the dahlias, chrysanthemums have also been grouped according to their type and size. The types of blooms are incurved, reflexed, intermediate, single, anemone-centred, pompons, and 'other types' into which are set the varieties with spidery blooms.

Varieties have been further divided and given numbers, which will often appear in catalogues by the sides of the listed varieties. These have been classified by the National Chrysanthemum Society.

### What to buy and when

Healthy, stocky plants with fresh, green leaves are best. Avoid plants with yellow, brown or dying leaves at the base. Good plants will be pot-grown and the pots well filled with roots.

Chrysanthemums are hardier than dahlias, which are easily damaged by frosts and best not planted in the garden until about the first week in June. Chrysanthemums, however, can be planted out in early May – or even late April in mild areas – after being hardened off under a garden frame or cold greenhouse. Dahlia tubers can be planted from mid-April because it will take several weeks before the tender shoots appear above the soil.

Dahlia specialists tend to sell rooted cuttings, but pre-packed tubers are freely available from garden centres and general horticultural suppliers. Tubers tend to be more expensive than plants but can be started into growth in a warm greenhouse in March and the new shoots made into cuttings. Alternatively the dormant tubers can be planted out in April. One advantage of tubers is that you don't need the greenhouse or frame facilities you might require to grow on the green plants. Large clumps of old tubers can be divided before planting, but each portion must have part of the crown.

## Stopping and disbudding

These techniques are used to encourage plants to produce a good number of sideshoots and to develop larger and better-quality blooms. Stopping (mainly done to chrysanthemums) involves nipping out the terminal bud, together with part of the stem. The sideshoots, which at that stage may be dormant, then develop into strong shoots which will bear flowers.

All large-flowered varieties of chrysanthemums should be stopped by the beginning of the second week in June.

With spray varieties of chrysanthemums, disbudding is not carried out, as their beauty lies in the mass of small blooms covering the entire plant.

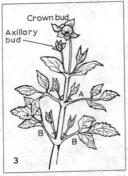

1. *Chrysanthemums are 'stopped' by pinching out the growing tip.*

2. *Stopping makes a bushier plant, with more stems.*

3. *Dahlias grown for garden display require no disbudding, although they often benefit from having the highest sideshoots (A) pinched out. For cutting, the two axillary flower buds should be removed while still small. For exhibition, remove axillary buds and sideshoots (A and B).*

## If you want to know more . . .

It is worth considering joining the National Dahlia Society or the National Chrysanthemum Society. Both societies are keen to aid and advise novices. The Secretary of the National Dahlia Society is Mr. Philip Damp, 26 Burns Road, Lillington, Leamington Spa, Warwickshire. The Secretary of the National Chrysanthemum Society is Mr. S. G. Gosling, 65 St. Margaret's Avenue, Whetstone, London, N20 9HT.

### Giant Decorative

'Hamari Girl': Lavender-pink fls of immense size.
Ⓘ H:1.2m (4ft) S:75cm (2½ft)   Stks: Widely available

'Lavengro': Deep lavender overlaid bronze.
Ⓘ H:1.2m (4ft) S:75cm (2½ft)   Stks: Widely available

'Playboy': Clear bright yellow.
Ⓘ H:1.5m (5ft) S:75cm (2½ft)   Stks: Widely available

### Small-flowered Decorative

'Biddenham Fire': Brilliant flame, on good strong stems.
H:90cm (3ft) S:60cm (2ft)   Stks: AY

'Flutterby': Water-lily type blooms, gold with touch of scarlet.
✕ H:1.3m (4½ft) S:75cm (2½ft)   Stks: AY

'Gerrie Hoek': Clear silvery-pink, yellow flush at centre.
✕ H:1.2m (4ft) S:75cm (2½ft)   Stks: AY

'Hamari Fiesta': Yellow tipped vermilion. Eyecatching.
✕ H:90cm (3ft) S:60cm (2ft)   Stks: HH

'Yellow Frank Hornsey': An outstanding clear yellow.
✕ Ⓘ H:1m (3½ft) S:60cm (2ft)   Stks: Widely available

### Miniature-flowered Decorative

'David Howard': Deep bronze fls on strong stems. Very dark lvs.
✕ Ⓘ H:1m (3½ft) S:60cm (2ft)   Stks: Widely available

'Mistill Delight': Immaculate pure white blooms.
✕ Ⓘ H:1.3m (4½ft) S:75cm (2½ft)   Stks: Widely available

'Schweitzer's Korkarde': Shades of orange, on long stems.
✕ Ⓘ H:1.3m (4½ft) S:75cm (2½ft)   Stks: Widely available

### Ball

'Crichton Honey': Blends of salmon, peach, gold and red.
Ⓘ H:1m (3½ft) S:60cm (2ft)   Stks: HH

### Miniature Ball

'Rothesay Superb': Masses of bright scarlet blooms.
✕ Ⓘ H:1m (3½ft) S:60cm (2ft)   Stks: AY

### Pompon

'Hallmark': Pinkish-lavender shade.
✕ Ⓘ H:90cm (3ft) S:60cm (2ft)   Stks: Widely available

'Noreen': Pure pink of outstanding quality.
✕ Ⓘ H:90cm (3ft) S:60cm (2ft)   Stks: Widely available

'Whale's Rhonda': Dark purple. Good shape.
Ⓘ H:1m (3½ft) S:60cm (2ft)   Stks: Widely available

### Small-flowered Semi-cactus

'Cheerio': Deep cerise, tipped white.
✕ H:1m (3½ft) S:60cm (2ft)   Stks: AY

'Margie': Salmon-bronze, deep formation.
✕ Ⓘ H:1m (3½ft) S:60cm (2ft)   Stks: HH

'Piper's Pink': Dwarf bedding type. Deep pink.
✕ H:60cm (2ft) S:45cm (1½ft)   Stks: AY

'Wootton Wedding': White blooms of good formation.
✕ H:1m (3½ft) S:60cm (2ft)   Stks: OD

### Collerette

'Claire de Lune': Light sulphur yellow with cream collar.
H:1m (3½ft) S:60cm (2ft)   Stks: AY

'Easter Sunday': Creamy white, on good strong stems.
Ⓘ H:1m (3½ft) S:60cm (2ft)   Stks: AY

DAHLIA TYPES: *1. Decorative; 2. Cactus; 3. Semi-cactus; 4. Collerette; 5. Pompon; 6. Decorative (waterlily type)*

### Small-flowered Cactus

'Doris Day': Deep cardinal red. An old favourite.
✕ H:1m (3½ft) S:60cm (2ft)    *Stks*: HH

'Klankstad Kerkrade': Sulphur-yellow with lighter tips.
✕ ☉ H:1.2m (4ft) S:75cm (2½ft)    *Stks*: Widely available

'Richard Marc': Bright pink over a lemon base.
✕ ☉ H:1m (3½ft) S:60cm (2ft)    *Stks*: Widely available

'Shirley Alliance': Soft orange over a gold base.
✕ ☉ H:1m (3½ft) S:60cm (2ft)    *Stks*: Widely available

'White Klankstad': White, sometimes with faint lavender flush.
✕ ☉ H:1.2m (4ft) S:60cm (2ft)    *Stks*: Widely available

---

### SPECIALIST SUPPLIERS

**AY**  Aylett's Nurseries Ltd., North Orbital Road, London Colney, St. Albans, Herts. Tel: Bowmansgreen 22255.

**HH**  W. N. Hall & Sons Ltd., West Heddon Nurseries, Heddon-on-the-Wall, Newcastle upon Tyne, NE15 0JS. Tel: Wylam 2245.

**OD**  Oscroft's Dahlias, Sprotborough Road, Doncaster, Yorkshire, DN5 8BE. Tel: Doncaster (0302) 49026.

**TC**  Terry Clarke, Braintris Dahlia Nursery, Beccles, Suffolk, NR34 7RL. Tel: 0502 715728.

---

*For key to symbols, see page 7*    81

## CHRYSANTHEMUMS

**Garden Spray Varieties** (*flowering August to October*)

'Anna Marie': Compact white sprays. Aug.–Sept. Easy to grow.
H:90cm (3ft) S:45cm (1½ft)    *Stks*: Widely available

'Lilian Hoek': Orange-bronze sprays. Cut early for second crop.
H:90cm (3ft) S:45cm (1½ft)    *Stks*: Widely available

'Lucida': Bright yellow, pert fully double fls, Sept.
H:90cm (3ft) S:45cm (1½ft)    *Skts*: Widely available

'Pinnochio': Fully double, amber-yellow fls. Long, strong stems.
H:90cm (3ft) S:45cm (1½ft)    *Stks*: HW

'Pennine Crimson': Deep red. Well-formed double. Sept.
H:1m (3½ft) S:45cm (1½ft)    *Stks*: Widely available

'Pennine Dancer': Deep pink, yellow centre. Semi-double. Sept.
H:1m (3½ft) S:45cm (1½ft)    *Stks*: Widely available

'Pennine Pink': Double pink, back of young petals bronze.
H:1m (3½ft) S:45cm (1½ft)    *Stks*: Widely available

'Pennine Signal': Single, bright red, yellow centre.
H:1m (3½ft) S:45cm (1½ft)    *Stks*: Widely available

'Pennine Silver': Fully double white. Sept.–Oct.
H:1m (3½ft) S:45cm (1½ft)    *Stks*: Widely available

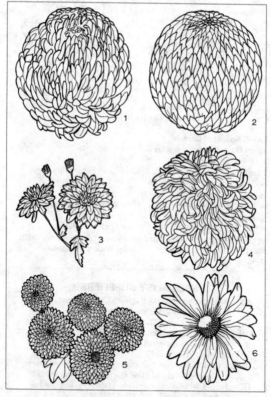

CHRYSANTHEMUM TYPES: *1. Intermediate; 2. Incurved; 3. Garden spray; 4. Reflexed; 5. Garden pompon; 6. Single*

*For key to stockists, see page 83*

**Garden Pompon Varieties** (*flowering August to October*)

'Cameo': Small globular white fls, opens yellow in centre.
H:60cm (2ft) S:45cm (1½ft)   Stks: Widely available

'Denise': Bright yellow semi-pompon on bushy plants.
H:40cm (16in) S:45cm (1½ft)   Stks: Widely available

'Fairie': A bright pink, one of the best pompons.
H:40cm (16in) S:45cm (1½ft)   Stks: Widely available

**Early-flowering Garden Varieties** (*flowering August and September*)

'Breitner': Pink. Also bronze, cream, gold, peach, yellow sports.
✗ H:1m (3½ft) S:45cm (1½ft)   Stks: Widely available

'Derek Bircumshaw': Immense, golden yellow, tightly incurved.
H:1m (3½ft) S:38cm (15in)   Stks: Widely available

'Evelyn Bush': Large incurved white. Sept. Stop mid–May.
① H:1.2m (4ft) S:45cm (1½ft)   Stks: Widely available

'Keystone': Royal purple, silver reverse. Incurved. Sept.
✗ ① H:1m (3½ft) S:38cm (15in)   Stks: Widely available

'Pinksmoor': Weather-resistant rose-pink fls, slightly reflexed.
✗ H:1.2m (4ft) S:45cm (1½ft)   Stks: Widely available

'Regalia': Vivid, rosy-purple reflexed fls. Weather resistant.
H:90cm (3ft) S:45cm (1½ft)   Stks: HW

'Tracy Waller': Large rich pink reflexed fls. Stop mid–May.
① H:1m (3½ft) S:45cm (1½ft)   Stks: Widely available

**Greenhouse Varieties** (*flowering October to December*)

'Balcombe Perfection': Bronze intermediate decorative. Dec.
H:1.2m (4ft) S:45cm (1½ft)   Stks: Widely available

'Daily Mirror': Incurving, plum-purple, silvery reverse. Nov.
H:1.5m (5ft) S:45cm (1½ft)   Stks: Widely available

'Fair Lady': Large clear pink with wide petals. Intermediate. Nov.
H:1.2m (4ft) S:45cm (1½ft)   Stks: HH

'Fred Shoesmith': Large creamy-white. Intermediate decorative.
H:1.2m (4ft) S:45cm (1½ft)   Stks: Widely available

'Golden Fred Shoesmith': Yellow form of above variety.
H:1.2m (4ft) S:45cm (1½ft)   Stks: Widely available

'Heather James': Bronze incurved decorative. Stop early June.
H:1m (3½ft) S:45cm (1½ft)   Stks: Widely available

'Mayford Perfection': Salmon overlaid apricot. Large incurved.
H:1.2m (4ft) S:45cm (1½ft)   Stks: Widely available

'Neil Zwager': Large buttercup yellow incurved fls. Oct.
H:1.2m (4ft) S:45cm (1½ft)   Stks: HW

'Rivalry': Deep golden yellow, large fls. Late Nov.
H:1.2m (4ft) S:45cm (1½ft)   Stks: HW

---

## SPECIALIST SUPPLIERS

**HH**   W. N. Hall & Sons Ltd., West Heddon Nurseries,
Heddon-on-the-Wall, Newcastle upon Tyne, NE15
0JS. Tel: Wylam 2245.

**HW**   Harold Walker, Oakfield Nurseries, Huntington,
Chester, CH3 6EA. Tel: Chester 20731.

**RY**   Riley's Chrysanthemums, Alfreton Nurseries,
Woolley Moor, Derby, DE5 6FF.

**WM**   H. Woolman (Dorridge) Ltd., Grange Road,
Dorridge, Solihull, B93 8QB. Tel: Knowle (05645)
6283.

# Geraniums

These attractive but tender plants are more correctly known as pelargoniums, as the word 'geranium' also applies to the hardy herbaceous plants of the genus *Geranium*.

### Types and uses

The best type for summer bedding are the zonals. Some of the $F_1$ hybrid seed-raised varieties are particularly useful, as they are compact and very floriferous. Raising them from seed also enables the number required for bedding to be obtained more cheaply than buying plants, and ensures disease-free plants.

For home and greenhouse decoration, the regals are best, with their larger, more showy flowers, softer leaves and bushier habit.

The miniatures are also suitable for growing on the window-sill, as well as in window-boxes and other containers outdoors.

Ivy-leaved geraniums are ever-popular for hanging baskets, where their trailing habit and long flowering period makes them particularly useful.

### When and what to buy

When buying these plants it is worth indicating to the nursery if you have the facility of a heated greenhouse, especially when buying them early in the year. Those for bedding cannot be planted out until the risk of frost has passed, and even then will need hardening off to acclimatize them to outdoor life.

If you are not able to sow the seed-raised types, local bedding plant retailers will have stocks from April onwards. Some national seed companies are also supplying seedlings.

### Overwintering the plants

Geraniums can be overwintered by taking cuttings in late summer and early autumn, growing them on in frost-proof greenhouse or home window-sill. Alternatively, cuttings can be taken from overwintered plants during March, but the subsequent plants tend to flower later. Cuttings 7.5cm (3in) long taken from the tips of the plants and inserted in a mixture of equal parts peat and sand will produce roots within a couple of weeks. If the growing tips are pinched out the plants will remain strong and bushy.

### If you want to know more . . .

Anyone keen on these plants should consider joining the British Pelargonium and Geranium Society. The Secretary is Mr. H. J. Wood, 129 Aylesford Avenue, Beckenham, Kent.

## Zonal Pelargoniums

'Flower of Spring': Lvs margined white. Contrasting red fls.
⌀ H:30cm (1ft) S:23cm (9in)    *Stks*: CG

'Irene': Semi-double rose red. Vigorous and free-flowering.
H:30cm (1ft) S:23cm (9in)    *Stks*: Widely available

'Mrs. Henry Cox': Single salmon fls. Gold/red variegated lvs.
⌀ H:30cm (1ft) S:23cm (9in)    *Stks*: Widely available

'Sincerity': Dark orange-red. Strong-growing, free-flowering.
H:30cm (1ft) S:23cm (9in)    *Stks*: TN

'Springtime': Salmon-pink. Double, weather-resistant large fls.
H:30cm (1ft) S:23cm (9in)    *Stks*: Widely available

### Miniature

'Red Black Vesuvius': Bright scarlet single fls, dark lvs.
⊖ H:23cm (9in) S:15cm (6in)    *Stks*: Widely available

### Ivy-leaved Pelargoniums

'Enchantress': Semi-double rose pink. Compact.
⊖ Trailing    *Stks*: TN

'Galilee': Bright rose-pink double fls. Free-flowering.
⊖ Trailing    *Stks*: Widely available

'La France': Semi-double lilac with maroon markings.
⊖ Trailing    *Stks*: Widely available

'Mexicanerin': Single white, edged and splashed crimson.
⊖ Trailing    *Stks*: Widely available

'Rouletta' see 'Mexicanerin'

'Ville de Paris': Profusion of single salmon-pink fls.
⊖ Trailing    *Stks*: Widely available

### Regal Pelargoniums

'Aztec': Pinkish-red blotches over white ground. Compact.
⊖ H:45cm (1½ft) S:30cm (1ft)    *Stks*: Widely available

'Grand Slam': Bright red, upper petals with brown marks.
⊖ H:45cm (1½ft) S:30cm (1ft)    *Stks*: Widely available

'Lavender Grand Slam': Bright lavender with purple marks.
⊖ H:45cm (1½ft) S:30cm (1ft)    *Stks*: Widely available

'Strawberry Sundae': Strawberry-red petals with white centre.
⊖ H:45cm (1½ft) S:30cm (1ft)    *Stks*: CG

### Seed-raised Zonal Pelargoniums

(can be bought as bedding plants – stockists are for seed)

'Cherie Improved': Salmon-pink. Compact and bushy.
▣ H:30cm (1ft) S:23cm (9in)    *Stks*: DB, SS, UW

'Mustang': Sizzling scarlet. Dark leaf zone. Outstanding.
⌀▣ H:30cm (1ft) S:23cm (9in)    *Stks*: SS, UW

'Ringo': Scarlet. Dark zone on lvs. Early and prolific.
⊖⌀▣ H:30cm (1ft) S:23cm (9in)    *Stks*: SS, UW

'Ringo Salmon': Pink. Dark zone on lvs. Excellent for bedding.
⌀▣ H:30cm (1ft) S:23cm (9in)    *Stks*: UW

---

### SPECIALIST SUPPLIERS

**AP**  Accelerated Propagation Ltd., Vines Cross,
Heathfield, Sussex. Tel: Horam Road 2033.

**CG**  The Clifton Geranium Nurseries, Cherry Orchard
Road, Whyke, Chichester, Sussex, PO19 2BX.
Tel: (0243) 782010.

**TN**  Thorp's Nurseries, 257 Finchampstead Road,
Wokingham, Berks. Tel: Wokingham (0734) 781181.

NOTE: The addresses for seed-raised zonal pelargonium
varieties will be found on page 19.

---

# Fuchsias

There are few plants so easy to grow, so free-flowering, and so resistant to pests and diseases when grown outside as fuchsias. None of the different kinds will stand the really severe frost of a very hard winter, but many will survive quite hard frosts if originally set several inches deep into the soil.

Hardier kinds are ideal in a small shrub border or among herbaceous plants, or even as hedges in maritime climates. Those with the largest and most attractively coloured flowers, however, tend to be best in pots.

Choose varieties with a trailing, pendulous habit for hanging baskets, the edges of window-boxes, tubs or similar containers. If you have the patience to train a young plant upright for a foot or two to produce a trunk, the trailing kinds also make good weeping standards. It will be necessary to keep these varieties firmly staked, as they take longer than vigorous kinds to form a stout trunk.

Upright-growing kinds are the easiest standards to grow, and also make the best window-sill pot plants.

Fuchsias perform best as young plants and after three or four years, as a general rule, they are best replaced by either rooting cuttings or buying in young plants.

When it is necessary to overwinter pot-grown plants a year or more old, reduce the watering in October. The compost should be virtually dry through the winter and the pots stored in a shed or garage. Remove the old leaves as they yellow. Given a mild winter, the plants will grow again in the spring after cutting back hard and watering.

Rooting new cuttings in August and overwintering them on a window-sill is the best method of keeping a stock.

## What to buy

Whitefly can be a serious pest on *indoor* pot-grown plants. Always avoid buying plants with any sign of this pest.

Plants should be growing vigorously, with lush green leaves. Thin, woody, leafless specimens will have had a severe check and take some time to recover. If pot plants drop their flowers within a few days of purchase this indicates a check, probably due to insufficient water. Water well and add liquid fertilizer, then they should soon form new flower buds.

## If you want to know more . . . .

If you fall victim to the charms of fuchsias, you might consider joining the British Fuchsia Society. The Secretary is Mr. R. Ewart, The Bungalow, Brookwood Military Cemetery, Brookwood, Surrey, GU24 0BL.

'Bon Accorde': Single. White tube and sepals, purple corolla.
🝕 Bedding. Upright growth.    Stks: Widely available

'Brutus': Single. Cerise tube and sepals. Corolla purple.
Greenhouse or outdoor standard (almost hardy)    Stks: CL

'Cascade': Single. White flushed carmine tube, carmine corolla.
🝕 Greenhouse. Trailing. Baskets.    Stks: Widely available

'Checkerboard': Single. Red tube, red/white sepals, red corolla.
① Greenhouse or bedding. Standard.    Stks: Widely available

'Citation': Single. Rose tube/sepals, white corolla veined pink.
① Greenhouse or bedding. Upright.    Stks: Widely available

'Display': Single. Pink tube and sepals, deeper pink corolla.
🝕 Greenhouse or bedding. Upright.    Stks: Widely available

'Dollar Princess': Double. Cerise tube/sepals, purple corolla.
🝕 Greenhouse. Upright    Stks: Widely available

'Fascination': Double. Pink tube/sepals, paler corolla.
🝕 ① Greenhouse or bedding.    Stks: Widely available

'Golden Marinka': Single. As 'Marinka', but lvs marked gold.
🝕 Greenhouse. Baskets.    Stks: Widely available

'Heidi Ann': Double. Red tube and sepals, corolla light mauve.
🝕 Greenhouse or bedding. Bushy.    Stks: Widely available

'Marinka': Single. Rich red tube/sepals, deeper corolla.
🝕 Greenhouse. Baskets.    Stks: Widely available

'Mieke Meursing': Single. Red tube/sepals, pink corolla.
① Greenhouse or bedding.    Stks: Widely available

'Ming': Single. Pink, paling at tips, and cerise.
🝕 Greenhouse. Upright. Standard.    Stks: CL

'Mrs Marshall': Single. White tube and sepals, clear red corolla.
Greenhouse or bedding (almost hardy).    Stks: Wdly avail.

'Pink Galore': Double. Pink tube/sepals, candy-pink corolla.
🝕 Greenhouse. Trailing. Baskets.    Stks: Widely available

'R.A.F.': Double. Red tube/sepals, white corolla flushed pink.
Greenhouse or bedding. Bushy. Standard.    Stks: CL

'Red Spider': Large single fls. Narrow red sepals, rose corolla.
Greenhouse. Trailing. Baskets.    Stks: Widely available

'Royal Velvet': Huge double. Crimson sepals, purple corolla.
🝕 Greenhouse. Standard.    Stks: Widely available

'Rufus The Red': Single. Turkey-red throughout.
Greenhouse or bedding. Standard.    Stks: Widely available

'Snowcap': Semi-double. Red tube and sepals, white corolla.
🝕 ① Greenhouse or bedding. Standard.    Stks: Wdly avail.

'Swingtime': Double. Rich red tube/sepals, white corolla.
🝕 Greenhouse. Semi-trailing. Baskets.    Stks: Widely available

'Texas Longhorn': Huge semi-double. Red sepals, white corolla.
Greenhouse. Standard.    Stks: Widely available

'Tom Thumb': Miniature. Red and pink fls.
🝕 Greenhouse or bedding (almost hardy).    Stks: Wdly avail.

---

### SPECIALIST SUPPLIERS

**CL**    C. S. Lockyer, 70 Henfield Road, Coalpit Heath, Bristol, BS17 2UZ. Tel: Winterbourne 772219.

**ON**    Oakleigh Nurseries, Petersfield Road, Monkwood, Alresford, Hants., SO24 0HB. Tel: Ropley 3344.

**VN**    V. T. Nuttall, Markham Grange Nursery, Long Lands Lane, Brodsworth, Doncaster. Tel: Doncaster 722390.

**WF**    Wills Fuchsias Ltd., Chapel Lane, West Wittering, Chichester, West Sussex.

# Delphiniums

It would hardly be summer in Britain without delphiniums. They have those lovely blue flowers which, with early June roses, epitomize cottage garden summers. You can also have a good show of flowers in the autumn by either cutting hard back immediately after flowering, adding fertilizer and watering well, or alternatively by sowing seeds in early spring.

These plants look best in mixed flower borders and, if you have no time to stake and tie, choose varieties 1m (3½ft) or less in height. Keen gardeners, including those growing for exhibition, are advised to purchase rooted cuttings of named varieties. The seed-raised strains are, however, more than adequate for garden decoration.

Named varieties have been selected by experienced enthusiasts from literally hundreds of thousands of seedlings. They have the edge on most home-raised seedlings, although you do always have the chance of raising an outstanding flower from seed.

## What to buy

Cuttings are taken from carefully selected plants in early spring. Shoots 10cm (4in) high are cut off with a small piece of root at the base. These will root easily in a jam-jar with 12mm (½in) sand and 2.5m (1in) of water in the base. Place the jar on a north facing window-sill until roots form and then pot up singly in potting compost.

Well-rooted cuttings, with thick stems, are the best buy. Plant these to build up a good root system the first summer, then good flowers will be produced the next year and for several successive summers. It is advisable to rejuvenate stocks by rooting new cuttings after three or four years.

Seed should always be *foil* packed when bought. Loose delphinium seed in paper packets loses viability quickly and should be sown immediately. If you need to store delphinium seeds place them, dry, in an airtight tin and keep in the fridge until ready to sow.

Special note should be made of the two seed-raised varieties 'Blue Fountains' (mixed colours) and 'Blue Heaven' (mid-blue with white eye). These recent introductions produce full-sized spikes on short stout stems and do not need staking. Where particularly good seedlings are produced, say from 'Blue Fountains', they can be increased and retained by taking cuttings as already described for named kinds.

## If you want to know more . . .

The Delphinium Society will provide information, help and encouragement. The Secretary is Mr. J. Seager, Birklands, Douglas Grove, Lower Bourne, Farnham, Surrey, GU10 3HP.

**Large-flowered** (*vegetatively propagated*)

'Blue Nile': Brilliant, pure mid-blue, white eye. Mid-season.
H:1.5m (5ft) S:45cm (1½ft)    *Stks*: BL, CE

'Cream Cracker': Creamy, yellow eye. Mid-season.
H:1.5m (5ft) S:45cm (1½ft)    *Stks*: CE

'Fanfare': Silvery light mauve. Early-flowering.
H:1.8m (6ft) S:60cm (2ft)    *Stks*: BL, CE

'Gordon Forsyth': Almost pure amethyst. Mid-season.
H:1.8m (6ft) S:60cm (2ft)    *Stks*: BL, CE

'Icecap': Pure white throughout. Mid-season.
H:2m (6½ft) S:60cm (2ft)    *Stks*: BL, CE

'Loch Leven': Pale mid-blue with white eye. Mid-season.
H:1.5m (5ft) S:45cm (1½ft)    *Stks*: BL, CE

'Loch Nevis': Pure pale blue with white eye. Early.
H:1.8m (6ft) S:60cm (2ft)    *Stks*: CE

'Mighty Atom': Huge florets, deep lavender-violet. Mid-season.
H:1.4m (4½ft) S:30cm (1ft)    *Stks*: BL, CE

'Molly Buchanan': Gentian-blue with a black eye. Mid-season.
H:1.5m (5ft) S:45cm (1½ft)    *Stks*: BL

'Nimrod': Rich royal purple with white eye. Late.
H:2m (6½ft) S:60cm (2ft)    *Stks*: BL, CE

'Olive Poppleton': Off-white with a gold eye. Mid-season.
H:1.5m (5ft) S:45cm (1½ft)    *Stks*: CE

'Purple Ruffles': Purple, almost fully double fls. Late.
H:1.8m (6ft) S:60cm (2ft)    *Stks*: CE

'Sabrina': Bright mid-blue with a white eye. Mid-season.
H:1.2m (4ft) S:30cm (1ft)    *Stks*: BL, CE

'Sentinel': Purple with a black eye. Early.
H:2m (6½ft) S:60cm (2ft)    *Stks*: BL, CE

'Shimmer': Bright mid-blue with a white eye. Late.
H:2m (6½ft) S:60cm (2ft)    *Stks*: BL, CE

'Silver Jubilee': Large white florets with dark eye. Mid-season.
H:1.5m (5ft) S:45cm (1½ft)    *Stks*: BL, CE

'Strawberry Fair': Rich mulberry-rose. Mid-season.
H:1.5m (5ft) S:45cm (1½ft)    *Stks*: BL, CE

'Tiddles': Almost double, slate-mauve florets. Late.
H:1.5m (5ft) S:45cm (1½ft)    *Stks*: BL, CE

'Tiny Tim': Deep blue with a hint of mauve. Mid-season.
H:1m (3½ft) S:30cm (1ft)    *Stks*: BL, CE

'Turkish Delight': Very pale pinkish-mauve. Mid-season.
H:1.5m (5ft) S:45cm (1½ft)    *Stks*: BL, CE

'Vespers': Blue and mauve with a white eye. Mid-season.
H:1.5m (5ft) S:45cm (1½ft)    *Stks*: BL

**Seed-raised strains and varieties**

'Pacific Giants Mixed': Double fls up to 7.5cm (3in) across.
H:1.5m (5ft) S:45cm (1½ft)    *Stks*: Available from seedsmen.

'Blue Fountains': Dwarf, sturdy stems, and good colour mixture.
H:75cm (2½ft) S:30cm (1ft)    *Stks*: Available from seedsmen.

'Blue Heaven': Double, mid-blue with contrasting white eye.
H:75cm (2½ft) S:30cm (1ft)    *Stks*: Available from seedsmen.

---

## SPECIALIST SUPPLIERS

**BL**   Blackmore & Langdon Ltd., Pensford, Nr. Bristol.
Tel: (0275) 892300.

**CE**   Colin Edwards, 11 Long Grove, Seer Green,
Beaconsfield, Bucks, HP9 2YN.
Tel: Beaconsfield 6315.

# Sweet Peas

A few years ago sweet peas were very much just a flower to cut from tall hedges of plants supported on bushy sticks. Now we have every height from the true dwarfs, a mound of low flower in a wide range of colours, and the intermediate, so called 'Knee High' types, as well as the traditional tall kinds.

If you plant the three kinds with the tallest at the back of the bed or border, and the shortest at the front, it will produce a sheet of flower from the ground upwards for the summer months.

The recent introduction of 'Snoopea', a type in full colour range with small leaves replacing tendrils, makes bedding out for summer display possible, as there is no need for support.

All are hardy and the best results will be achieved by sowing in late September or early October. They can be sown in pots and overwintered in cold frames and cold greenhouses to plant in spring.

Even better results are achieved where seed is sown in the flowering position in the autumn and protected overwinter under cloches.

Seeds can be sown in a temperature of 15–20°C (60–70°F) in early spring and then grown on under cold glass. Sowing under *cold* glass (and even in poorly heated greenhouses) in early spring is likely to give poor germination. Finally seed can be sown where required to flower in spring, but these sowings will flower later and the plants will need watering well if late spring and early summer weather is dry.

All but the low type seedlings are best with the growing tip pinched out after two pairs of leaves have formed. The side-shoots will grow stronger than the main central tip.

## What to buy

Sweet peas are self pollinating and all seed is acceptable. Do not reject the small wrinkled seed in mixtures, those are likely to be the blue and lavender shades. Home-saved seeds will produce plants identical to the parent.

## Cordon sweet peas

One stem per plant, tied at every other leaf to a cane and all side-shoots and tendrils pinched out, produces 'cordon' training and long-stemmed, large flowers for cutting and exhibition.

## If you want to know more . . .

Sweet pea enthusiasts should consider joining the National Sweet Pea Society. The Secretary is Mr. L. Williams, Acacia Cottage, Down Ampney, Nr. Cirencester, Glos., GL7 5QW.

### Spencer Type

'Beaujolais': Four to six maroon fls per stem.
⌇✕ H:2.4m (8ft) S:30cm (1ft)   *Stks*: Widely available

'Carlotta': Bright carmine. Very strong grower.
⌇✕ H:2.4m (8ft) S:30cm (1ft)   *Stks*: Widely available

'Cream Beauty': Four or five very frilly fls per stem.
✕ H:2.4m (8ft) S:30cm (1ft)   *Stks*: LE, SS

'Gipsy Queen': Rich crimson. Very large, well-placed fls.
⌇①✕ H:2.4m (8ft) S:30cm (1ft)   *Stks*: Widely available

'Herald': Deep rose-pink, suffused orange. Strong-grower.
①✕ H:2.4m (8ft) S:30cm (1ft)   *Stks*: DB, RB

'Honeymoon': Pale blue fls of exhibition standard.
①✕ H:2.4m (8ft) S:30cm (1ft)   *Stks*: LE

'Leamington': Frilled rosy-lavender fls on long, stiff stems.
⌇①✕ H:2.4m (8ft) S:30cm (1ft)   *Stks*: Widely available

'Noel Sutton': Rich deep blue fls on long, strong stems.
⌇①✕ H:2.4m (8ft) S:30cm (1ft)   *Stks*: Widely available

'Rosy Frills': White ground with deep pink picotee edge.
⌇✕ H:2.4m (8ft) S:30cm (1ft)   *Stks*: Widely available

'Southbourne': Almond-blossom pink, white base.
⌇✕ H:2.4m (8ft) S:30cm (1ft)   *Stks*: Widely available

'White Leamington': Bold, frilly white fls on long stems.
✕ H:2.4m (8ft) S:30cm (1ft)   *Stks*: Widely available

'Winston Churchill': Bright crimson, frilled and fluted fls.
✕ H:2.4m (8ft) S:30cm (1ft)   *Stks*: Widely available

### Hedge Type

'Jet Set Mixed': Large fls in many shades, usually frilled.
⌇✕ H:90cm (3ft) S:30cm (1ft)   *Stks*: Widely available

'Knee High': Five or six fls on strong stems. Mixed colours.
✕ H:75cm (2½ft) S:30cm (1ft)   *Stks*: Widely available

### Low-growing Type

'Burpee's Patio': Up to four large, waved fls per stem.
⌇⊝ H:30cm (1ft) S:45cm (1½ft)   *Stks*: DB

'Early Dwarf Bijou': Large, frilled fls. Good edging plant.
⊝ H:30cm (1ft) S:45cm (1½ft)   *Stks*: TM, WU

'Snoopea': Masses of fls in mixed colours. Ideal for bedding.
⌇✕⊝ H:30–45cm (1–1½ft) S:45cm (1½ft)   *Stks*: TM

### Outdoor Cutting Type (not for cordon growing)

'Multiflora Galaxy Mixed': Five to seven fls on long stems.
⌇✕ H:1.8m (6ft) S:45cm (1½ft)   *Stks*: Widely available

### Greenhouse Type

'Early Multiflora Gigantea Mixed': Up to ten large fls, long stems.
✕ H:1.8m (6ft) S:30cm (1ft)   *Stks*: RB, SS

---

## SPECIALIST SUPPLIERS

**DB**   Samual Dobie & Son Ltd., Upper Dee Mills,
Llangollen, Clwyd, LL20 8SD. Tel: (0978) 860119.

**LE**   L. Everitt, Meadow Cottage Nursery, Little Clacton,
Essex. Tel: Clacton-on-Sea 24310.

**RB**   Robert Bolton & Son, Birdbrook, Nr Halstead,
Essex, CO9 4BQ. Tel: Ridgewell 246.

**SS**   Suttons Seeds, Hele Road, Torquay, Devon, TQ2
7QJ. Tel: Torquay (0803) 62011.

**TM**   Thompson & Morgan Ltd., London Road, Ipswich,
Suffolk, IP2 0BA.

**WU**   W. J. Unwin Ltd., Histon, Cambridge.
Tel: Histon 2270.

---

# Houseplants

Plants grown in pots in the home are quite rightly universally popular, but they should be enjoyed as they are, and not expected to live for ever (even though many will thrive in the house for years, often increasing in size and value as they grow).

Try to use plants as part of the house decor, rather than solitary specimens sitting like china ornaments on ledges. Grouped together they will benefit from the extra humidity and rearrangement will show each plant off to its best effect. Where a few lower leaves age and yellow or fall from taller, older plants, you can arrange them at the back of a group to mask the loss.

Bathrooms and kitchens have a more humid atmosphere and this benefits many plants. Avoid soft felty leaved plants in bathrooms because they attract dust and powder and prove difficult to clean.

Hangers, including attractive macrame kinds, fixed to pelmets and curtain rails look attractive and hang the plant in a nice light position. Very few plants suffer from too much light, except on the occasional scorching hot day in mid-summer on a window-sill facing due south.

Virtually all growing plants will benefit from moving into lighter positions in winter when the days are short and the sunshine weak.

Cooler rooms, bedrooms, spare rooms and occasionally used rooms are best reserved for plants preferring colder temperatures.

If you want plants in very dark corners, have three specimens of a kind able to withstand shade, and rotate them every three to seven days, giving them two-thirds of their life in a lighter position.

## How to grow

Each plant has a potting compost recommendation in the list. Where both John Innes potting compost and peat-based potting compost are listed good results will be obtained by mixing half of each kind.

All-peat composts get very light as they dry and large plants in these composts are likely to topple over unless put in a wide-based pot. Plants in John Innes compost are more able to survive neglect, but the surface of the compost can become hard. Mixing the two kinds gives the best of both worlds for many houseplants.

Correct watering comes with practice; it is better to let the compost dry out somewhat and then water well – avoid having plants standing constantly wet (this is especially important in winter). Wet compost is very heavy and checking the weight of pot plants is one way of assessing their need for water.

If you tend to forget to water plants, then the automatic watering systems and wicks are made for you.

**1.** *Water well, leave to absorb, then remove from the pot. If necessary, tap the rim of the pot against a table to loosen.*

**2.** *Place the old pot in one a size or two larger. Pack compost between the two pots.*

**3.** *Remove the small pot, drop the root-ball into the hole, firm, then water thoroughly.*

When plants are growing they will need feeding. New compost will have several weeks' supply of plant food, and then fortnightly or weekly feeding will be necessary. The smaller the pot and the faster the growth, the more regular feeding ought to be.

Very dark green, even unusually wrinkled leaves, indicate excessive feeding. When this happens just stop for a while, then once leaf colour pales feeding can be re-started.

### What to buy

Look for strong-growing, fresh-leaved plants. The sooner the plants are transported from nursery to the position in your home, the better. For this reason the best buys are often found in the *glasshouses* of garden centres and retail nurseries.

Select plants of a size in balance with the pot; large plants in small pots are difficult to water adequately.

Avoid plants with any sign of insect pests.

When buying year-round pot chrysanthemums from November to March make sure the flowers are at least half open. Tight buds do not open very well in the light of ordinary homes at this time. See that tiny poinsettia flowers in the centre of the coloured bracts are still in place. If these have dropped it is a sure sign of a recent check to growth.

### If you want to know more . . .

A useful and readable book is *Woman's Own Book of Houseplants*, by William Davidson (Hamlyn).

**Acalypha** (15°C/59°F) Intermediate    J.I./P.B.    ○
*hispida* (red-hot cat's tail): Long, tassel-shaped crimson fls.
❀ H:1.2m (4ft) S:45cm (1½ft)    *Stks*: Widely available

**Achimenes** (15°C/59°F) Intermediate    P.B.    ◐
Hybrids: Colours of fls include red, pink, white, mauve.
❀ H:25cm (10in) S:20cm (8in)    *Stks*: Widely available

**Adiantum** (10°C/50°F) Intermediate    P.B.(M)    ◐
*raddianum* (maidenhair): Green fronds on black, wiry stems.
⌀ H:30cm (1ft) S:45cm (1½ft)    *Stks*: Widely available

**Aechmea** (urn plant) (16°C/61°F) Intermediate    P.B.    ○–◐
*fasciata*: Pink, long-lasting bracts, and 'vase' of silver lvs.
⌀ ❀ H:60cm (2ft) S:45cm (1½ft)    *Stks*: Widely available

**Aglaonema** (10°C/50°F) Intermediate    J.I./P.B.    ◐
'Silver Queen': Beautiful lvs with silvery markings.
⌀ H:23cm (9in) S:30cm (1ft)    *Stks*: Widely available
*treubii*: Dark green lance-shaped lvs, marked silver-grey.
⌀ H:23cm (9in) S:30cm (1ft)    *Stks*: KN

**Ananas** (pineapple) (18°C/65°F) Easy    P.B.(D)    ○
*sativus*: Pointed, strap-shaped, arching grey-green lvs.
⌀ H:1m (3½ft) S:60cm (2ft)    *Stks*: Widely available

**Anthurium** (15°C/59°F) Difficult    P.B.(M)    ◐
*scherzerianum*: Unusual scarlet spathe around yellow fl spike.
❀ H:60cm (2ft) S:30cm (1ft)    *Stks*: Widely available

**Aphelandra** (15°C/59°F) Intermediate    J.I./P.B.(M)    ○–◐
*squarrosa* 'Dania': Ivory markings along side veins/mid-rib.
⌀ ❀ H:30cm (1ft) S:30cm (1ft)    *Stks*: Widely available

**Araucaria** (Norfolk Island pine) (5°C/41°F) Easy    J.I.    ◐
*excelsa*: Like a miniature pine tree with 'needle' lvs.
⌀ H:1–2.1m (3½–7ft) S:90cm (3ft)    *Stks*: Widely available

**Aspidistra** (cast iron plant) (10°C/50°F) Easy    J.I.(D)    ○–◐
*elatior*: Bright green lvs. Some varieties are variegated.
⌀ H:45cm (1½ft) S:30cm (1ft)    *Stks*: Widely available

**Asparagus** (10°C/50°F) Easy    J.I./P.B.    ○–◐
*densiflorus*: Attractive, trailing stems. Needle-like lvs.
⌀ H:90cm (3ft) S:60cm (2ft)    *Stks*: Widely available
*plumosus* see *A. setaceus*
*setaceus*: Sprays of feathery fern-like growth.
⌀ H:45–90cm (1½–3ft) S:30cm (1ft)    *Stks*: Widely available
*sprengeri* see *A. densiflorus*

**Asplenium** (12°C/54°F) Easy/Intermediate    P.B.    ○–◐
*bulbiferum* (Easy): Fern-like lvs, with bulbils at their ends.
⌀ H:45cm (1½ft) S:30cm (1ft)    *Stks*: KN, TB
*nidus* (Intermediate): Strap-like glossy lvs, forming a 'vase'.
⌀ H:45cm (1½ft) S:30cm (1ft)    *Stks*: Widely available

**Azalea** (13°C/55°F) Intermediate    P.B.(M)    ○–◐
*indica*: Masses of double pink, white or red fls.
❀ H:30cm (1ft) S:30cm (1ft)    *Stks*: Widely available

**Begonia** (temp: see text) Easy/Intermediate    P.B.    ○–◐
*elatior* (15°C/59°F); Intermediate: red, pink, yellow fls.
❀ H:30cm (1ft) S:30cm (1ft)    *Stks*: Widely available
*rex* (13°C/55°F); Intermediate: Very colourful lvs.
⌀ H:30cm (1ft) S:38cm (15in)    *Stks*: Widely available
*semperflorens* (15°C/59°F); Easy: Small but plentiful fls.
❀ H:20cm (8in) S:20cm (8in)    *Stks*: Widely available

× *tuberhybrida* (21°C/70°F); Easy: Beautiful, large double fls.
❀ H:38cm (15in) S:30cm (1ft)     *Stks*: Widely available

**Belloperone** (10°C/50°F) Easy     J.I./P.B.     ○–◑
*guttata*: Long-lasting pinkish bracts, fls resembling shrimps.
❀ H:60cm (2ft) S:45cm (1½ft)     *Stks*: Widely available

**Bougainvillea** (7°C/45°F) Intermediate     J.I.
*glabra*: Red and purple bracts in late summer, early autumn.
❀ H:1.8m (6ft) S:75cm (2½ft)     *Stks*: Widely available

**Bouvardia** (13°C/55°F) Intermediate     J.I./P.B.     ○
× *domestica*: Clusters of tubular fls, June–Nov.
❀ H:60cm (2ft) S:45cm (1½ft)     *Stks*: KN, TB

**Brunfelsia** (13°C/55°F) Intermediate     J.I./P.B.     ◑
*calycina*: Fragrant, large, mauve fls, borne April-Aug.
�™❀ H:60cm (2ft) S:30cm (1ft)     *Stks*: Widely available

**Caladium** (21°C/70°F) Intermediate     P.B.(M)     ◑
× *bicolor* 'Candicum': Beautiful white lvs with green veins.
∅ H:30cm (1ft) S:23cm (9in)     *Stks*: Widely available

**Calathea** (18°C/65°F) Difficult     P.B.     ◑
*makoyana*: Variegated lvs, silvery green above, purple below.
∅ H:45cm (1½ft) S:30cm (1ft)     *Stks*: Widely available

**Calceolaria** (slipper flower) (7°C/45°F) Easy     J.I./P.B.     ◑
× *herbeohybrida*: An annual with beautiful pouched fls.
❀ H:30cm (1ft) S:25cm (10in)     *Stks*: Widely available

**Campanula** (10°C/50°F) Easy     J.I./P.B.     ○–◑
*isophylla* (star of Bethlehem): Masses of sky-blue fls.
❀ Trailing     *Stks*: Widely available
*isophylla* 'Alba': Delightful white flowers, slightly larger.
❀ Trailing     *Stks*: Widely available

**Capsicum** (pepper) (10°C/50°F) Easy     J.I./P.B.     ○–◑
*annuum*: Annual with attractive orange or yellow fruits.
⚹ H:30cm (1ft) S:23cm (9in)     *Stks*: Widely available

**Ceropegia** (hearts entangled) (7°C/45°F) Easy     J.I.     ◑
*woodii*: Trailing, greyish, mottled succulent lvs.
∅ Trailing     *Stks*: Widely available

**Chamaedorea** (13°C/55°F) Intermediate     P.B.     ◑–●
*elegans*: An attractive palm, especially for small homes.
∅ H:1m (3½ft) S:45cm (1½ft)     *Stks*: Widely available

**Chlorophytum** (7°C/45°F) Easy     J.I./P.B.(M)     ○–◑
*comosum variegatum*: Narrow, green and cream lvs.
∅ H:30cm (1ft) S:30cm (1ft)     *Stks*: Widely available

**Chrysanthemum** (10°C/50°F) Easy     J.I./P.B.     ○–◑
Year-round flowering type: Single or double. Many colours.
❀ H:30cm (1ft) S:25cm (10in)     *Stks*: Widely available

**Cineraria** see *Senecio*

**Cissus** (kangaroo vine) (10°C/50°F) Easy     J.I./P.B.     ◑–●
*antarctica*: Attractive, light green lvs, climbing stems.
∅ H:1.5m (5ft) S:45cm (1½ft)     *Stks*: Widely available

**Citrus** (13°C/55°F) Intermediate     J.I./P.B.     ○–◑
*mitis*: Fragrant white fls, and small orange fruits.
�™⚹ H:45cm (1½ft) S:30cm (1ft)     *Stks*: Widely available

**Clivia** (Kaffir lily) (16°C/61°F) Intermediate     J.I.     ○–◑
*miniata*: Evergreen strap-like lvs. Orange heads of fls.
❀ H:45cm (1½ft) S:30cm (1ft)     *Stks*: Widely available

*For key to symbols, see page 7*

**Cocos** (16°C/61°F) Intermediate    P.B.    ◐
*weddeliana*: Beautiful small palm with mid-green lvs.
⌀ H:1.5m (5ft) S:1m (3½ft)    Stks: Widely available

**Codiaeum** (croton) (15°C/59°F) Intermediate    J.I./P.B.    ◐
*variegatum* (Joseph's coat): Attractively coloured glossy lvs.
⌀ H:75cm (2½ft) S:45cm (1½ft)    Stks: Widely available

**Coffea** (18°C/65°F) Intermediate    P.B.    ○–◐
*arabica* (coffee plant): Attractive, shiny lvs. Red coffee beans.
⌀ H:1.2–3m (4–9ft) S:0.6–1.2m (2–4ft)    Stks: HE, KN

**Coleus** (flame nettle) (15°C/59°F) Easy    J.I./P.B.    ○–◐
*blumei*: Vividly coloured lvs. Easily raised from seed.
⌀ H:30cm (1ft) S:23cm (9in)    Stks: Widely available

**Columnea** (13°C/55°F) Intermediate    P.B.    ○–◐
*microphylla*: Small lvs, trailing stems. Orange-scarlet fls.
⌀ ❁ Trailing    Stks: KN, TB

**Cordyline** see *Dracaena terminalis*

**Crassula** (7°C/45°F) Easy    J.I.    ○–◐
*argentea*: Succulent plant with fleshy lvs and pink fls.
⌀ H:60cm (2ft) S:45cm (1½ft)    Stks: Widely available
*coccinea* see *Rochea coccinea*

**Crypthanthus** (earth star) (13°C/55°F) Easy    P.B.    ◐
*bivittatus*: Rosettes of attractively striped lvs.
⌀ H:7.5cm (3in) S:10cm (4in)    Stks: Widely available

**Cuphea** (cigar flower) (7°C/45°F) Easy    J.I./P.B.    ◐
*ignea*: Bright scarlet tubular fls, with black 'ash' on tips.
❁ H:45cm (1½ft) S:30cm (1ft)    Stks: Widely available

**Cyclamen** (10°C/50°F) Intermediate    J.I./P.B.    ○–◐
*persicum*: Range of cultivars, many colours. Oct.–April.
❁ H:25cm (10in) S:20cm (8in)    Stks: Widely available

**Cyperus** (13°C/55°F) Intermediate    P.B.(M)    ○–◐
*alternifolius*: Long shoots with 'umbrella' of grass-like lvs.
⌀ H:75cm (2½ft) S:45cm (1½ft)    Stks: Widely available

**Cyrtomium** (7°C/45°F) Easy    P.B.    ◐–●
*falcatum* (holly fern): Holly-like, rich, dark and shiny lvs.
⌀ H:45cm (1½ft) S:45cm (1½ft)    Stks: Widely available

**Dieffenbachia** (13°C/55°F) Intermediate    J.I./P.B.    ◐
*picta* (dumb cane): Large green lvs, marbled creamy-white.
⌀ H:60cm (2ft) S:30cm (1ft)    Stks: Widely available

**Dipladenia** (13°C/55°F) Intermediate    J.I./P.B.    ◐
*splendens*: Rose-pink trumpet-shaped fls, June–Sept.
❁ H:2.1m (7ft) Climber    Stks: Widely available

**Dizygotheca** (13°C/55°F) Intermediate    J.I./P.B.    ◐
*elegantissima*: Coppery-red to green thin wavy-edged lvs.
⌀ H:1.2m (4ft) S:45cm (1½ft)    Stks: Widely available

**Dracaena** (13°C/55°F) Intermediate    J.I./P.B.    ○–◐
*fragrans* 'Massangeana': Green margins to lvs, gold centre.
⌀ H:90cm (3ft) S:45cm (1½ft)    Stks: Widely available
*marginata*: Narrow, grass-like lvs, striped green, cream, pink.
⌀ H:90cm (3ft) S:45cm (1½ft)    Stks: Widely available
*marginata* 'Tricolor': Beautiful, grass-like tricoloured lvs.
⌀ H:90cm (3ft) S:45cm (1½ft)    Stks: Widely available
*terminalis*: Lvs flushed cream, red or purple.
⌀ H:75cm (2½ft) S:30cm (1ft)    Stks: Widely available

**sanderiana**: Grey-green lvs with silver or ivory edges.
⌀ H:45cm (1½ft) S:38cm (15in)   *Stks*: Widely available

**Epiphyllum** (5°C/41°F) Easy   J.I./P.B.   O – ❶
Hybrids: Flat, succulent stems. Massive fls in many colours.
❀ H:90cm (3ft) S:60cm (2ft)   *Stks*: Widely available

**Euonymus** (2°C/35°F) Easy   J.I./P.B.   O – ❶
**japonicus** 'Aureo-picta': Dark green lvs. with gold centre.
⌀ H:38cm (15in) S:38cm (15in)   *Stks*: Widely available

**Euphorbia** (15°C/59°F) Intermediate   J.I./P.B.   O – ❶
**pulcherrima** (poinsettia): Red, white or pink. Nov. – May.
❀ H:90cm (3ft) S:30cm (1ft)   *Stks*: Widely available

**Exacum** (Persian violet) (13°C/55°F) Easy   J.I./P.B.   ❶
**affine**: Annual with small purple-blue fls; yellow 'eye'.
⚘❀ H:25cm (10in) S:20cm (8in)   *Stks*: Widely available

**Fatsia** (false castor oil plant) (6°C/43°F) Easy   J.I.   ❶ – ●
**japonica**: Large, attractive, hand-shaped glossy lvs.
⌀ H:1.5m (5ft) S:1.2m (4ft)   *Stks*: Widely available

× **Fatshedera** (4°C/40°F) Easy   J.I./P.B.   ❶ – ●
**lizei**: Shiny, deep-green, hand-shaped lvs.
⌀ H:1.8m (6ft) S:45cm (1½ft)   *Stks*: Widely available

**Ficus** (temp: see text)   J.I./P.B.   O – ❶
**elastica** 'Robusta' (16°C/61°F); Easy: Improved rubber plant.
⌀ H:1m+ (3½ft+) S:45cm+ (1½ft+)   *Stks*: Widely available
**elastica** 'Tricolor' (16°C/61°F); Intermediate: Flushed pink.
⌀ H:1.2m+ (4ft+) S:45cm+ (1½ft+)   *Stks*: Widely available
**benjamina** (weeping fig) (15°C/59°F); Easy: Hanging, narrow lvs.
⌀ H:1.2m+ (4ft+) S:45cm (1½ft)   *Stks*: Widely available
**lyrata** (13°C/55°F); Intermediate: Large, fiddle-shaped lvs.
⌀ H:1.2m+ (4ft+) S:1m (3½ft)   *Stks*: Widely available
**pumila** (7°C/45°F); Intermediate: Small dark green lvs.
⌀ Trailing   *Stks*: Widely available
**radicans** 'Variegata' (15°C/59°F); Intermediate: Variegated lvs.
⌀ Trailing   *Stks*: HE, KN

**Fittonia** (16°C/61°F) Intermediate   P.B.   ❶ – ●
**verschaffeltii**: Attractive lvs with carmine-red veins.
⌀ H:15cm (6in) S:25cm (10in)   *Stks*: HE, KN

**Fuchsia** see page 86

**Gardenia** (16°C/61°F) Intermediate   J.I./P.B.   O – ❶
**jasminoides**: Scented, white, rose-like fls.
⚘❀ H:1m (3½ft) S:45cm (1½ft)   *Stks*: Widely available

**Gesneria** (12°C/54°F) Intermediate   P.B.   ❶
**macrantha**: Scarlet fls, early summer to mid-autumn.
❀ H:25cm (10in) S:20cm (8in)   *Stks*: Widely available

**Gloxinia** see *Sinningia speciosa*

**Grevillea** (7°C/45°F) Easy   J.I.   O
**robusta** (silk oak): Feathery, light green lvs. Raised from seeds.
⌀ H:1.5m+ (5ft+) S:45cm (1½ft)   *Stks*: Widely available

**Guzmania** (16°C/61°F) Intermediate   P.B.   ❶ – ●
**lingulata**: Scarlet fls (bracts) remaining for many weeks.
⌀❀ H:30cm (1ft) S:23cm (9in)   *Stks*: Widely available

**Gynura** (13°C/55°F) Intermediate   J.I.   O
**aurantiaca**: Stems and lvs covered in violet-purple hairs.
⌀ H:45cm (1½ft) S:45cm (1½ft)   *Stks*: Widely available

**Hedera** (ivy) (7°C/45°F) Easy    J.I./P.B.    ◑–●
  *canariensis* 'Gloire de Marengo': Large lvs, variegated.
  ⌀ H:1.2m+ (4ft+) S:30cm (1ft)    *Stks*: Widely available
  *canariensis* 'Variegata' see *Hedera C*. 'Gloire de Marengo'
  *helix* 'Chicago': Attractive, with small plain green lvs.
  ⌀ H:45cm+ (1½ft+) S:23cm (9in)    *Stks*: Widely available
  *helix* 'Glacier': Small lvs, frosted white and silver.
  ⌀ H:30cm+ (1ft+) S:20cm (8in)    *Stks*: Widely available
  *helix* 'Gold Heart': Neat growth. Yellow centres to small lvs.
  ⌀ H:30cm+ (1ft+) S:20cm (8in)    *Stks*: Widely available
  *helix* 'Green Ripple': Shiny dark green lvs, lighter veins.
  ⌀ H:45cm+ (1½ft+) S:23cm (9in)    *Stks*: Widely available
  *helix* 'Sagittaefolia: Attractive, arrow-shaped green lvs.
  ⌀ H:45cm+ (1½ft+) S:23cm (9in)    *Stks*: Widely available

**Hibiscus** (16°C/61°F) Easy    J.I./P.B.    ○–◑
  *rosa-sinensis*: Trumpet-shaped, single or double fls.
  ✿ H:1.5m (5ft) S:30cm (1ft)    *Stks*: Widely available

**Howeia** (10°C/50°F) Intermediate    J.I./P.B.    ◑–●
  *forsteriana*: Large, attractive palm, with pendulous leaflets.
  ⌀ H:2.4m (8ft) S:1.5m (5ft)    *Stks*: Widely available

**Hoya** (16°C/61°F) Intermediate-Difficult    J.I./P.B.    ◑
  *bella*: Clusters of star-shaped, fragrant, waxy white fls.
  ꒰✿ H:45cm (1½ft) S:30cm (1ft)    *Stks*: Widely available
  *carnosa*: Fragrant, star-shaped, white to flesh-pink fls.
  ꒰✿ H:45cm (1½ft) S:30cm (1ft)    *Stks*: Widely available

**Hippeastrum** (amaryllis) (13°C/55°F) Easy    J.I.
  Hybrids: Huge, trumpet-shaped fls on stout stems.
  ✿ H:45cm (1½ft) S:30cm (1ft)    *Stks*: Widely available

**Hydrangea** (13°C/55°F) Easy    J.I.    ○–◑
  *macrophylla* (mop-head type): Pink to blue fls, April–June.
  ✿ H:45cm (1½ft) S:30cm (1ft)    *Stks*: Widely available

**Hypocyrta** (10°C/50°F) Easy    P.B.
  *glabra* (clog plant): Thick, glossy, dark green lvs, orange fls.
  ⌀✿ H:25cm (10in) S:25cm (10in)    *Stks*: HE, KN

**Hypoestes** (polka dot plant) (10°C/50°F) Easy    J.I./P.B.    ○
  *sanguinolenta*: Lvs spotted pink. Can be raised from seed.
  ⌀ H:30cm (1ft) S:23cm (9in)    *Stks*: Widely available

**Impatiens** (13°C/55°F) Easy    J.I./P.B.    ○–◑
  Hybrids: Floriferous. Fls in various colours, over months.
  ✿ H:60cm (2ft) S:30cm (1ft)    *Stks*: Widely available

**Jasminum** (5°C/41°F) Intermediate    J.I./P.B.    ◑
  *polyanthum*: White fls, Nov.–April, pink in bud.
  ꒰✿ H:1.8m (6ft) S:45cm (1½ft)    *Stks*: Widely available

**Kalanchoe** (5°C/41°F) Easy    J.I.    ○
  *blossfeldiana*: Scarlet fls borne in dense clusters.
  ✿ H:23cm (9in) S:20cm (8in)    *Stks*: Widely available

**Kentia** see *Howeia*

**Maranta** (prayer plant) (10°C/50°F) Intermediate    P.B.    ◑
  *leuconeura* 'Erythroneura': Lvs have dark crimson veins.
  ⌀ H:18cm (7in) S:25cm (10in)    *Stks*: KN, TB
  *leuconeura* 'Kerchoveana': Dark blotches between lf veins
  ⌀ H:18cm (7in) S:25cm (10in)    *Stks*: Widely available

**Mimosa** (18°C/65°F) Easy    J.I./P.B.    ◑
  *pudica*: Feathery lvs fold up when touched. Seed-raised.
  ⌀ H:30cm (1ft) S:25cm (10in)    *Stks*: Widely available

**Monstera** (10°C/50°F) Easy    J.I./P.B.    ❶–❷
  *deliciosa* (Swiss cheese plant): Shiny, green lvs, deeply cut.
  ∅ H:1.8m+ (6ft+) S:1m (3½ft)    *Stks*: Widely available

**Neoregelia** (13°C/55°F) Intermediate    P.B.    ❶
  *carolinae* 'Tricolor': Rosette of red-cream-green lvs.
  ∅ ✿ H:30cm (1ft) S:25cm (10in)    *Stks*: Widely available
  *spectabilis*: Leathery lvs, dark green with white bands.
  ∅ ✿ H:30cm (1ft) S:25cm (10in)    *Stks*: KN

**Nephrolepis** (10°C/50°F) Intermediate    P.B.(M)    ❶–❷
  *exaltata* 'Bostoniensis' (Boston fern): Fringed fronds.
  ∅ H:45cm (1½ft) S:30cm (1ft)    *Stks*: Widely available
  *exaltata* 'Teddy Junior': Fronds form a compact plant.
  ∅ H:30cm (1ft) S:30cm (1ft)    *Stks*: Widely available

**Neanthe bella** see *Chamaedorea elegans*

**Nertera** (bead plant) (5°C/41°F) Easy    J.I./P.B.    ○
  *granadensis*: Compact plant, covered with orange berries.
  ✾ H:13cm (5in) S:15cm (6in)    *Stks*: HE, KN

**Pachystachys** (10°C/50°F) Intermediate    J.I./P.B.    ❶
  *lutea*: Succession of golden-yellow bracts in summer.
  ✿ H:30cm (1ft) S:25cm (10in)    *Stks*: Widely available

**Pandanus** (screw pine) (13°C/55°F) Intermediate    J.I.    ❶
  *veitchii*: Attractively striped, cream-variegated lvs.
  ∅ H:60cm (2ft) S:30cm (1ft)    *Stks*: Widely available

**Pelargonium** see page 84

**Pellaea** (7°C/45°F) Easy    P.B.    ❶
  *rotundifolia*: Fern with small, rounded segments to fronds.
  ∅ H:20cm (8in) S:20cm (8in)    *Stks*: Widely available

**Peperomia** (13°C/55°F) Easy    J.I./P.B.    ❶
  *caperata*: White spikes of fls. Wrinkled, dark green lvs.
  ∅ H:18cm (7in) S:15cm (6in)    *Stks*: Widely available
  *hederifolia*: Quilted surface to olive-green lvs, darker veins.
  ∅ H:15cm (6in) S:15cm (6in)    *Stks*: Widely available
  *magnoliifolia*: Ovate, glossy green lvs.
  ∅ H:20cm (8in) S:23cm (9in)    *Stks*: Widely available
  *scandens*: Climbing and trailing. Heart-shaped creamy lvs.
  ∅ H:75cm (2½ft) S:25cm (10in)    *Stks*: Widely available

**Philodendron** (16°C/61°F) Easy    J.I./P.B.    ●
  *bipinnatifidum*: Deep green lvs, lobed and deeply incised.
  ∅ H:1.2m+ (4ft+) S:90cm (3ft)    *Stks*: Widely available
  *erubescens* 'Burgundy': Distinctive, coppery-red young lvs.
  ∅ H:1.5m+ (5ft+) S:1m (3½ft)    *Stks*: HE, KN
  *scandens*: Climber. Heart-shaped, mid to dark green lvs.
  ∅ H:1.5m (5ft) S:30cm (1ft)    *Stks*: Widely available

**Phoenix** (10°C/50°F) Intermediate    J.I.    ○–❶
  *canariensis*: Arching palm fronds with spiky leaflets.
  ∅ H:3m (10ft) S:1.2m (4ft)    *Stks*: Widely available

**Pilea** (10°C/50°F) Easy    J.I./P.B.    ❶–❷
  *cadierei* (aluminium plant): Lvs green with silvery blotches.
  ∅ H:23cm (9in) S:15cm (6in)    *Stks*: Widely available
  *mollis*: Velvety lvs, having a coleus-like appearance.
  ∅ H:23cm (9in) S:15cm (6in)    *Stks*: KN

**Platycerium** (13°C/55°F) Difficult    P.B.(M)    ◐
  *bifurcatum* (stag's horn fern): Beautiful, large, antler-like fronds.
  ∅ H:60cm (2ft) S:45cm (1½ft)    *Stks*: Widely available

**Primula** (7°C/45°F) Easy    J.I./P.B.    ○–◑

*malacoides*: Delicate heads of fls in various colours.
✿ H:25cm (10in) S:20cm (8in)    *Stks*: Widely available

*obconica*: Bold heads in orange, purple, blue, red, pink.
✿ H:30cm (1ft) S:25cm (10in)    *Stks*: Widely available

*vulgaris*: Hardy, well-known plant for winter and spring fls.
🌢✿ H:20cm (8in) S:20cm (8in)    *Stks*: Widely available

**Pteris** (7°C/45°F) Easy    P.B.    ◑–●

*cretica*'Alboplineata': White central band on each leaflet.
∅ H:30cm (1ft) S:23cm (9in)    *Stks*: Widely available

**Rhipsalidopsis** see *Schlumbergera*

**Rhoicissus** (grape ivy) (7°C/45°F) Easy    J.I.    ◑

*rhomboidea*'Ellen Danica': Climber. Deeply-cut lvs.
∅ H:1.2m+ (4ft+) S:45cm (1½ft)    *Stks*: Widely available

**Rhoeo** (boat lily) (7°C/45°F) Easy    J.I.    ◑

*discolor*: Attractive, sword-shaped green and purple lvs.
∅ H:30cm (1ft) S:30cm (1ft)    *Stks*: Widely available

**Rochea** (5°C/41°F) Easy    J.I.    ○–◑

*coccinea*: Attractive, leathery, green lvs. Pink fls.
✿ H:38cm (15cm) S:30cm (1ft)    *Stks*: KN, TB

**Saintpaulia** (16°C/61°F) Intermediate    P.B.    ◑

*ionantha*: Clusters of violet-blue fls over rosettes of lvs.
✿ H:15cm (6in) S:20cm (8in)    *Stks*: Widely available

**Sansevieria** (16°C/61°F) Intermediate    J.I.(D)    ○

*trifasciata*'Laurentii': Sword-shaped lvs; creamy edges.
∅ H:45cm (1½ft) S:20cm (8in)    *Stks*: Widely available

**Saxifraga** (7°C/45°F) Easy    J.I.(D)    ○–◑

*stolonifera*'Tricolor': Attractively variegated lvs.
∅ H:20cm (8in) S:25cm (10in)    *Stks*: Widely available

**Schefflera** (13°C/55°F) Easy    J.I./P.B.    ○–◑

*actinophylla*(umbrella plant): Glossy umbrella-like leaflets.
∅ H:1.8m (6ft) S:45cm (1½ft)    *Stks*: Widely available

**Schizanthus** (8°C/46°F) Easy    J.I./P.B.    ○–◑

'Star Parade': Annual. Multi-coloured butterfly-like fls.
✿ H:25cm (10in) S:23cm (9in)    *Stks*: HE, KN

**Schlumbergera** (13°C/55°F) Easy    J.I.    ○–◑

*gaertneri*(Easter cactus): Bright red fls, March–April.
✿ H:23cm (9in) S:45cm (1½ft)    *Stks*: Widely available

*truncatus* see *Zygocactus truncatus*

**Scindapsus** (13°C/55°F) Intermediate    P.B.    ◑

*aureus*'Golden Queen': Beautiful, cream-variegated lvs.
∅ H:1.2m (4ft) S:30cm (1ft)    *Stks*: Widely available

**Sedum** (5°C/41°F) Easy    J.I.(D)    ○

*sieboldii*'Medio-variegatum': Cream and green-blue lvs.
∅ H:7.5cm (3in) S:30cm (1ft)    *Stks*: Widely available

**Senecio** (10°C/50°F) Easy    J.I.    ○–◑

*cruentus*(cineraria): Annual with colourful daisy-like fls.
✿ H:45cm (1½ft) S:30cm (1ft)    *Stks*: Widely available

*macroglossus*'Variegatus': Cream and green ivy-like lvs.
∅ H:45cm (1½ft) S:30cm (1ft)    *Stks*: HE, KN

**Sinningia** (18°C/65°F) Intermediate    P.B.    ◑

*speciosa*(gloxinia): Velvety lvs. Trumpet-shaped fls.
✿ H:25cm (10in) S:30cm (1ft)    *Stks*: Widely available

**Solanum** (7°C/45°F) Easy   J.I.   ○
  *capsicastrum*: Scarlet berries, Dec.–Jan. Raised from seed.
  ⚘ H:30cm (1ft) S:25cm (10in)   *Stks*: Widely available

**Spathiphyllum** (peace lily) (10°C/50°F) Easy J.I./P.B. ◑–●
  *wallisii*: Rich, shiny lvs topped by arum-like white fls.
  ❁ H:25cm (10in) S:20cm (8in)   *Stks*: Widely available

**Stephanotis** (15°C/59°F) Intermediate   J.I./P.B.   ○–◑
  *floribunda*: Dark green lvs. Climbing. Fragrant, white fls.
  ⤴❁ H:45cm (1½ft) S:25cm (10in)   *Stks*: Widely available

**Syagrus** see *Cocos*

**Syngonium** (goosefoot plant) (15°C/59°F) Easy   P.B.   ◑
  *podophyllum*: Light green, arrow-shaped lvs.
  ∅ H:90cm (3ft) S:30cm (1ft)   *Stks*: Widely available

**Thunbergia** (15°C/59°F) Easy   J.I./P.B.   ○
  *alata*: Annual climber. Yellow fls, with black centres.
  ❁ H:1.8m (6ft) S:23cm (9in)   *Stks*: Widely available

**Tradescantia** (7°C/45°F) Easy   J.I./P.B.   ○–◑
  *fluminensis* 'Variegata': Green lvs striped white, flushed pink.
  ∅ H:20cm (8in) S:30cm (1ft)   *Stks*: Widely available

**Vreisia** (13°C/55°F) Intermediate   P.B.   ◑
  *splendens*: Light and dark green striped lvs. Red fls.
  ∅❁ H:30cm (1ft) S:20cm (8in)   *Stks*: Widely available

**Zebrina** (wandering Jew) (7°C/45°F) Easy   J.I.   ○–◑
  *pendula*: Lvs silvery above, rich purple beneath.
  ∅ H:15cm (6in) S:23cm (9in)   *Stks*: Widely available

**Zygocactus** (13°C/55°F) Intermediate   J.I.   ○–◑
  *truncatus*: The distinctive and well-known Christmas cactus.
  ❁ H:23cm (9in) S:45cm (1½ft)   *Stks*: Widely available

---

## SPECIALIST SUPPLIERS

Houseplants are not normally available as growing plants
by mail order, although there are a few exceptions. The
majority are distributed by wholesale companies
specializing in houseplants, and with the exception of
Thomas Butcher Ltd (who will dispatch by post or
passenger train) the companies below are wholesalers.
However, if you find a shop or garden centre stocking
their plants it is usually possible to order them in for you –
subject to season.

    Messrs Butcher, Evans, Kennedys, and Rochford also
have plants available from their garden centres.

**GE**   Geest Horticultural Group Ltd., Horseshoe Road,
      Spalding, Lincolnshire, PE11 1NB.

**HE**   H. Evans & Sons Ltd., Ruxley Manor Nursery,
      Sidcup, Kent. Tel: 01–300 2128.

**KN**   Kennedys Garden Centres, Kingsdown Nurseries,
      Stratton St. Margaret, Swindon, Wilts., SN2 6SE.

**NR**   The New Ruaton Garden Co. Ltd., Earls Hall Drive,
      St. John's Road, Clacton-on-Sea, Essex, CO16 8BP.

**TB**   Thomas Butcher Ltd., 60 Wickham Road, Shirley,
      Croydon, Surrey, CR9 8AG. Tel: 01–654 3720.

**TR**   Thomas Rochford & Sons Ltd., Turnford Hall
      Nurseries, Broxbourne, Hertfordshire, EN10 6BH.

# Fruit

Apple trees represent the best possible investment and value for money spent on the garden. It may take a few years for them to establish, but after that the easy-to-grow varieties will give masses of attractive flowers in spring and good yields of fruit for up to 50 years.

'Conference' pear and 'Victoria' plum run the apple a close second – and the soft fruit bushes, especially gooseberries and red currants, will crop repeatedly with very little attention for 15 years or more.

Where the soil is well dug and improved by adding well-rotted manure and/or garden compost before planting, growth will be very much better. This preparatory treatment cannot be too strongly emphasized. Subsequent pruning will also help improve yields and fruit quality. It is important to prune all fruits correctly in the first few years – and every year for blackcurrant, blackberry, loganberry and raspberry.

## Where to plant

Trees are usually best planted around the outer perimeter of the garden and used as specimens. Select fan-trained trees and trees with tiered branches (called espaliers) to plant against walls and fences. Even north-facing walls are suitable for a 'Morello' cherry and 'Victoria' plum. Reserve the warm south and west walls for peaches, gages and pears. Wire fences between properties provide the ideal place for cordon apples and pears planted 90cm (3ft) apart in a single row.

All the soft fruits are best grouped to allow netting in one go to protect from birds. Where the fruit plot is adjacent to one or two fences, the fence can be used as part support for the net, and will also serve to support cane fruits like loganberries and blackberries.

Keep a one-metre (one-yard) diameter area of soil cultivated around young trees if at all possible. The competition from grass and weeds will severely check growth in the first two years.

## What to buy

All that is recommended for trees (page 45) applies equally to fruit trees, and recommendations for shrubs (page 57) apply to soft fruit bushes.

When buying fruit *trees*, the kind of roots each tree has is as important as the variety. Nurserymen have a range of rootstocks of different vigour; small apple trees, for instance, are obtained by grafting on to dwarfing rootstocks like Malling 9. Where apple trees are required eventually to reach greater size, then Malling Merton 111 rootstock is often used.

Trees on the dwarfing rootstocks, because they are not so vigorous, need secure staking, some for the

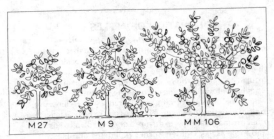

*The effect of rootstock on growth is demonstrated clearly in this illustration of six-year-old apple trees. All are dwarfing, but M27 is a new very dwarf stock useful for very vigorous varieties such as 'Bramley's Seedling', a variety otherwise too large for a small garden. Malling 9 is usually used for small trees.*

whole of their life, and fertile soils. Medium vigour apple stocks like MM 106 and MM 111 are advisable for the average garden soil and for most garden uses. The dwarfing Malling 9 is ideal for cordons, but on poor soil the stronger-growing stocks are better – even for cordons.

Inexperienced gardeners are well advised to seek advice on the right stock to suit their soil and purpose. If trees are found with a reference to 'EMLA', this means they have come from especially healthy and carefully selected rootstocks and mother trees.

Healthy stock is important with all new plants, but is especially so for blackcurrants, loganberries, raspberries and strawberries. All these plants can be infected with virus diseases, and your protection against buying diseased specimens is the government-controlled 'Certification' scheme.

Always buy 'Certified' stock. Container and pot-grown soft fruits are often offered for sale, and here the term used is 'grown from certified stock'.

Avoid at all costs soft fruit plants with yellow, mottled or twisted leaves. Blackcurrants should have *no* overlarge swollen round buds, which would be caused by disease-carrying big bud mites.

There is little point in introducing disease-free stock into the garden if you have infected plants there already. Where disease is causing poor growth and low crops, the old plants must be dug up, all leaves and branches collected up and burnt before thoroughly preparing a new site and introducing new disease-free plants.

All soft fruits are best planted as strong-growing one-year-old, at most two-year-old, plants. Trees are best planted as two- or three-year-olds with the nurseryman establishing the main branch framework.

**If you want to know more . . .**

An authoritative, well-illustrated book, useful for beginners and experienced alike, is *The Fruit Garden Displayed*, published by The Royal Horticultural Society.

## POLLINATION OF APPLES

To ensure a good crop, it is necessary for apples to be
fertilized with pollen from another variety. For that reason it is
better to plant two trees that flower at the same or similar time.
There will, however, be some overlap between adjacent
groups. As a guide, the varieties listed in the chart are
repeated below according to flowering season.

Because 'Blenheim Orange' and 'Bramley's Seedling' are
triploid varieties, however, it is necessary to have at least two
other ordinary varieties to ensure a good set on all trees. The
crab apple Malus 'Golden Hornet' pollinates all apples.

| Early flowering | Mid-season flowering | Late flowering |
|---|---|---|
| 'Egremont Russet' | 'Arthur Turner' | 'Howgate Wonder' |
| 'Idared' | 'Ashmead's Kernel' | 'Lord Derby' |
| 'Rev. W. Wilks' | 'Blenheim Orange'* | 'Newton Wonder' |
| | 'Bramley's Seedling'* | 'Red Ellison's Orange' |
| | 'Charles Ross' | 'Spartan' |
| | 'Cox's Orange Pippin' | 'Worcester Pearmain' |
| | 'Discovery' | (late-flowering |
| | 'Epicure' | reduces the chance |
| | 'Fortune' | of frost |
| | 'Grenadier' | damage) |
| | 'James Grieve' | |
| | 'Sunset' | |

*= triploid variety, see note above.*

---

**Apple**   LMH   O   ***

'Arthur Turner' (C): Large, yellowish with brown-red flush.
*Season*: Oct.–Nov.   *Stks*: RR, SN

'Ashmead's Kernel' (D): Small to medium, greenish-yellow.
F *Season*: Nov.–March   *Stks*: HN, SN

'Blenheim Orange' (C/D): Large, crisp orange-yellow fruits.
*Season*: Nov.–Jan.   *Stks*: Widely available

'Bramley's Seedling' (C): Very large green to yellow fruits.
*Season*: Nov.–March   *Stks*: Widely available

'Charles Ross' (C/D): Round, pale yellow with light flush.
*Season*: Oct.–Dec.   *Stks*: Widely available

'Cox's Orange Pippin' (C/D): Fruits have a yellow flesh.
F *Season*: Nov.–Jan.   *Stks*: Widely available

'Discovery' (D): Scarlet fruit, delicious fresh from tree.
*Season*: Aug.–Sept.   *Stks*: Widely available

'Egremont Russet' (D): Medium size, brownish and russetted.
F *Season*: Oct.–Nov.   *Stks*: Widely available

'Epicure' (D): Yellow, with red stripes. Juicy.
F *Season*: Sept.   *Stks*: RR, SN

'Fortune' (D): Greenish yellow, with red flush.
F *Season*: Oct.–Nov.   *Stks*: Widely available

'Grenadier' (C): Irregular-shaped green fruits, yellowing.
*Season*: Aug.–Sept.   *Stks*: Widely available

'Howgate Wonder' (C): Huge fruits; neat and compact
growth.
*Season*: Nov.–Feb.   *Stks*: Widely available

'Idared' (C): Colour turns yellow flushed scarlet when ripe.
*Season*: Jan.–April.   *Stks*: HN, SN

'James Grieve' (C/D): Medium-sized, pale yellow, red flush.
F *Season*: Sept.–Oct.   *Stks*: Widely available

'Lord Derby' (C): Green, flesh turns pink when cooked.
*Season*: Oct.–Dec.   *Stks*: Widely available

'Newton Wonder' (C): Yellow with a red flush. Stores well.
*Season*: Nov.–March   *Stks*: Widely available

'Red Ellison's Orange' (D): Deep red fruits. Easy to grow.
🄵 *Season*: Sept.–Oct.   *Stks*: Widely available

'Rev. W. Wilks' (C): Large, creamy fruits. Heavy cropping.
*Season*: Sept.–Nov.   *Stks*: RR, SN

'Spartan' (D): Medium-sized, dark crimson fruits.
*Season*: Nov.–Jan.   *Stks*: Widely available

'Sunset' (D): Small to medium sized fruits, golden-yellow.
🄵 *Season*: Nov.–Dec.   *Stks*: Widely available

'Worcester Pearmain' (D): Fruits yellow with scarlet flush.
*Season*: Aug.–Sept.   *Stks*: Widely available

## VARIETIES FOR NORTHERN DISTRICTS

Not all apple varieties thrive in the cooler northern climate, but the following will succeed in these areas:

| | | |
|---|---|---|
| 'Arthur Turner' | 'Epicure' | 'Lord Derby' |
| 'Charles Ross' | 'Fortune' | 'Red Ellison's Orange' |
| 'Discovery' | 'Grenadier' | 'Rev. W. Wilks' |
| 'Egremont Russet' | 'James Grieve' | 'Worcester Pearmain' |

**Apricot**   MH(C)   O   **

'Moorpark' (D): Round, brownish-orange with brown flush.
🄵 *Season*: late Aug.   *Stks*: Widely available

**Blackberry**   LMH   O–◑   ***

'Bedford Giant' (C/D): Large berries. Medium vigour.
*Season*: late July–Aug.   *Stks*: Widely available

'Himalaya Giant' (C/D): Sharp-flavoured fruit. Heavy cropper.
*Season*: mid Aug.–Oct.   *Stks*: Widely available

'Oregon Thornless' (C/D): Thornless. Near-evergreen lvs.
🄵 *Season*: late Aug.–Oct.   *Stks*: KM, SN

'Smooth Stemmed' (C/D): Thornless, heavy cropping.
*Season*: Sept.–Oct. *Stks*: KM

**Blackcurrant**   LMH   O–◑   ***

'Blackdown' (C): Large easy-to-pick fruits. High yield.
*Season*: mid July   *Stks*: KM

'Baldwin' (C): Large to medium-sized fruits. Compact bush.
🄵✻ *Season*: late July   *Stks*: Widely available

'Ben Lomond' (C): Large fruits. Good crop. Mildew resistant.
🄵 *Season*: early July   *Stks*: KM

'Boskoop Giant' (C): Large berries, good for bottling.
🄵 *Season*: early July   *Stks*: RR, SN

'Malling Jet' (C): Long trusses. Heavy crop.
✻ *Season*: late July–Aug.   *Stks*: KM

'Tenah' (C): Heavy crops. Evenly-sized berries.
*Season*: late July   *Stks*: KM

'Wellington XXX' (C): Medium to large berries.
🄵 *Season*: July   *Stks*: Widely available

**Blueberry** (D)   LMH(A,P)   O–◑   ***

'Earliblue' see 'Early Blue'

'Early Blue' (C): Light blue and very firm.
🄵 *Season*: Aug.–Sept.   *Stks*: KM, SN

'Goldtraube' (C): Small berries, light blue in colour.
🄵 *Season*: Aug.–Sept.   *Stks*: KM

'Jersey' (C): Very large, light blue berries.
*Season*: Aug.–Sept.   *Stks*: KM, SN

Note: It is advisable to plant two varieties to produce a better crop.

*For key to symbols, see page 7*

## POLLINATION OF CHERRIES

The varieties 'Morello' and 'Stella' are self-fertile and will set a good crop with their own pollen (as well as being a pollinator for most other varieties). All other cherries listed will require a suitable pollinator, and a key to these is given below.

| Variety | Pollinate with: |
|---|---|
| 'Merton Bigarreau' | 'Merton Glory'<br>'Stella' |
| 'Merton Glory' | 'Merton Bigarreau'<br>'Van' |
| 'Van' | 'Merton Glory'<br>'Stella' |

**Cherry**   MH   ○   \*\*\*
  'Merton Bigarreau' (D): Large, purplish-crimson to black.
  🄵 *Season*: mid to late July   *Stks*: SB, SN
  'Merton Glory' (D): Large, round, yellow with orange flush.
  🄵 *Season*: mid–July   *Stks*: Widely available
  'Morello' (C) ○–●: Large, fruits, deep red to jet black.
  🄵 *Season*: Aug.–Sept.   *Stks*: Widely available
  'Stella' (D): Heart-shaped, late, dark red fruits.
  *Season*: late July   *Stks*: Widely available
  'Van' (D): Dark red-black, sweet fruits.
  *Season*: mid to late July   *Stks*: HN, SN

**Damson**   LMH   ○   \*\*\*
  'Merryweather' (C): Large, black fruits with a thin bloom.
  *Season*: early Sept.   *Stks*: SN
  'Prune Damson' see 'Shropshire Damson'
  'Shropshire Damson' (C): Small, oval, blue-black fruits.
  🄵 *Season*: mid to late Sept.   *Stks*: SB, SN
  Note: These are self-fertile.

**Fig**   LMH   ○   \*\*
  'Brown Turkey' (D): Pear-shaped, brown tinged purplish.
  *Season*: Sept.–Oct.   *Stks*: HN, RR

**Gooseberry**   LMH   ○–◑   \*\*\*
  'Careless' (C): Large, oval fruits, green to creamy-white.
  *Season*: June–July   *Stks*: Widely available
  'Keepsake' (C/D): Medium to large fruits, pale green.
  *Season*: July   *Stks*: RR, SN
  'Leveller' (C/D): Large fruits, greenish-yellow in colour.
  🄵 *Season*: July–Aug.   *Stks*: Widely available
  'May Duke' (C/D): Medium size, deep crimson fruits.
  🄵 *Season*: June–July   *Stks*: RR, SN
  'Whinham's Industry' (C/D): Medium to large fruits, dark red.
  🄵 *Season*: July   *Stks*: Widely available
  'Whitesmith' (C/D): Pale yellowish-white, medium to large.
  🄵 *Season*: July   *Stks*: Widely available

**Grape (indoor)**   MH   ○   \*\*\*
  'Black Hamburg' (D): Large berries in good-sized bunches.
  ◔ *Season*: Aug.–Oct.   *Stks*: Widely available

**Grape (outdoor)**   MH   ○   \*\*\*
  'Brant' (D): Small, late, black berries. Nice autumn lvs.
  *Season*: Sept.–Oct.   *Stks*: Widely available
  'Mueller-Thurgau': Mainly grown for wine production.
  *Season*: Sept.–Oct.   *Stks*: HN

'Reisling Sylvaner' see 'Mueller-Thurgau'
'Seyve-Villard 5/276': Excellent for wine or eating.
*Season*: Sept.–Oct.   *Stks*: HN

**Loganberry**   LMH   ○–◐   \*\*\*
'LY 59' (C/D): Large, oblong, dark claret-red fruits.
*Season*: July–Aug.   *Stks*: Widely available
'LY 654' (C): Thornless canes, but less vigorous than above.
*Season*: July–Aug.   *Stks*: HN, KM

**Nectarine**   LMH(C)   ○   \*\*
'Early Rivers' (D): Greenish-yellow fruits, streaked scarlet.
*Season*: mid to late July   *Stks*: SN
'Lord Napier' (D): Large, pale yellowish-green, red flush.
*Season*: early Aug.   *Stks*: HN, SB

**Peach**   LMH(C)   ○   \*\*
'Duke of York' (D): Large fruits. Rich crimson skin.
*Season*: mid–July   *Stks*: HN, SN
'Peregrine' (D): Large, round fruits. Brilliant crimson skin.
Ⓕ *Season*: early to mid Aug.   *Stks*: Widely available
'Rochester' (D): Medium sized, yellow flushed red fruits.
*Season*: early Aug.   *Stks*: HN, SN

---

## POLLINATION OF PEARS

All pears set an unsatisfactory crop with their own pollen, and
compatible varieties should be planted together. 'Conference'
will set fruit on its own, but crops better in the company of
'Onward' or 'Williams' Bon Crétien'.

Plant together those varieties that will be in flower at the same
or similar times. There is bound to be some overlap in flowering
period. The flowering group to which each of the listed varieties
belongs is given below.

| *Early flowering* | *Mid-season flowering* | *Late flowering* |
|---|---|---|
| Louise Bonne of Jersey* | 'Beurré Hardy' | 'Bristol Cross' |
| | 'Conference' | 'Doyenné du Comice' |
| | 'Williams' Bon Chrétien'* | 'Onward' |

\* = *will not pollinate each other*

---

**Pear**   MH   ○   \*\*\*
'Beurré Hardy' (D): Vigorous and disease-resistant.
*Season*: Oct.   *Stks*: Widely available
'Bristol Cross' (D): Fruits yellow with a golden russet.
Ⓕ *Season*: Oct.–Nov.   *Stks*: SN
'Conference' (D): Fruits dark green with a brown russet.
*Season*: Oct.–Dec.   *Stks*: Widely available
'Doyenné du Comice' (C/D): Pale yellow with a fine russet.
Ⓕ *Season*: Nov.–Dec.   *Stks*: Widely available
'Louise Bonne of Jersey' (D): Yellow-green, flushed deep red.
Ⓕ *Season*: Oct.   *Stks*: RR, SN
'Onward' (D): Oval, pale yellow with a russet. Easy to grow.
Ⓕ *Season*: Sept.   *Stks*: HN
'Williams' Bon Chrétien' (D): Oval, golden-yellow with russet.
Ⓕ *Season*: Sept.   *Stks*: Widely available

Pear rootstocks: *Most pears are grafted on to Quince A
rootstock, which is a good all-round stock for tree forms. For a
more dwarfing stock, Quince C should be chosen.*

# POLLINATION OF PLUMS AND GAGES

Some plums and gages fail to set a good crop with their own pollen. Some, such as 'Jefferson' will not set any crop. To ensure a good yield, plant 'Jefferson' with a variety from one of the other groups. Those which set a poor crop with their own pollen should be planted with another variety from the same group, or with any from the self-fertile list. Self-fertile varieties will set a satisfactory crop with their own pollen.

*Self-sterile*
  'Jefferson' (*early flowering*)
*Poor crop with own pollen*
  'Cambridge Gage' (*late flowering*)
  'Early Laxton' (*mid-season flowering*)
  'Rivers' Early Prolific' (*mid-season flowering*)

*Self-fertile*
  'Czar' (*mid-season flowering*)
  'Majorie's Seedling' (*late flowering*)
  'Victoria' (*mid-season flowering*)
  'Warwickshire Drooper' (*early to mid-season flowering*)

---

**Plums and Gages**   LMH   O   ***
  'Cambridge Gage' (D): Vigorous tree. Green fruit.
  ⓕ *Season*: end of Aug.   *Stks*: SN
  'Czar' (C): Medium, purple fruits. Heavy cropping.
  *Season*: early Aug.   *Stks*: Widely available
  'Early Laxton' (C/D): Round to oval, bright yellow flushed red.
  *Season*: late July   *Stks*: SN
  'Jefferson' (D): Large, oval, yellowish fruits.
  ⓕ *Season*: early Sept.   *Stks*: RR, SN
  'Majorie's Seedling' (C): Large, round, blue-black fruits.
  *Season*: late Sept.–Oct.   *Stks*: HN, SN
  'Rivers' Early Prolific' (C/D): Oval, dark violet-purple.
  *Season*: late July   *Stks*: RR, SN
  'Victoria' (C/D): Large, oval fruits, bright red and speckled.
  ⓕ *Season*: late Aug.   *Stks*: Widely available
  'Warwickshire Drooper' (C): Medium-sized fruits, yellow.
  *Season*: mid-Sept.   *Stks*: SN

**Quince**   MH   O   ***
  'Vranja' (D): Large, pear-shaped fruits, golden-yellow skin.
  *Season*: Oct.   *Stks*: HN, SN

**Raspberry**   LMH   O–◑   ***
  *Summer-fruiting*
  'Delight' (C/D): Huge berries. Very heavy yielding.
  ① ✳ *Season*: June–July   *Stks*: Widely available
  'Glen Clova' (C/D): Large berries, easy to grow and pick.
  ⓕ ✳ *Season*: July   *Stks*: Widely available
  'Malling Admiral' (C/D): Medium-sized fruits; heavy cropper.
  ✳ *Season*: July–Aug.   *Stks*: Widely available
  'Malling Jewel' (C/D): Medium-sized, bright red berries.
  ⓕ ✳ *Season*: June–July   *Stks*: Widely available
  'Malling Promise' (C/D): Large, conical, bright fruits.
  ⓕ ✳ *Season*: June–July   *Stks*: RR, SN
  'Orion' (C/D): Large to medium fruits. Late.
  ✳ *Season*: July–Aug.   *Stks*: RR

*Autumn-fruiting*
'Fallgold' (C/D): Pale gold. Light yield, but very sweet.
*Season*: July and Sept.–Oct.   Stks: KM

'September' (C/D): Medium size, firm berries. Heavy cropper.
*Season*: Sept.–Oct.   Stks: KM, SN

'Zeva' (C/D): Large fruits, dark red and very juicy.
*Season*: Sept.–Oct.   Stks: HN, KM

**Red currant**   LMH   O–●   ***
'Jonkheer van Tets' (C/D): Early and very prolific.
*Season*: early July   Stks: KM

'Red Lake' (C/D): Large berries hang in long, loose bunches.
① *Season*: mid-July   Stks: Widely available

**Rhubarb**   LMH   O–◐   ***
'Timperley Early' (C): Good garden variety, fine for forcing.
*Season*: Jan.–June   Stks: Widely available

'Cawood Delight' (C): Brilliant scarlet and fleshy stems.
①Ⓕ *Season*: March–Aug.   Stks: TM (address page 121)

**Strawberry**   LMH   O–◐   ***
'Baron Solemacher' (C/D): Alpine strawberry. Small fruits.
*Season*: June–Oct.   Stks: KM, SN

'Cambridge Favourite' (D): Large berries. Easy to grow.
✱ *Season*: June–July   Stks: Widely available

'Cambridge Vigour' (D): Large, conical fruits.
Ⓕ☾ *Season*: June   Stks: Widely available

'Gento' (D): Large crimson berries. Perpetual-fruiting.
Ⓕ *Season*: July-Oct.   Stks: HN, KM

'Grandee' (D): The largest fruits of all.
Ⓕ *Season*: June-July   Stks: KM

'Hapil' (D): Abundant fruits of large size.
*Season*: June-July   Stks: KM

'Pantagruella' (D): Very early, ideal for cloches.
Ⓕ☾ *Season*: June-July   Stks: HN, KM

'Redgauntlet'(D): Ideal for cropping under cloches.
☾ *Season*: June–July, Sept.–Oct.   Stks: Widely available

'Royal Sovereign' (D): Scarlet berries. Light yielding.
Ⓕ *Season*: June–July   Stks: Widely available

'Tamella' (D): All all-purpose variety, cropping heavily.
Ⓕ *Season*: June–July   Stks: KM

**White currant**   LMH   O–◐   ***
'White Dutch' (C/D): Large milky-yellow berries.
*Season*: July   Stks: SN

'White Versailles' (C/D): Large, round, pale yellow berries.
*Season*: July   Stks: HN, KM

---

## SPECIALIST SUPPLIERS

**HN**   Highfield Nurseries, Whitminster, Gloucester, GL2 7PL. Tel: Gloucester (0252) 740266.

**KM**   Ken Muir, Honeypot Farm, Weeley Heath, Clacton-on-Sea, Essex, CO16 9BJ. Tel: Weeley (0255) 830181.

**RR**   R. V. Roger Ltd., The Nurseries, Pickering, North Yorkshire, YO18 7HG. Tel: Pickering (0751) 72226.

**SB**   W. Seabrook Ltd., Little Leighs Hall, Little Leighs, Chelmsford, Essex, CM3 1PG. Tel: Gt. Leighs 221.

**SN**   Scotts Nurseries (Merriott) Ltd., Merriott, Somerset, TA16 5PL. Tel: Crewkerne (0460) 72306.

# Vegetables

Growing vegetables in the home garden and allotment gives great satisfaction and provides produce fresher and tastier than you can ever buy. Where cost of food is of prime importance money can also be saved by growing your own. To save the maximum amount, care needs to be exercised in not sowing too much seed at a time and not spending on flashy tools and gadgets.

Experienced gardeners and those gardeners with large plots will inevitably have gluts of some kinds of vegetables in mid to late summer. Careful planning of what to grow will keep over-production to a minimum. Deep-freeze owners will not have this problem because many of the surpluses can be frozen for winter use.

Some form of protection for the soil early and late in the year will extend the cropping season for several vegetables and salads. It will also allow earlier sowing in warmed soil. Polythene tunnel cloches give the largest covered area for the least cost.

## Where to grow

Limited space need be no obstacle with the fertilized peat-filled growing bag providing the ideal medium for many crops. Growing bags are often used as loss-leaders by retailers to attract trade, and they are often cheaper than ordinary bags of peat.

It is possible to grow several crops in the one bag, but as with soil husbandry the crops must be different each year. Bags used for tomatoes, peppers or aubergines can be used a second time for lettuces, courgettes or French beans, and then finally for strawberries and flowering plants before the root-filled peat is dug into soil as you would an ordinary bag of peat.

All soils can be used to grow vegetables but much better crops will be gathered if the soil is improved by digging in well-rotted garden compost and dressed with a general fertilizer each spring.

Where the soil is heavily shaded, leafy crops are the best bet. Vegetables in shade are unlikely to produce tight hearts or good root crops.

## What to buy

Onions are easiest grown from sets, sold by weight. The small sets will give you more for your money and will produce a much heavier yield than large sets of the same variety. Large sets are more likely to run to seed.

Large shallot bulbs will produce a greater number of small bulbs at harvest time. Each small shallot will produce less bulbs but they will be larger. Sold by weight, small shallot planting bulbs will give a heavier yield.

Much the same goes for potatoes. Small egg-sized tubers are the ideal size and give maximum yield.

The best seed is usually the cheapest in the end, excepting current introductions which carry a novelty premium. Good strains (a term that indicates careful selection by the seedsmen and good quality in every respect) are especially important for root crops such as carrots, radishes and beetroot, and for cabbages (especially spring-maturing varieties) and cauliflowers.

Vegetables sold as $F_1$ hybrids will cost more but the resulting plants will be more uniform, stronger-growing, heavier yielding and, in a number of cases, more resistant to disease.

It is important to store seed carefully if you are to get full value for money. Most packets contain more seed than is needed at one sowing. Surplus seed is best stored in an airtight tin in a cool temperature.

Seeds packed in foil will retain good germination for three years and are the best buy if you are likely to miss sowing for any reason. Loose-filled packets are likely to give more seeds for your money, and once foil packs are opened the seed life is the same.

Some old and well tried varieties, like lettuce 'Tom Thumb' and leek 'Musselburgh', have been grown for a hundred years and still give good results. As a general rule, however, the more recent varieties will give better yield, flavour and pest and disease resistance.

The increase in starch and fibre and reduction in sugars found in winter-hardy varieties affect vegetable quality. For this reason hardy round-seeded early peas, broad beans like 'Aquadulce' for autumn sowing, and winter-hardy strains of 'White Lisbon' onion should be used only for early crops gathered while still young.

### If you want to know more ...

For comprehensive cultural instructions for all the vegetables described in this book, read *The Complete Vegetable Gardener*, by Peter Seabrook (Cassell).

Anyone really interested in vegetables, particularly if growing for exhibition, should consider joining the National Vegetable Society. The Secretary is Mr W. Hargreave, 29 Revidge Road, Blackburn, Lancs., BB2 6JB.

*A little protection can advance crops and bring them in when they are most appreciated. Cloches are ideal, but even clear plastic containers can usefully protect early lettuce and similar crops. Cut out the base and 'screw' the edge into the soil for at least 12mm (½in). Unscrew the top for ventilation.*

111

**Artichoke, globe**  LM  ○  **

'Green Ball': Large, fleshy heads of good size.
*Sow*: March–April *Plant*: following spring.  *Stks*: DB, SS

**Artichoke, Jerusalem**  LMH  ○–◐  ***

'Silver Skinned': White-skinned tubers. A popular variety.
*Plant*: Feb.–March  *Stks*: Local garden centres

**Aubergine**  LM/growing bag  ○  *

'Black Prince': Large purple-black fruits, very early.
✳ ◯ ⊞ *Sow*: Feb.–March, under glass  *Stks*: SM, TM, WU
'Moneymaker': Very early cropping, dark purple fruits.
✳ ◯ ⊞ *Sow*: Feb.–March, under glass  *Stks*: SS
'Oriental Egg Plant': Creamy-white, almost round fruits.
◯ *Sow*: Feb.–March, under glass  *Stks*: TM

**Asparagus**  LMH  ○–◐  ***

'Connover's Colossal': Plump shoots with slender tips.
✳ *Sow*: April *Plant*: next April  *Stks*: Widely available

**Bean, broad**  LMH  ○–◐  ***

'Aquadulce Claudia': Succulent pods, up to 38cm (15in) long.
*Sow*: late Oct.–Nov.  *Stks*: Widely available
'Beryl' see 'Ite'
'Cavalier': A long-pod variety; about eight white seeds.
*Sow*: Oct. and Feb.–March  *Stks*: GP, TB
'Exhibition Longpod'; Good pods, eight or nine beans.
① ✳ *Sow*: Feb.–April  *Stks*: GP, SS, WJ
'Express': An early long-pod. Very heavy cropper.
⊞ *Sow*: Feb.–April  *Stks*: Widely available
'Green Windsor': Later cropping. Four or five green beans.
✳ *Sow*: March–April  *Stks*: Widely available
'Hylon': Longest pods of all. Ten beans.
*Sow*: March–April  *Stks*: SS
'Imperial Green Longpod': Long pods; up to nine beans.
*Sow*: Feb.–April  *Stks*: DB, TM
'Ite': Late cropping, small beans ideal for mixed vegetables.
✳ *Sow*: March–May  *Stks*: TM

**Bean, French**  LMH/growing bag  ○  *

'Kinghorn Wax': Round, yellowish pods, slightly curved.
*Sow*: late April–May  *Stks*: SS
'Loch Ness': Straight, round stringless pods. Upright plants.
⊞ ✳ *Sow*: late April–May  *Stks*: Widely available
'Masterpiece': An early variety, heavy yielding. Straight pods.
⊞ ✳ ◯ *Sow*: late April–May  *Stks*: Widely available
'Tendergreen': Round stringless pods, medium length. Early.
⊞ ✳ *Sow*: March–May  *Stks*: Widely available
'The Prince': Straight, long slender fleshy pods. Early.
① ✳ *Sow*: March–May  *Stks*: Widely available

**Bean, French (climbing)**  LMH  ○  *

'Blue Lake White Seeded': Small, round stringless pods.
⊞ ✳ ◯ *Sow*: late April–May  *Stks*: DB, TB, WJ
'Selka Improved': Wide flat pods. Use like runners, sliced.
⊞ *Sow*: April–May  *Stks*: TM

**Bean, runner**  LMH  ○  *

'Achievement': Long, straight pods of good colour.
① ✳ *Sow*: late April–May *Plant*: June  *Stks*: Widely available
'Desiree': Almost stringless. High quality and yield.
⊞ ✳ *Sow*: late April–May *Plant*: May–June  *Stks*: TM

'Prizewinner': Medium length pods. Heavy cropper.
*Sow*: late April–May *Plant*: May–June    *Stks*: GP, SS, TB

'Mergoles': White seeded and stringless. Excellent quality.
ⓕ✳ *Sow*: late April–May *Plant*: May–June    *Stks*: DB, GP

'Scarlet Emperor': Old, reliable variety. A heavy cropper.
*Sow*: late April–May *Plant*: May–June    *Stks*: Widely avail.

'Streamline': Long, smooth pods. Good colour.
✳ *Sow*: April–May *Plant*: May–June    *Stks*: Widely available

**Beetroot**    LMH    ○    **
'Avonearly': Round. Bolt-resistant. Ideal as baby beet.
✳ *Sow*: March–June    *Stks*: GP, SM, SS

'Boltardy': Deep, blood-red. Bolt-resistant.
✳◐ *Sow*: March–June    *Stks*: Widely available

'Cheltenham Green Top': A long-rooted variety. Stores well.
*Sow*: May–June    *Stks*: DB, SS, TB

'Crimson Globe' see 'Detroit'

'Cylindra': Cylindrical roots, good for slicing.
*Sow*: April–June    *Stks*: Widely available

'Detroit–Little Ball': Small, ball-shaped, blood-red roots.
①ⓕ *Sow*: April–July    *Stks*: DB, SM, SS

'Detroit–New Globe': Very uniform and good colour.
① *Sow*: April–July    *Stks*: DB, GP, WJ

**Beet, spinach**    LMH    ○–◐    ***
'Perpetual Spinach': Succulent, spinach-like lvs.
✳ *Sow*: March–July    *Stks*: Widely available

**Beet, seakale (Swiss chard)**    LMH    ○–◐    ***
'Rhubarb Chard': Attractive, long, bright-red stalks.
*Sow*: April–July    *Stks*: Widely available

'Silver': Fleshy leaf-stems, with white midribs.
*Sow*: April–July    *Stks*: Widely available

**Borecole (curly kale)**    MH    ○–◐    ***
'Cottagers': Crimpled-edged, purple-tinged lvs.
*Sow*: April–May *Plant*: July    *Stks*: SS, TM

'Pentland Brig': Extremely hardy. Tasty shoots Feb.–May.
*Sow*: April–May *Plant*: July    *Stks*: SM, SS, TM

'Tall Green Curled': Deeply curled lvs.
*Sow*: April–May *Plant*: July    *Stks*: Widely available

'Tall Scotch Curled' see 'Tall Green Curled'

**Broccoli**    LMH    ○    ***
'Purple Sprouting': Small purple 'cauliflowers', April–May.
*Sow*: April *Plant*: May–June    *Stks*: Widely available

'White Sprouting': Small white 'cauliflowers' in April–May.
*Sow*: April *Plant*: May–June    *Stks*: Widely available

**Brussels sprout**    LMH    ○    ***
'Achilles': Medium height, deep green sprouts, Oct.–Feb.
✳ⓕ *Sow*: March–April *Plant*: May–June    *Stks*: DB, TM

'Citadel': Medium height. Dark green sprouts, Jan–April.
✳ⓕ *Sow*: March *Plant*: May    *Stks*: Widely available

'King Arthur': Fairly tall. Smooth, solid sprouts. Jan–March.
✳ⓕ *Sow*: March–April *Plant*: May–June    *Stks*: GP, WU

'Peer Gynt': Medium-sized, dark green buttons. Oct.–Dec,
ⓕⓕ *Sow*: March–April *Plant*: May–June    *Stks*: Wdly avail.

'Perfect Line': Medium-sized, solid buttons. Dec.–Jan.
ⓕⓕ *Sow*: March–April *Plant*: May–June    *Stks*: SS

'Zid': Dark green, medium-sized sprouts, Jan.–April.
ⓕ✳ⓕ *Sow*: March–April *Plant*: May–June    *Stks*: DB

## Cabbage (spring cutting)    LMH    O–◑    ***

'April': Neat, pointed hearts. Few outer lvs. Ready April.
🅕 *Sow*: July–Aug. *Plant*: Sept.–Oct.    *Stks*: Widely available

'Avoncrest': Good colour. Medium-sized pointed heads.
*Sow*: July–Aug. *Plant*: Sept.–Oct.    *Stks*: GP

'Offenham – Flower of Spring': Compact, pointed hearts.
🅕 *Sow*: July–Aug. *Plant*: Sept.–Oct.    *Stks*: Widely available

'Wheeler's Imperial – Ellams Early Dwarf': Spring greens.
*Sow*: July–Aug. *Plant*: Sept.–Oct.    *Stks*: GP, WJ, WU

## Cabbage (summer and autumn cutting)    LMH    O    ***

'Golden Acre': Firm, round heads. Compact.
🅕 *Sow*: March–May *Plant*: May–June    *Stks*: Wdly avail.

'Greyhound': An early pointed cabbage with a compact head.
*Sow*: March–May: *Plant*: May–June    *Stks*: Widely available

'Hispi': Compact habit with pointed heads. Quick-growing.
🅕🅕 *Sow*: Feb.–May *Plant*: May–June    *Stks*: Widely avail.

'Minicole': Small, round to slightly oval hearts. Fast-growing.
🅕 *Sow*: March–May *Plant*: May–June    *Stks*: Widely avail.

'Primo' see 'Golden Acre'

'Winnigstadt': Large, pointed heart. Late summer cropping.
① *Sow*: March–May *Plant*: May–June    *Stks*: Wdly avail.

## Cabbage (red)    LMH    O    ***

'Niggerhead': Very solid hearts. Blood-red. Dwarf.
*Sow*: March–April. *Plant*: May–June    *Stks*: Wdly avail.

'Ruby Ball': Ball-shaped, solid heads, with few outer lvs.
🅕 *Sow*: March–April *Plant*: May–June    *Stks*: SM, WU

## Cabbage (winter cutting)    LMH    O    ***

'Celtic': Round, solid heads. Ready Dec., holds till April.
🅕 *Sow*: May *Plant*: June–July    *Stks*: Widely available

## Cabbage (for winter storage)    LMH(C)    O    ***

'Holland Late Winter': Solid. Cut and store Nov.–March.
*Sow*: April–May *Plant*: June–July    *Stks*: Widely available

## Cabbage (savoy)    LMH    O    ***

'January King': Coarse outer lvs. Matures Dec.–Feb.
🅕 *Sow*: April–May *Plant*: July    *Stks*: Widely available

## Cabbage, Chinese    LM(M)    O    **

'Nagaoka': Tight, cylindrical heads.
🅕 *Sow*: June–July    *Stks*: TM, WU

'Sampan': Large, conical hearts. Bolt-resistant.
🅕 *Sow*: April or June–July    *Stks*: SS

## Calabrese    LMH    O    ***

'Express Corona': Dark green heads of fine quality.
🅕 *Sow*: March–May *Plant*: April–June    *Stks*: SS, TB

'Green Comet': Deep green heads; few laterals.
🅕✳🅕 *Sow*: March–May *Plant*: June    *Stks*: Widely available

## Capsicum    LM/growing bag    O    *

'Canape': Matures early. One of the best to try outdoors.
⬚🅕 *Sow*: March, indoors. *Plant*: June.    *Stks*: Wdly avail.

'New Ace': Very large fruits. Grow in greenhouse.
⬚🅕 *Sow*: Feb.–March, indoors. *Plant*: May–June.    *Stks*:
SM, SS, WJ

## Carrot    LM    O–◑    ***

'Amsterdam Forcing': Small, stump-rooted variety for forcing.
✳⬚ *Sow*: Feb.–July    *Stks*: Widely available

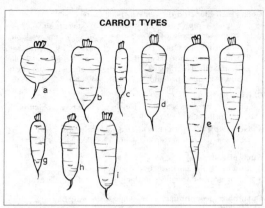

**CARROT TYPES**

CARROT SHAPES: *a. round; b. 'Chantenay'; c. 'Amsterdam Forcing'; d. 'Autumn King'; e. long; f. intermediate; g. slender 'Nantes'; h. 'Early Nantes'; i. large 'Nantes'*

'Autumn King': Large roots, heavy yield. Orange flesh.
*Sow*: April–June    *Stks*: Widely available

'Chantenay Red Cored': Intermediate length, stump-rooted.
Ⓕ *Sow*: March–June    *Stks*: Widely available

'Early Nantes': Stump-rooted and cylindrical.
Ⓕ✳☼ *Sow*: Feb.–July    *Stks*: Widely available

'St. Valery': Long, tapering roots.
Ⓘ *Sow*: April–June    *Stks*: Widely available

**Cauliflower (autumn)**    MH    ○    \*\*
'Kangaroo': Firm, white heads for cutting Sept.–Oct.
Ⓘ Ⓕ *Sow*: April–May *Plant*: June–July    *Stks*: GP, SS
'Snowcap': Quality heads, ready Nov.–Dec.
✳ *Sow*: May *Plant*: June    *Stks*: SM, TB, WU
'South Pacific': Solid, pure white heads, ready Oct.–Nov.
✳ *Sow*: April–May *Plant*: June–July    *Stks*: DB, WU

**Cauliflower (summer)**    MH    ○    \*\*
'All The Year Round': Compact heads with good curds.
✳ *Sow*: Feb.–May *Plant*: March–June    *Stks*: Widely avail.
'Lecerf' see 'All The Year Round'
'Snowball – Early Snowball': Close, white heads. Medium size.
*Sow*: Oct./Feb.–May *Plant*: March–June    *Stks*: Wdly avail.
'Snow Crown': Large, rounded, snow-white heads. Uniform.
Ⓕ *Sow*: March–May *Plant*: March–July    *Stks*: SM, WU

**Cauliflower (winter and spring)**    MH    ○    \*\*/\*\*\*
'Angers No. 2' (\*\*): Grow in South-west. Feb.–March.
✳ *Sow*: May *Plant*: June    *Stks*: SM, SS
'English Winter – Late Queen' (\*\*\*): Large heads. Ready May.
Ⓕ✳ *Sow*: May *Plant*: June    *Stks*: Widely available

**Celeriac**    LM(M)    ○–◐    \*\*\*
'Marble Ball': Large, globular-shaped. Stores well.
*Sow*: March, indoors *Plant*: June    *Stks*: Widely available

**Celery**    MH(M)    ○    \*\*\*
'Giant Pink': A pink variety that blanches easily. Crisp.
Ⓘ *Sow*: March, indoors *Plant*: June    *Stks*: Widely available
'Giant White': Solid, crisp, white stems.
Ⓘ Ⓕ *Sow*: March, indoors *Plant*: June    *Stks*: Wdly avail.

**Celery (self-blanching)**  MH(M)  O–◐  \*\*

'American Green': Solid, stringless stems stay green.
Ⓕ *Sow*: March, indoors *Plant*: June  *Stks*: Widely available

'Golden Self-blanching': Crisp and creamy sticks, Sept.–Dec.
Ⓒ *Sow*: March, indoors *Plant*: June  *Stks*: Widely available

'Lathom Self-blanching': Crisp, stringless stems. Slow to bolt.
Ⓕ *Sow*: March–April, indoors *Plant*: May–June  *Stks*: SM

**Chicory**  LMH  \*\*\*

'Crispa': Lift roots Nov. and store in peat – force as chicons.
*Sow*: April–May  *Stks*: GP, TB

'Normato': White chicons force easily early Nov.–Feb.
Ⓕ *Sow*: late April-early May  *Stks*: SM, WU

**Cucumber (frame)**  LM  O–◐  \*

'Butcher's Disease Resisting': Heavy cropper.
Ⓒ *Sow*: April-early June (under glass)  *Stks*: Wdly avail.

**Cucumber (greenhouse)** peat compost/growing bag  \*

'Fembaby': Ideal to grow on windowsills in 20–25cm pot.
*Sow*: Feb.–Aug. *Plant*: 4 weeks from sowing.  *Stks*: DB, TM

'Femdan': All female fls. Dark green bitter-free fruits.
Ⓕ *Sow*: Feb.–April, indoors *Plant*: April–June  *Stks*: TB

'Topsy': Large crop of all-female fls, juicy cucumbers
Ⓕ *Sow*: Feb.–April, indoors *Plant*: April–June  *Stks*: GP

'Uniflora D': Self-pruning. Grows a crop for six months.
Ⓕ *Sow*: Feb.–April *Plant*: April–June  *Stks*: TM

**Cucumber (ridge–outdoor)**  LM  O–◐  \*

'Bedfordshire Prize': Hardy and prolific. Prickly skin.
*Sow*: April–May *Plant*: June  *Stks*: DB, TB

'Burpless': Easy to grow and heavy yielding.
ⒻⒻ *Sow*: April–May *Plant*: June  *Stks*: WJ

'Burpless Tasty Green': Mildew-resistant. Prickly fruits.
Ⓕ *Sow*: April–May *Plant*: June  *Stks*: Widely available

'Long Green Ridge' see 'Bedfordshire Prize'

**Kohl rabi**  LMH  O  \*\*\*

'Green Vienna': White flesh. Early. Pull when small.
*Sow*: April–July  *Stks*: TB, WJ

'White Vienna': see 'Green Vienna'

**Leek**  LMH  O–◐  \*\*\*

'Lyon': Tender, solid white stems. Frost-resistant.
Ⓘ *Sow*: March–April *Plant*: June  *Stks*: Widely available

'Musselburgh': Long, thick stems. Weather-resistant.
ⒾⒻ *Sow*: March-April *Plant*: June  *Stks*: Widely available

'Titan': Medium green. Tall, with long blanched stem.
Ⓕ *Sow*: March–April *Plant*: May–July  *Stks*: GP

**Lettuce (butterhead type)**  LMH  O  \*\*\*

'All The Year Round': Very compact. Slow to run to seed.
Ⓕ *Sow*: Feb.–July *Plant*: April  *Stks*: Wdly avail.

'Avondefiance': Solid, tender hearts. Mildew-resistant.
*Sow*: Feb.–Aug. *Plant*: April, or thin  *Stks*: Widely available

'Buttercrunch': Small, dark green heads. Crisp.
*Sow*: March–July *Plant*: April, or thin  *Stks*: Widely avail.

'Cobham Green': Large, dark green, solid hearts.
Ⓕ *Sow*: Feb.–July *Plant*: March–April, or thin  *Stks*: DB, TB

'Fortune' see 'Hilde II'

'Hilde II': Large, tight heads. Light green colour.
Ⓒ *Sow*: Jan.–July *Plant*: March–April, or thin  *Stks*: SM, SS

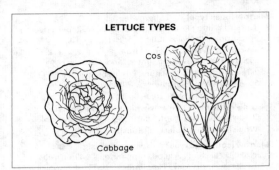

**LETTUCE TYPES**

Cos

Cabbage

'Suzan': Early hearting and very slow to bolt.
*Sow*: March–July *Plant*: April–Aug.   *Stks*: SS, TB, WJ

'Tom Thumb': Very small, crisp, sweet, solid hearts.
*Sow*: Jan.–April *Plant*: Feb.–April   *Stks*: Widely available

**Lettuce (crisphead)**   LMH   O   \*\*

'Avoncrisp': Crisp heads. Good for hot, dry soils.
*Sow*: March–July   *Stks*: Widely available

'Great Lakes': Very large hearts. Slow to bolt.
*Sow*: March–July   *Stks*: Widely available

'New York': see 'Webb's Wonderful'

'Webb's Wonderful': Crisp and very sweet. Robust.
*Sow*: March–July   *Stks*: Widely available

**Lettuce (winter-maturing)**   LMH   O   \*\*/\*\*\*

'Arctic King' (\*\*\*): One of the hardiest varieties to overwinter.
*Sow*: Aug.   *Stks*: Widely available

'Dandie' (\*\*): Best cold greenhouse lettuce.
⌂ *Sow*: Aug.–Nov.   *Stks*: GP, SS, TB

'Kloek' (\*\*): Produces large heads about the end of March.
⌂ *Sow*: Sept.–Oct. (cool greenhouse)   *Stks*: DB, SS, WU

'Valdor' (\*\*\*): Large, deep green, crisp hearts in spring.
*Sow*: Aug.–Sept.   *Stks*: DB, SM, SS

**Lettuce (cos)**   LMH   O   \*\*

'Little Gem': Self-hearting. Crisp, sweetly flavoured.
F *Sow*: March–July   *Stks*: Widely available

'Lobjoit's Green': Large, dark green heads. Needs loose tie.
*Sow*: March–July *Plant*: April–Aug.   *Stks*: Widely available

'Paris White': Good, crisp, solid hearts. Needs loose tie.
*Sow*: March–July. *Plant*: April–Aug.   *Stks*: Widely available

'Valmaine': Self-folding cos type. Thin to 6in, keep cutting.
*Sow*: March–July   *Stks*: TM

'Winter Density': Self-hearting. Very sweet and crisp.
*Sow*: March–July. *Plant*: April–Aug.   *Stks*: Widely available

**Lettuce (loose-leaf type)**   LMH   O–◑   \*\*

'Salad Bowl': Endive-like lvs. No real heart.
*Sow*: March–July   *Stks*: Widely available

**Marrow (trailing type)**   LM/growing bag   O   \*

'Long Green Trailing': Cylindrical, with light stripes.
① *Sow*: April–May *Plant*: June   *Stks*: Widely available

'Long White Trailing': Free-cropping; large white fruits.
① *Sow*: April–May *Plant*: June   *Stks*: Widely available

'Vegetable Spaghetti': After boiling inside is like spaghetti.
*Sow*: April–May *Plant*: June   *Stks*: Widely available

**Marrow (bush type)**   LM/growing bag   O   *
  'Custard White': Round, flattened fruits, scalloped edges.
  *Sow*: April–May *Plant*: June   *Stks*: DB, SS, TB
  'Epicurean': Very early, green fruit.
  🄵 *Sow*: April–May *Plant*: June   *Stks*: GP
  'Green Bush': Early to mature. Prolific but compact.
  *Sow*: April–May *Plant*: June   *Stks*: Widely available
  'Long Green Bush' see 'Green Bush'
  'Long White Bush': Creamy-white fruits, medium size.
  ① *Sow*: April–May *Plant*: June   *Stks*: Widely available
  'White Bush': see 'Long White Bush'

**Marrow (courgette type)**   LM/growing bag   O   *
  'Golden Zucchini': A good cropper; long, golden fruits.
  🄵🄵 *Sow*: April–May *Plant*: June   *Stks*: Widely available
  'Zucchini': Very heavy cropper, with emerald-green fruits.
  🄵🄵 *Sow*: April–May *Plant*: June   *Stks*: Widely available

**Melon**   LM/growing bag   O   *
  'Sweetheart': Easiest variety. Small fruits, pink flesh.
  🄲🄵 *Sow*: April, indoors *Plant*: June   *Stks*: Widely available

**Onion**   LMH   O   ***
  'Ailsa Craig': Globe-shaped, with a rich straw colour.
  ① *Sow*: Sept. or March–April.   *Stks*: Widely available
  'Hygro': Very high yielding, with a uniform globe shape.
  🄵 *Sow*: March–April   *Stks*: SM, WJ, WU

**Onion (salad)**   LMH   O   ***
  'White Lisbon': Quick-growing. Silvery-white base.
  *Sow*: Any time (cloches Sept.–Feb.)   *Stks*: Widely available

**Onion (sets)**   LMH   O   ***
  'Sturon': Large, round, thin-necked, straw-coloured bulbs.
  *Plant*: March–May   *Stks*: Widely available

**Onion (pickling)**   LM   O   **
  'Barletta': A small, white-skinned variety.
  *Sow*: March–April   *Stks*: Widely available
  'Paris Silver Skin': Excellent for cocktail pickles.
  *Sow*: March–April   *Stks*: SM, SS, WJ

**Onion, Japanese**   LMH   O   ***
  'Express Yellow': A flattish shape, ready to harvest in June.
  🄵 *Sow*: Aug.   *Stks*: Widely available

**Parsnip**   LMH   O   ***
  'Avonresister': Small conical roots, resistant to canker.
  *Sow*: Feb.–April   *Stks*: Widely available
  'Hollow Crown Improved': Long, smooth and tapering roots.
  ①🄵 *Sow*: Feb.–April   *Stks*: Widely available
  'Tender and True': Long, tapering roots, with smooth skins.
  ①🄵 *Sow*: Feb.–April   *Stks*: Widely available

**Peas (first early)**   LMH   O   ***
  'Hurst Beagle': Dwarf, very early small-podded variety.
  *Sow*: Feb.–March, and June   *Stks*: Widely available
  'Kelvedon Wonder': Dwarf. Early and of good quality.
  ✱ *Sow*: Feb.–March, and June   *Stks*: Widely available
  'Little Marvel': Dwarf. Stump-ended pods, in pairs.
  *Sow*: Oct.–Nov., March or June   *Stks*: Widely available

**Peas (second early)**   LMH   O   **
  'Early Onward': Dwarf. Blunt, large, dark green pods.
  ✱ *Sow*: March–April   *Stks*: Widely available

'Hurst Green Shaft': Medium height. Long, slender pods.
F ✱ *Sow*: March–April   *Stks*: Widely available

**Pea (maincrop)**   LMH   O   \*\*
'Lord Chancellor': Medium height. Heavy crop of dark pods.
*Sow*: April–May   *Stks*: SS, WU
'Onward': Medium height. Dark green, blunt-nosed pods.
F ✱ *Sow*: April–May   *Stks*: Widely available

**Pea (edible pod type)**   LMH   O   \*\*
'Sugar Snap': Thick, fleshy pods. Eat pods and peas. Tall.
*Sow*: March–April   *Stks*: Widely available

**Potato**   LMH   O   \*
'Desiree' (early maincrop): Red-skinned, kidney-shaped.
① F *Plant*: Late March–May   *Stks*: DB, TB
'Maris Bard' (early): Very early, long/oval white tubers.
F ◔ *Plant*: March–April   *Stks*: DB, TB
'Maris Piper' (maincrop): High quality, white-skinned, oval.
*Plant*: late March–May   *Stks*: DB
'Pentland Javelin' (early): Heavy crop. White tubers.
① F *Plant*: March–April   *Stks*: DB, TB
'Vanessa' (second early): Long, pink tubers. Yellow flesh.
① *Plant*: Late March–May   *Stks*: TB

| Variety | POTATO QUALITIES | | |
| | Scab Resistance | Drought Resistance | Moist/Waxy Mealy/Floury |
|---|---|---|---|
| 'Desiree' | Poor | Good | ✓ |
| 'Maris Bard' | Average | Average | ✓ |
| 'Maris Piper' | Poor | Poor | ✓ |
| 'Pentland Javelin' | Good | Average | ✓ |
| 'Vanessa' | Average | Good | ✓ |

**Radish**   LMH   O   \*\*\*
'Cherry Belle': Brilliant red, smooth, round globes.
*Sow*: Feb.–July   *Stks*: Widely available
'French Breakfast': Cylindrical, scarlet roots, white tips.
*Sow*: Feb.–July   *Stks*: Widely available
'Prinz Rotin' see 'Red Prince'
'Red Prince': Large round scarlet roots. Slow to go hollow.
◔ *Sow*: March–July   *Stks*: TM, WU
'Scarlet Globe': Brilliant red, with crisp, white flesh.
*Sow*: Feb.–July   *Stks*: Widely available
'Sparkler': Bright scarlet, globe-shaped, tipped white.
*Sow*: Feb.–July   *Stks*: Widely available
'White Long Icicle': Crisp, tender, long, tapering roots.
*Sow*: March–July   *Stks*: Widely available

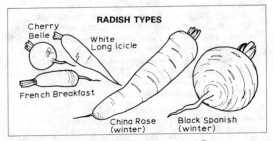

**RADISH TYPES**

Cherry Belle
White Long Icicle
French Breakfast
China Rose (winter)
Black Spanish (winter)

**Radish (winter)**   LM   O   \*\*\*
'Black Spanish Round': Black skin, white flesh. Round.
*Sow*: July–Aug.   *Stks*: DB, SM
'China Rose': Oval roots. Skin deep rose, with a white tip.
*Sow*: July–Aug.   *Stks*: Widely available

**Salsify**   LM   O   \*\*\*
'Giant': Pale, slender, dandelion-like roots.
*Sow*: March–April   *Stks*: SS

**Scorzonera**   LM   O   \*\*\*
'Russian Giant': Similar to salsify, but with black roots.
*Sow*: March–April   *Stks*: DB, SS, TB

**Shallot**   LMH   O   \*\*\*
'Giant Yellow': Large bulbs with a mild, agreeable flavour.
F *Plant*: Feb.–March   *Stks*: SS, TB, WJ
'Hative de Niort': Very large, reddish-skinned bulbs.
① F *Plant*: Feb.–March   *Stks*: SM, SS

**Spinach**   LMH   O–◗   \*\*\*
'Broad-leaved Prickly': Dark green, thick and fleshy lvs.
*Sow*: Aug.–Sept.   *Stks*: Widely available
'Greenmarket': Large, dark green lvs. Yields very heavily.
✳ *Sow*: Sept. or March–April.   *Stks*: SS
'Longstanding Round': Quick growing, with dark green lvs.
✳ *Sow*: Feb.–July   *Stks*: SS, WJ

**Spinach, New Zealand**   LMH   O   \*\*
New Zealand Spinach: Fleshy lvs, doesn't bolt in hot weather.
✳ *Sow*: May   *Stks*: Widely available

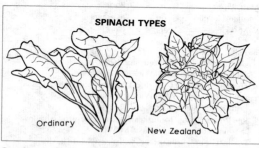

SPINACH TYPES

Ordinary          New Zealand

**Swede**   MH   O   \*\*\*
'Marian': Yellow flesh. Resists mildew and club-root.
F *Sow*: May–June   *Stks*: Widely available
'Purple Top': Yellow-fleshed, small necked, purple skinned.
*Sow*: May–June   *Stks*: TM, WT, WU

**Sweet corn**   LMH   O   \*\*
'Earliking': Large cobs. Early maturing, medium height.
✳ F *Sow*: May, indoors *Plant*: June   *Stks*: Widely available
'Early Xtra Sweet': Very early variety, with sweet cobs.
F ✳ F *Sow*: May, indoors *Plant*: June   *Stks*: SM, TM, WU
'Kandy Cob': Early, sweeter than traditional varieties.
F ✳ F *Sow*: May, indoors *Plant*: June   *Stks*: GP
'Kelvedon Glory': High quality and yield. Large, pale cobs.
✳ F *Sow*: May, indoors *Plant*: June   *Stks*: Widely available

**Tomato** peat compost/growing bag   O   \*
'Alicante': Smooth-skinned red fruits, greenback-free.
◔ *Sow*: see footnote   *Stks*: Widely available

'Arla': Medium-fruits. Earliest bush type. For outdoors.
*Sow*: see footnote   *Stks*: GP

'Big Boy': Very large, scarlet-red fruits, for greenhouses.
🄴🄳🄵 *Sow*: see footnote   *Stks*: Widely available

'Curabel': High yielding, disease resistant. Greenhouse.
🄴🄳🄵 *Sow*: see footnote   *Stks*: GP

'Gardeners Delight': Small-fruited, finest flavour.
🄴🄳 *Sow*: see footnote   *Stks*: Widely available

'Golden Sunrise': Golden-yellow, medium-sized fruits.
🄳 *Sow*: see footnote   *Stks*: Widely available

'Grenadier': Heavy yield, good quality, disease resistant.
🄴🄳🄵 *Sow*: see footnote (indoors only).   *Stks*: SS

'Marmande': Large, irregular-shaped fruits. Outdoor.
🄵 *Sow*: see footnote   *Stks*: Widely available

'Outdoor Girl': Potato-like lvs, medium-sized red fruits.
*Sow*: see footnote   *Stks*: Widely available

'Pixie': Compact and fast-ripening. Ideal for patio pots.
🄵🄵 *Sow*: see footnote   *Stks*: TM, WJ

'Sleaford Abundance': Bush type, for cloches and outdoors.
🄵 *Sow*: see footnote   *Stks*: Widely available

*Indoor varieties can be sown in heat from February onwards,
depending on the warmth available (a minimum of 15°C/60°F is
necessary). For outdoors, sow in heat during late March or April
and plant out in late May or June.*

**Turnip**   LMH   ○   ***
'Golden Ball': Round, yellow-skinned. Stores well.
① *Sow*: March–May.   *Stks*: Widely available

'Jersey Navet': Long, white roots with a good flavour.
🄳 *Sow*: Feb., under glass; March–May, outdoors.   *Stks*: SS

'Snowball': Round white roots, mild flavour. Early.
① *Sow*: March–May.   *Stks*: Widely available

'White Milan': Fast growing. Medium sized, smooth flat roots.
🄳 *Sow*: March–May.   *Stks*: Widely available

---

## SPECIALIST SUPPLIERS

**DB**   Samuel Dobie & Son Ltd., Upper Dee Mills,
Llangollen, Clwyd. LL20 8SD. Tel: (0978) 860119.

**GP**   'Garden Pride' (Hurst Gunson Cooper Taber Ltd).,
Witham, Essex, CM8 2DX. Tel: Witham 516600.

**SM**   S. E. Marshall & Co Ltd., Regal Road, Wisbech,
Cambs., PE13 2RF. Tel: Wisbech 407.

**SS**   Suttons Seeds Ltd., Hele Road, Torquay, Devon,
TQ2 7QJ. Tel: Torquay (0803) 62011.

**TB**   Thomas Butcher Ltd., 60 Wickham Road, Shirley,
Croydon, Surrey, CR9 8AG. Tel: 01–654 3720.

**TM**   Thompson & Morgan Ltd., London Road, Ipswich,
Suffolk, IP2 0BA.

**WJ**   W. W. Johnson & Son Ltd., Boston, Lincolnshire,
PE21 8AD.

**WU**   W. J. Unwin Ltd., Histon, Cambridge, CB4 4LE.
Tel: Histon (022023) 2270.

**Important**: 'Garden Pride' and W. W. Johnson seeds are
distributed through local shops and garden centres –
they are not available by mail order. However, in cases of
difficulty the companies will be able to tell you the
nearest stockist.

# Herbs

Herbs can bring an added dimension to food and cooking, and although originally used to cloak incipient decay and to stimulate the appetite during gargantuan feasts, they now play a useful role in garnishing meat and vegetables. Mint, parsley, thyme, chives and garlic are well known, but also useful to adventuresome cooks are caraway, borage, basil, angelica, horseradish and many others recommended here.

## Where to grow

Herbs are very adaptable, and may be grown on the grand scale in separate beds, or clustered together in a pot on a window-sill. Basil, parsley, chives, chervil and marjoram suit small pots, while mint, which is more invasive, is best in a larger container but where its spread can be restricted.

Many flat dwellers are able to grow these plants in small parsley pots placed on a window-sill. There are separate openings, through which the different herbs can be set. Clip back any that tend to dominate their neighbours.

Plants in the garden or containers positioned outside are best planted in the spring, when they have a long period in which to establish themselves, although pot-grown specimens can be planted at any time during the growing season.

Set the plants firmly in place and give a thorough watering. Once established the plants need little attention, apart from weeding and ensuring that the soil does not dry out.

*Strawberry pots can be used for a small collection of herbs.*

For stockists, see page 124

## Harvesting and storing

The leaves are usually picked fresh for immediate use or dried and stored. If used fresh, select the young and fresh leaves, as old ones tend to develop a bitter taste and to lose their flavour.

Herbs for later use can be hung upside down in bunches in a dry and airy place for 10 to 15 days. Enclose the separate bunches in paper bags or muslin. Those herbs with a high moisture content, such as basil, balm and tarragon, need to be dried rapidly and are best spread in trays and placed over a radiator or in an airing cupboard. Turn the stems every day until they are dry, then remove the leaves, crush them and place in stoppered jars with dark sides.

*Dry herbs by hanging them in bunches or spreading on trays. Rub small-leaved kinds such as mint between the hands to remove stalks and large pieces. Bay leaves are dried separately.*

Many herbs can be raised from seed – parsley and dill being popular examples – but most of them are also widely available as plants at garden centres. If buying plants always look for young plants with rich, vigorously-growing leaves. Avoid plants with lower and older leaves browning – an indication of a check to growth.

In the event of a particular plant not being available locally, there are several reputable mail-order nurseries that specialize in herbs.

**Angelica**  HP   MH(M)   ●   ***
Seed-raised perennial. Lives for 4–5 years. Fern-like lvs.
H:1.8m (6ft) S:1.2m (4ft)   *Stks*: Widely available

**Basil, sweet**  HHA   LMH   ○–◑   *
Fleshy stems and thick lvs with a strong aroma of cloves.
◒ H:60cm (2ft) S:30cm (1ft)   *Stks*: Widely available

**Bay** see *Laurus nobilis*, page 62

**Borage**  HA   LMH   ○   ***
Bristly lvs. Cucumber flavour. Bright blue, star-like fls.
H:45cm (1½ft) S:23cm (9in)   *Stks*: Widely available

**Caraway**  HB   LMH   ○   ***
Frond-like lvs. Tiny, white fls. Seeds ripen July–Aug.
H:60cm (2ft) S:30cm (1ft)   *Stks*: Widely available

**Chives**  HP   LMH   ○–◑   ***
Grass-like lvs. Rose-purple fls in May.
◒ H:25cm (10in) S:23cm (9in)   *Stks*: Widely available

*For key to symbols, see page 7*

**Dill**    HA    LMH    ○    ***
Minute, starry fls, June–Aug. Lace-like, blue-green lvs.
H:45–75cm (1½–2½ft) S:30cm (1ft)    *Stks*: Widely available

**Fennel**    HP    LMH    ○    ***
Bluish-green, glossy and feathery lvs. Yellow fls.
H:1.5m (5ft) S:45cm (1½ft)    *Stks*: Widely available

**Garlic**    HP    (Bulb)    LMH    ○    ***
Cloves of this herb are planted Oct.–Nov., or March.
H:30–90cm (1–3ft) S:30cm (1ft)    *Stks*: Widely available

**Horseradish**    HP    LMH    ○–◑    ***
Invasive plant, grown for its roots. Dock-like lvs.
H:60cm (2ft) S:60cm (2ft)    *Stks*: Widely available

**Lemon balm**    HP    LMH    ○–◑    ***
Almost circular, wrinkled lvs, intensely lemon scented.
H:75cm (2½ft) S:45cm (1½ft)    *Stks*: Widely available

**Marjoram, sweet**    HHA    LMH    ○    ***
Bushy plant, grey-green lvs. Pale lilac, pink or white fls.
♥ H:30cm (1ft) S:30cm (1ft)    *Stks*: Widely available

**Mint**    HP    LMH    ○–●    ***
Spearmint: The usual type grown, and used for mint sauce.
H:25cm (10in) S:30cm (1ft)    *Stks*: Widely available
Peppermint: Distinctive peppermint flavour.
H:25cm (10in) S:25cm (10in)    *Stks*: Widely available
'Bowles Mint': Attractive woolly lvs. Lilac fls.
H:60cm (2ft) S:60cm (2ft)    *Stks*: Widely available

**Parsley**    HB or HA    LMH    ○–◑    ***
Curled and divided lvs, much used for decoration.
♥ H:15cm (6in) S:23cm (9in)    *Stks*: Widely available

**Rosemary** (*Rosmarinus officinalis*) see page 64

**Sage** (*Salvia officinalis*) see page 64

**Savory, summer**    HA    LMH    ○    ***
Dark green, strongly aromatic lance-shaped lvs.
H:30cm (1ft) S:23cm (9in)    *Stks*: Widely available

**Sorrel, French**    HP    LMH    ○–◑    ***
Dock-like, sour-tasting lvs. Rather like spinach.
H:30cm (1ft) S:15cm (6in)    *Stks*: Widely available

**Tarragon, French**    HP    LM    ○    **
Bushy. Dies down in autumn, evergreen in mild areas.
H:75cm (2½ft) S:30cm (1ft)    *Stks*: Widely available

**Thyme**    HP    LM(C)    ○    ***
Common or French Thyme: Creeping evergreen, purple fls.
H:23cm (9in) S:30cm (1ft)    *Stks*: Widely available
Lemon Thyme: Lemon-scented broader lvs. Less hardy.
H:30cm (1ft) S:23cm (9in)    *Stks*: Widely available

---

### SPECIALIST SUPPLIERS

Yorkshire Herbs, The Herb Centre, Middleton Tyas, Richmond, North Yorkshire. Tel: Barton 686.

The Herb Garden, Thunderbridge, Nr Huddersfield, Yorkshire. Tel: Kirkburton 2993.

# Common Name Index

If you encounter a plant under a common name, and you cannot find it in the relevant chapter, the following index should enable you to track down the right plant. No common name index can ever be complete – there are even regional variations – but the following list includes those you are most likely to come across when shopping for the plants described in this book.

# Peter Seabrook's Colour Parade

The plants illustrated here in colour represent only a small fraction of the superb plants to be found within the pages of this book. But it is impossible to encapsulate the beauty of any plant in half a dozen words, and the illustrations on the following pages help to bring alive just a few of the many joys to be found in the garden.

If you find the lists a little daunting at first glance, then the pictures should whet your appetite and give a hint of the treasures stored within these pages.

The selection reflects the range of ornamental plants covered by the book, and is a cross-section of some of the plants I would want to grow in my own garden.

Looking through these pictures, colourful though they are, the plants in reality will look even more attractive in your own garden. You can have something of interest and beauty in your garden every day of the year.

*The author with the new dwarf calendula 'Family Circle'.*

### Begonia 'Non-stop Orange'

A recently introduced fully double tuber-forming type. The flowers are medium sized and the plants really do flower without stopping throughout the summer. They grow best in peat compost. Keep it damp to avoid flower drop.

### Camellia × williamsii 'Donation'

This evergreen and exotic flowering shrub is often considered tender, but in practice will grow in quite cold districts. If a little protection can be given against wind it grows vigorously in peaty soils. It is excellent for tub and pot culture.

### Clematis jackmanii

A valuable climber to flower in late summer (July/August), and one of the easiest and most vigorous of the large-flowered varieties. It will grow best if pruned hard back each spring. Cut all stems back to 38cm (15in) above the ground.

### Cyclamen

An ever-popular plant, best given a very light, cool position indoors for the best growth. Too much warmth or darkness causes the leaves to yellow and flowers to drop. Plants with masses of flower buds will need regular feeding.

130

### Dahlia 'Gerrie Hoek'

The medium-sized decorative dahlias like this old stager are excellent to cut and arrange in water. To get large individual flowers on strong stems it is advisable to disbud – that is, to pinch out side buds below the main bud on each stem.

### Euphorbia polychroma

One of the best hardy border flowers. It grows well in almost all soils and the early yellow flowers are followed by attractively coloured flower bracts. The autumn foliage is also pleasantly coloured. Growth is neat and rounded and does not need support.

### Forsythia

This is one of the brightest of all shrubs, and always a welcome spring sight. Prune hard back after flowering to encourage strong young growth to carry the next year's flowers. Well-budded branches can be cut in winter and placed indoors in water for early flowers.

### Hedera canariensis 'Variegata'

This large-leaved variegated ivy can be used in many ways. It is a good houseplant to grow in pots, it can be used to furnish banks and is a good wall or fence cover. Plant large-flowered clematis with this ivy for year-round interest.

131

### Hosta fortunei 'Albopicta'

A lovely plant that revels in damp peat-enriched soils – but watch out for slugs that eat the attractive cream and green leaves. It is an attractive plant to grow in pots in a cold greenhouse as well as the usual flower border or pool-side position.

### Impatiens

Busy-lizzies, as these plants are commonly known, are among the most popular pot plants, but are not so well known for their quality as bedding plants. They do best if the soil is improved with peat. If the soil is kept damp they thrive in both sun and shade.

### Iris reticulata

This dwarf iris is one of the earliest spring bulbs. There are bright and dark blue varieties, and they have a sweet fragrance. If growing in pots, keep them outside until the buds show colour. Bringing into warmth too soon will cause the flowers to die in the leaves.

### Juniperus communis 'Depressa Aurea'

This is one of the most attractive low-growing conifers. It has rich yellow young growth that turns a dark green and then reddish through the winter. This juniper needs full sun but others are less demanding and thrive in poor soil and conditions.

## Lupin

Lupins produce so much beauty that they deserve more frequent sowing. It is better to buy good strains of seed, as cheap mixtures will not have the variety or richness of colour. Cut the stems hard back after flowering, to encourage a late second flush of flower spikes.

## Mahonia aquifolium

Commonly called the Oregon grape, this shrub has bright yellow flowers in April, rich purple berries in the autumn and attractive evergreen foliage the year round. Prune hard after flowering, to encourage strong, rich new growth.

## Muscari armeniacum

The robust grape hyacinth is a charming, trouble-free plant for spring. The bulbs multiply freely and soon provide bold clumps of deep blue flowers – equally successful in the rock garden or as an edging to a flower bed.

## Narcissus

Narcissi look pretty and give years of colourful flower when naturalized in grass, or left to form large clumps. Try to leave the leaves for at least six weeks after flowering before cutting back. If thick clumps stop flowering, lift in summer, divide, and replant in fresh sites.

133

### Prunus 'Kanzan'

The branches of this flowering cherry have the shape of an umbrella blown inside out, and the tree is rather upright in habit. Masses of double pink flowers are produced every spring.

### Pyracantha 'Orange Glow'

This is one of the finest of all self-supporting wall plants. It will grow against walls and fences facing any point of the compass. Always buy pot-grown plants because pyracanthas do not like root disturbance.

### Rhododendron 'Elizabeth'

The dwarf and lower growing rhododendrons are better suited to the smaller modern gardens. Once established in peaty soil they produce masses of flowers, which virtually cover the leaves in late spring. The evergreen leaves are attractive the year round.

### Rose 'Silver Jubilee'

This recent introduction has vigorous growth, large shapely flowers and shiny rich green leaves that show good resistance to disease. Large blooms like this are commonly referred to as hybrid tea roses. They can be used for bedding and for cutting for the home.

### Sedum 'Autumn Joy'

An excellent border plant for early autumn. The flower heads retain their colour for weeks, and the succulent leaves are attractive from spring onwards. The flower heads are also a great attraction for butterflies. There are several other good varieties, and all are easy.

### Sorbus aria 'Lutescens'

The whitebeams are robust trees that thrive even in windswept or industrial areas. The undersides of the leaves are whitish, and the variety 'Lutescens' has a white felty down on both surfaces. There is the added bonus of pleasant autumn tints and clusters of red berries.

### Salvia splendens

The bright red salvias are a traditional part of summer bedding, and massed together make a vivid splash of colour. They need to be raised under glass in spring in a minimum temperature of 15°C (60°F). Cooler temperatures result in late flowering.

### Stock, East Lothian

There are several different types of stocks, the East Lothian kind having a very high percentage of plants with double flowers. They flower well under cold glass in early spring from an August sowing, and if then planted out they continue to flower right through summer.

### Thuja plicata 'Atrovirens'

This conifer makes a superb hedge and responds well to quite hard clipping. It makes a tall, thick hedge in just a few years. Where a lower, smaller hedge is required, choose *Thuja occidentalis* 'Smaragd'. *Thuja plicata* has a pineapple smell when crushed.

### Tulipa greigii 'Red Riding Hood'

Many of the species tulips are ideal for windy sites, because of their low-growing habit. Some have the beauty of vivid flowers and bold, attractively marked leaves. They also tend to flower reliably in succeeding years after planting.

### Wallflowers

One of the prettiest, sweetest-smelling cottage garden flowers. Modern varieties are dwarf and compact. The higher-priced seed mixtures usually have the best colour range. It is advisable to sow in May or June for good flowering twelve months later.

### Weigela florida 'Foliis Purpureis'

Easy natured plants are often bypassed by gardeners, which is a pity. This one is very easy to grow, and is covered with masses of flowers in June. It does not grow too large. Prune immediately after flowering.